To Olivia
with love from Daddy
February 17, 1985

*Stories from the Bible*

KU-772-220

other books for children by Walter de la Mare

★

(*prose*)

COLLECTED STORIES FOR CHILDREN

ANIMAL STORIES

TALES TOLD AGAIN

THE THREE ROYAL MONKEYS

THE STORY OF JOSEPH

(*verse*)

COLLECTED RHYMES AND VERSES

PEACOCK PIE

# STORIES FROM THE
# BIBLE

by

## WALTER DE LA MARE

*illustrated by*

EDWARD ARDIZZONE

FABER AND FABER

3 Queen Square

London

First published in 1929
Reprinted in this edition 1961
Second impression 1967
First published in this edition 1977
by Faber and Faber Limited
3 Queen Square London W.C.1.
Printed in Great Britain by
Redwood Burn Limited
Trowbridge & Esher
All rights reserved

ISBN 0 571 11086 X (Faber Paperbacks)

To

FRIDY

**CONDITIONS OF SALE**

This book is sold subject to the condition that it shall not, by way of
trade or otherwise, be lent, re-sold, hired out or otherwise circulated
without the publisher's prior consent in any form of binding or cover
other than that in which it is published and without a similar condition
including this condition being imposed on the subsequent purchaser

© 1977 by the Literary Trustees of
Walter de la Mare

# Contents

# CONTENTS

## THE WILDERNESS

## SAMSON

## SAMUEL

## SAUL

## DAVID

# Introduction

The stories contained in this volume are versions of but a few of the narratives related in the first nine books of the Old Testament of the Bible, "that inestimable treasure which excelleth all the riches of the earth".

The Bible, it is said, is not being read nowadays so much as it used to be: while there *was* a time when, it is recorded, a load of hay would be paid gladly for the loan of a manuscript Testament for an hour a day. Wholly apart from the profound truth that "simple men of wit may be edified much to heavenly living by reading and knowing of the Old Testament", this statement, if true, implies a loss beyond measure to mind and heart, and particularly to the young—its wisdom and divination, truth and candour, simplicity and directness. All that man is or feels or (in what concerns him closely) thinks; all that he loves or fears or delights in, grieves for, desires and aspires to is to be found in it, either expressed or implied. As for beauty, though this was not its aim, and the word is not often used in it—it is "excellent in beauty"; and poetry dwells in it as light dwells upon a mountain and on the moss in the crevices of its rocks. In what other book—by mere mention of them—are even natural objects made in the imagination so whole and fair; its stars, its well-springs, its war-horse, its almond tree?

[ 9 ]

That there are difficulties for those unfamiliar with its pages no one with any knowledge of the subject would deny. The very simplicity and austerity of the Old Testament stories, their conciseness, the slight changes that have occurred in the meaning or bearing of English words, occasional obscurities and repetitions in the text, are among them. My small endeavour has been to lighten some of these difficulties, while yet keeping as close to the spirit of the text as I am capable of. In many passages I have kept even to the letter. Apart from that, remembrance of what the matchless originals in the Bible itself meant to me when I was a child is still fresh and vivid in mind, and these renderings are little more than an attempt to put that remembrance as completely as I can into words.

But words in their influence are subtle and delicate beyond all things known to man, and the least change in them when they are in company, or the least addition to that company, cannot but entail a change of meaning; a change, that is, in their complete effect on the mind and spirit of the reader. Comparison of some of the English translations, as they deal in turn with the same brief passage, will be evidence of this, however little evidence is needed.

Here, for example, are three familiar verses from the first chapter of the Book of Ruth. Having come to the parting of the ways, Naomi, wholly against her heart and will, entreats Ruth to return to her own people and venture no further into a strange land:

"The which answerde, Ne contrarye thou me, that Y forsake thee, and goo a wey; whider euere thou gost, I shal goo, and where thow abidist, and I togidre shal abyde; thi puple my puple, and thi God my God; what erthe the takith diynge, in it I shal die, and there I shal take place of biriynge; thes thingis God do to me, and thes thingis adde, if not oonly deth me and thee seuere. Seynge thanne Noemye, that with stedfast inwit Ruth hadde demed to goo with hir, wold not contrarye, ne more mouynge the turnynge agen to hyrs. And thei wenten forth to gidre, and thei camen into Bethlem . . ."     (Wycliffe: *c*. 1382)

"And sche answeride, Be thou not aduersarye to me, that Y forsake thee, and go awei; whidur euer thou schalt go, Y shal go, and where thou schalt dwelle, and Y schall dwelle togidere; thi puple is my puple, and thi God is my God; what lond schal resseyue thee diynge, Y schal die ther ynne, and there Y schal take place of biriyng; God do to me these thingis, and adde these thingis, if deeth aloone schal not departe me and thee. Therfor Noemy saw, that Ruth hadde demyde with stidefast soule to go with hir, and sche nolde be agens hir, nether counseile ferthere turnynge agen to her cuntrei men. And thei geden forth togidere, and camen in to Betheleem . . ."

(The "Wycliffe" translation revised by
John Purvey: 1386)

"Ruth answered: Speake not to me thereof, that I shulde forsake thee, and turne backe from the: whither so euer thou goest, thither wil I go also: and loke where thou abydest, there wil I abide also: Thy people is my people, and thy God is my God. Loke where thou diest, there wil I dye, and euen there wil I also be buried. The Lorde do this and that unto me, death onely shal departe vs.

"Now whan she sawe, that she was stedfastly mynded to go with her, she spake nomore to her therof. So they wente on both together, till they came vnto Bethleem."

(Miles Coverdale: 1536)

"And Ruth answered, Intreate mee not to leaue thee, nor to depart from thee: for whither thou goest, I will goe: and where thou dwellest, I will dwell: thy people shalbe my people, and thy God my God. Where thou diest, will I die, and there will I be buried. The Lord do so to me and more also, if ought but death depart thee and me.

"When she saw yt she was stedfastly minded to goe with her, shee left speaking vnto her. So they went both vntill they came to Beth-lehem . . ." (The Geneva Bible: 1560)

"She answered: Be not against me, to desire that I should leave thee and depart: for whithersoever thou shalt go, I will go: and where thou shalt dwell, I also will dwell. Thy people shall be my people, and thy God my God. The land that shall receive thee dying, in the same will I die; and there will I be buried. The Lord do so and so to me, and add more also, if aught but death part me and thee.

"Then Noemi seeing, that Ruth was steadfastly determined to go with her, would not be against it, nor persuade her any more to return to her friends: So they went together and came to Bethlehem." (The Douai Bible: 1609)

"And Ruth said, Entreat me not to leave thee, or to return from following after thee: for whither thou goest, I will go: and where thou lodgest, I will lodge: thy people shall be my people, and thy God my God: Where thou diest, will I die, and there will I be buried: the Lord do so to me, and more also, if ought but death part thee and me.

"When she saw that she was stedfastly minded to go with her, then she left speaking unto her. So they went until they came to Bethlehem . . ." (Authorized Version: 1611)

It is a lesson in much more than mere word-craft to consider each of these in turn. In one, the lovely simplicity of "that I forsake thee, and go away"; in another, "that Ruth had deemed with steadfast soul to go with her"; in another, "She spake no more to her thereof. So they went on both together"; and then, the sovran "Intreat me not to leave thee", and "the Lord do so to me and more also"; and last, in the Douai translation, "if aught but death part me and thee".

Here also is but a fragment from the second chapter of Genesis:

"And the Lord God brought forthe of the erthe eche tree fayre in sight, and swete to ete."　　　　(Wycliffe)

"And the Lorde God caused to sprynge out of the earth all maner trees, pleasant to loke upon, and good to eate."
(Miles Coverdale: 1536)

"For out of the ground made the Lorde God to grow euery tree pleasant to the sight and good for meate."
(The Geneva Bible: 1560)

"And the Lord God brought forth of the ground all manner of trees, fair to behold and pleasant to eat of."
(The Douai Bible: 1609)

"And out of the ground made the Lord God to grow every tree that is pleasant to the sight and good for food."
(Authorized Version: 1611)

If these are the varying achievements of the masters, what manifold dangers, then, await the "simple creature" who attempts in our own day to re-tell even a fraction of any particular chapter of the Old Testament in his own words.

To read, too, any book worthy of the name needs all the powers of understanding and imagination and spirit of which one is capable, and even then, what is made of the reading may fall far short of what was intended in the writing. How much so, then, when that book is the Bible! Its unique history is proof of it. Even the most usual of words in the most ordinary of circumstances may have many senses. We say, "Here I am, at home": meaning, "in my own familiar place": and, maybe, "the house where I was born". But as when striking a note softly on a piece of fine glass one may listen on to its chiming overtones, so, if we listen to the echoes of the word home in memory, they can hardly fail to remind us of the home that is the body, where the "I, myself", has its earthly dwelling. Next, maybe, of the "keeping in order" of that home. And last, of the home of the heart's desire, which has had almost as many names given to it as there are races of mankind.

"Worde," as Wycliffe says, "worde wynd and mannes mynd is full short, but letter written dwelleth." So too with the Bible. Its meanings or "understandings", as St. Thomas Aquinas declared, are fourfold. First the literal, which is "ground and foundement" of the other three—the allegorical, the moral and the analogical.

These words sound a little formidable, but no word is "long", when one knows the meaning of it. Thus the word Jerusalem may mean first, literally, the chief city of Palestine—seated beyond the barren hills between it and the sea, and of an age-long, unique and tragic history. Next, allegorically, it may signify also the Jerusalem that is the longed-for Zion, the place of peace, the Church on earth. Next, morally, it may signify the soul of man. And last, analogically, in what by retention it resembles, it is the place of paradise, "where there shall be bliss in body and soul without end". The Jerusalem of King David, that is; the Jerusalem of Christ, the Messiah; the Jerusalem mourned and desired in every human heart; the heavenly Jerusalem otherwhere. Or again, the literal refers to things that happen or have happened on earth, the allegorical to what is to be believed, the moral to what is to be done, and the analogical to what is to be hoped for in the life to come.

A word in the Old Testament in the inspiration of the man who wrote it, may be taken to bear only one of these interpretations, or more than one, or all. So, too, in differing respects, in other writings. William Blake's "Tiger", for example; is it to read too much into his poem if we see in it the tiger that ranges the forest of the night, the tiger that is the emblem of strength and ferocity, the tiger that is the exemplar of fearlessness, the tiger that is a revelation of the miracle of divine creativeness? And so, too, maybe, when Shakespeare wrote of "what we fear of death". But here I am venturing beyond my depth.

All this, at least, concerns the stories contained in this volume as they appear, once and for all, in the all-sufficing "bare text" of the Old Testament itself. My own versions of them, apart from what has been literally embodied from it (and even here the frame given to that must in some degree affect its meaning), is no more than my own conception of them, which cannot but be very partial, faulty, inaccurate, and far from complete.

Little evidence though there may be of it, and however inadequately I have taken advantage of their learning and insight, I am indebted to many authorities and commentators, though it would be only the poorest of tributes to specify them. My deepest thanks, however, may be expressed to friends who have generously helped me, to Sister Frances de Chantal for invaluable kindness and counsel, to Mr. Forrest Reid and to Mr. R. N. Green-Armytage for their kindness in reading and commenting on my proofs. Nevertheless the full responsibility for what is here—and I realize how serious a responsibility it is—cannot but remain entirely my own.

If, in spite of all its defects and shortcomings, this book persuades any of its young readers to return to the inexhaustible well-spring from which it came, it will have amply fulfilled its purpose.

# THE GARDEN OF EDEN

# The Creation of Man

In the beginning the Lord God created the heaven and
the earth. And the earth was without form, and void.
All was darkness, confusion and watery chaos. But the
spirit of the Lord God, in whose sight a thousand years
are but as yesterday, brooded in divine creation upon the

dark face of the waters. And God said: "Let there be light." And there was light. And God saw the light, that it was good.

And he divided the wondrous light called Day from the darkness that he called Night. And he parted asunder the waters of the firmament called heaven from the waters beneath upon the earth. And the dry land appeared, its desolate plains and drear ice-capped mountains. And he made the green seeding grass to grow, and herb and tree yielding fruit; and he saw that it was good.

In the heaven above, for sign of the seasons and of days and of years, and to divide the day from the night, he set the sun and the moon to shine and to lighten the whole earth. The sun, the greater light, ruled the day, and the moon, the lesser light, that waxes and wanes in radiance ever changing, ruled the night; and the wandering planets had each its circuit in heaven, and the stars their stations in the depth and height of space.

Then said the Lord God: "Let the waters bring forth abundantly moving creatures that have life, and winged birds of the air that may fly above the earth under the firmament of heaven." So there were fishes in the deep sea, and great whales had their habitation therein, and the air was sweet with birds.

And when the heavens and the earth and all the host of them were finished in the days that the Lord God appointed, he for ever blessed and hallowed the seventh day, because in joy and love he had stayed then and rested from all his work which he had created and made.

Of the power and wisdom of God was everything to which he had given life—tree and plant and flower and herb, from the towering cedar to the branching moss. All the beasts of the earth also, the fishes of the sea, the fowls of the air, the creeping things and the insects, each in the place where was its natural food and what was needful for its strength and ways and wants; from beasts so mighty and ponderous that they shook the ground with their tread, to the grasshopper shrilling in the sunshine on his blade of grass and the silent lovely butterfly sipping her nectar in the flower; from the eagle in the height of the skies to the wren flitting from thicket to thicket, each after its own kind.

The Lord God saw everything that he had made, and behold, it was very good. He blessed it, and bade all things living grow and increase and multiply upon the earth, wheresoever it was meet for them. But still in his power and wisdom he was not satisfied with the earth that he had created until, last of all things living, he made man. And he called him by name, Adam.

For dwelling-place meet for this man that he had made the Lord God planted a garden. It was a paradise of all delight, wherein he intended him to have bliss in body and soul without end. And though it was of the earth, it was yet of a beauty and peace celestial, wherein even the angels of heaven might find joy to stray.

This garden lay eastward in Eden; and a river went out of Eden to water it. Flowing thence, and beyond it, its waters were divided, and they became the four great rivers of the world, whose names have been many.

The name of the first river was Pison, which flows about and encompasses the whole land of Havilah, where there is gold. And the gold of that land is fine gold. There also is found the gum of spicery called bdellium, sweet to the taste and bitter to the tongue, and the clear green onyx or beryl stone. The name of the second river was Gihon, whose windings encompass the whole land of Ethiopia. And the name of the third river was Hiddekel, or Tigris, that

flows eastward of the land Assyria. And the fourth great
river of the world is the Euphrates.

But by any device of knowledge, desire, or labour, to return from beyond Eden by any one of these rivers into that
Garden is now for man a thing impossible. Its earthly paradise is no more.

Then, every beast and living thing that was in the Garden, and roved its shades and valleys and drank of its
waters, was at peace in the life that had been given it, without fear or disquietude or wrong. But as yet they had no
names. Trees grew in abundance on the hills and in the
valleys of the Garden, and every tree that sprang forth out
of the earth was fair in sight and good to eat.

In the crystal waters of its river swam fish curious and
marvellous in scale and fin and in their swift motion in the
water; and flowers of every shape and hue grew so close in
company upon its banks that the air was coloured with the
light cast back from their clear loveliness. The faintest
breeze that stirred was burdened with their fragrance. And
at certain seasons a mist went up out of the Garden; and
night-tide shed its dews, watering the whole face of the
ground, refreshing all things.

And in the very midst of the Garden were two trees,
secret and wondrous; the Tree of Life, and the Tree of the
Knowledge of Good and Evil. Their branches rose in a
silence so profound that no cry of bird or beast was heard
there, and no living thing shaped by the Lord God out
of the dust of the earth ever drew near.

Now the man whom the Lord God had created was different from every other living thing upon the earth. Miraculous in grace and life and strength, his lighted eyes, his
hair, his hands, the motion of his limbs, the mystery of his
beating heart, his senses to touch and taste and smell and

hear and see—miraculous also in the wonder of his mind that reflected in little all things of the great world around him—he too, like all else that had life in the Garden, had been fashioned and shaped of the dust. Yet was he in the image and likeness of the divine; the Lord God had breathed into him breath of life, and he became a living soul.

Since his body, like theirs, was also of the earth, Adam was at peace with all living creatures in the Garden. Nevertheless because in mind and spirit he was man and no beast, God made him the lord and master of the Garden, sovereign even to the fishes of the water, to the birds of heaven and the unreasonable beasts of earth. He had dominion over them all. And as the free and harmless creatures that for a happy dwelling-place shared the Garden with him were less than he, so he himself was a little lower than the angels of heaven, who are not of the earth, but of a different being and nature, and dwell in glory beyond thought or imagination in the presence of the Lord God.

Thus Adam, shaped of the dust and given life of the divine, came into this earthly paradise, and his eyes were opened, and the light of day shone in upon him as through windows, and joy and amazement filled his mind. He heard the voice of beast and bird and wind and water, and with his fingers he touched the flowers. He was clothed in the light and heat of the sun, and stood erect and moved his limbs and stretched his arms above his head. The Lord God looked on him with love and talked with him in the secrecy of his heart.

"Lo, all things that I have made to be of thy company I give into thy charge to keep and tend and to use. Do with them as thy heart desires. And behold, I have given thee also for food every herb whose seed is in itself of its own kind, and every tree yielding fruit and seed. Of every tree thou mayest freely eat except only the fruit of the Tree of the Knowledge of Good and Evil that is in the midst of the Garden. Of that thou mayest not eat. It is denied thee. For if thou eat of it, it will bring thee only grief and misery; deadly of its nature is this fruit unto thee, and in the day that thou eatest thereof thou shalt surely die."

Adam hearkened to these words with all his understanding, and in the will of the Lord God he found freedom and his peace. The days of his life went by, and the Lord God brought to him in his own season every beast of the field and every fowl of the air that he had made out of the dust, to see what Adam would call it, and to see which of them was most meet to him for company. And Adam gazed at them, marvelling as they moved before him, each in its own kind following the instinct and desire that was the secret of its life.

And as Adam watched them, it seemed that of his own insight and divination he shared in the life and being of each one of them in turn. They wandered amid the branching trees, browsing in the herbage, and on the gentle slopes at the river's brink stooped their heads to quench their thirst, or stretched themselves to drowse in the sunshine, or lay cleaning and preening their sleek coats, or sported in play one with another, and leaped and exulted.

Adam watched too the birds among the green-leafed branches, and the prudent and loving ways of the waterfowl. The swan with plumage markless as the snow was there, and the goose on high at evening arrowed the still air, winging in company of her kind. In the hush of dark the little owl called *a-whoo* into the warm silence, and the nightingale sang on whether the moon shone in the dark or no, though all through the day it had been singing too.

Adam listened, never wearying of their cries and songs. And whatsoever—according to the exclamations of wonder, surprise or delight that came to his lips at sight or hearing of them—Adam called them, such were their names. To every living thing he gave a name. Its image and its name were of one memory in his mind. At call of its name the creature to whom he had given it came fearlessly to his side. He rejoiced to see it, and at sound of his laughter the Garden itself seemed also to rejoice and to renew its life.

At evenfall the Lord God would return into the Garden and talk with Adam, communing with him in the secrecy of his heart. And even when Adam slept, his divine presence haunted him in dreams, and when he awoke to day again his love enfolded him. As naturally as the birds in their singing, Adam praised the Lord God in all that he did.

But though he had joy in the company of the creatures around him in the Garden, Adam had none like to himself with whom to share his own spirit and nature. He was in this apart from them and was alone. And the Lord God read this secret in Adam's heart and had compassion on his solitude.

"It is not good," he said, "that the man whom I have created should be alone; I will make him a help meet for him."

In the darkness of night he caused a deep sleep or trance to fall upon Adam, and out of his side as he slept he took a rib, and with a touch closed again and healed the wounded side. And as he had made all things living and Adam himself out of the dust, so in the mystery of his wisdom he made woman out of man. He breathed into her body the breath of life, and in the stillness of night she lay, as yet unawakened, beside Adam as he slept.

When daybreak lightened again over Eden and the shafts

of sunrise pierced its eastern skies, the voice of the bird of morning stole sweet and wildly in upon Adam's dreams, and the very rocks resounded. He awoke, and saw the woman. She lay quiet as a stone, the gold of the sun mingling with the gold of her hair, her countenance calm and marvellous.

Adam stooped in awe and wonder and with his finger touched her hand, as in the beginning the Lord God had with his divine touch bidden him rise and live. So too the woman's eyes opened and looked upon Adam, and out of one paradise he gazed into another. And love breathed in him, seeing that she was of his own form and likeness. As he looked upon her, he cried with joy: "This, this is now bone of my bones and flesh of my flesh!"

So Adam was no longer alone in the Garden. She whom he called woman because she had been created by the Lord God out of man, was his continual company and delight. She was Eve, Adam's wife. They two were one, and this is the reason why a man, leaving even his father and his mother, cleaves to his wife. And in the paradise of earth and mind which had been made for them, Adam and Eve were both of them naked, for they were of all innocence as are children, and they were not ashamed.

Happy and at peace together beyond the heart of man now to dream of or conceive, Adam and Eve dwelt in the Garden of Eden, tending and dressing it to keep it fair and well.

# The Fall from Grace

Now of all living creatures in Eden the serpent was more subtle than any other which the Lord God had made. And because of his subtlety there entered into him the knowledge and malice of an angel fallen because of pride from grace, and banished from the presence of the Lord God. This fallen angel's evil influence found harbourage within the serpent; and Adam knew it not.

Couched in his beauty upon his coils, cold and stealthy, the changing colour of his scales rippling his whole length through, the serpent with lifted head would of his subtlety seek their company and share with them a knowledge that was his only. He would drowse beside them in the sun's heat while they talked together, and as he listened, envy sprang up in him, and he hated them for their innocence and their peace in their happy obedience to him who had made them and set them free.

There came an hour in the fullness of morning when Adam was away from the woman, and the serpent, seeing it, approached her and was with Eve alone. She sat in dappled shade from the sun, whose light was on all around them, and whose heat was pleasant to her after the cold of the waters in which she had bathed. There she had seen her own image or reflex in its glass; and she had praised the Lord God at the thought she was so fair. The serpent lifted up his flat-browed head, fixed his eyes upon her as she sat sleeking her hair, and he said: "Where, now, is the man Adam?"

Eve told the serpent that he was gone into the glades of the Garden near at hand to gather fruit for them to eat.

The serpent couched lower, rimpling the scales upon his skin. "But is it not", he said, "that the Lord God hath forbidden thee and the man Adam, saying, 'You shall not eat of any of the trees in the Garden'?"

Eve smiled, marvelling that the serpent should so speak. "Nay," she said, "we may eat of the fruit of any of the trees in the Garden. Except only the fruit of the Tree that is in the midst of it. Of that the Lord God hath said: 'You shall not eat of it. Taste it not lest you die!' "

The Garden was still. Above them the wondrous blue of morning was brimmed with the light of day, and the shadows of tree and mountain moved with the sun. Except for the warbling of birds, there came no sound of any other voice between them, and the serpent drew back his head, and from his cold and changeless eyes steadfastly looked upon Eve, loveliest of all things on earth that the Lord God had made.

"Yea," he answered, "and so the Lord God has said! But of a surety thou shalt not die. For he himself knows well that in the day that thou eat of the fruit of this Tree, then shall thine eyes be opened to his wisdom and thou shalt be as the divine ones, the angels of heaven, knowing both good and evil. It is no wonder that the fruit of the Tree hath been forbidden thee, for even though thou share it not with me, thou hast thine own secret wisdom. I did but desire to show thee how sweet and delectable are the fruits that grow upon this strange Tree's branches."

Eve listened to the guile of the serpent. She stooped her head upon her shoulders and thought deeply within herself of what he had said. And the serpent watching her, held his peace.

At length she answered him. "I know not", she said, "where grows the Tree. And Adam my husband expressly told me not even to seek to look upon it unless he were with me. It is well that the Lord God hath forbidden us the Tree, if only evil come of it."

"Yea," said the serpent. "But verily Adam thy husband hath seen it. I know well where grows this Tree of Knowledge. Come, now, let us go together, and thou thyself shalt see with thine own eyes how harmless it is. Yea, verily, it far surpasses every other tree that is in the Garden; and when I myself quaffed in its fragrance there was none to say me nay. But it may be thou hast no thirst for this wisdom, and thy husband himself would keep it from thee."

The woman rose with trembling hands and looked hither and thither, seeking Adam. But in vain, and the serpent was already gone from her. With a faint cry she followed after him, and the serpent went on before her.

The way became strange to her. It narrowed in beneath lofty trees whose upper branches, interlacing their leaves together under the noon, shut out the day. The ground rose steeply, crag and boulder, but smooth with moss and pleasant to the foot. They descended into a ravine where streams of water brawled among rocks, meeting to part again. Birds of smouldering and fiery plumage, so small they seemed to be of flame, and butterflies, with damasked wings, hovered over the wide-brimmed flowers.

But soon these were few and showed no more. And there were now no birds or any living thing, and in silence they continued on their way ever going up now through the secret places of the Garden, and hidden in a shade so deep no star of night could pierce it, or the moon shine in. The air was cold as water from a well, and there was not even sighing of wind in the midst of the forest to cool Eve's cheek. But it seemed to her that she heard the music of voices afar off and as it were out of the midst of the morning, between the earth and the firmament.

She stayed her steps to listen. And the serpent tarried beside her while she rested, for she was weary with the steepness of the way. Her eyes entreated him, for her mind was troubled, but speech was over between them, and she followed again after him, to discover whence the music of the voices she heard was sounding.

They came out from the verge and shade of the forest into a hollow space of a marvellous verdure that fell away, then rose in slope towards a mountain that towered high beyond it, transfigured with a light that seemed too rare and radiant to be only the light of day. On either side of this mountain, its rocks illumined with the colours of their own bright stone and of the multitudinous flowers that mantled over them, Eve gazed into the vacancy of space. It was as though they had come to the earth's end.

And midway on the green of the mountain slope there was a Tree, the Tree of the Knowledge of Good and Evil, while above it, but well-nigh invisible in the light that dwelt upon it, there was another Tree, and that on the heights beyond.

The sounds as of voices and instruments of music faint and far, and of the rapture of thousands upon thousands beyond telling, had ceased; and it was as though the radiant blue were agaze with the eyes of a great multitude, lost to vision in the light of heaven.

"Lo, now," the serpent whispered in Eve's ear, "methought I heard the sound of voices, but all is still, and there is none to watch or hear us."

And Eve approached and drew near to the Tree, whose branches as of crystal shone in the light of day, ravishing her eyes. Buds and petalled flowers lay open upon them, and they were burdened also with their fruit, both ripening and ripe. A nectar-like fragrance lay upon the air, and the Tree was of a beauty and strangeness that made her heart pine within her.

And behold, the fruit that was upon the Tree seemed sweet and pleasant and desirable to the sight, a fruit to make one wise. Eve looked upon it, and thirsted, though a voice in her own mind called in warning to her of the deathly and infinite danger she was in. And though she remembered the words of Adam that the Lord God had spoken, yet she heeded them not.

The eyes of the serpent were fixed upon her, stealthy with malice, and an envy came upon her senses. She put out her hand and plucked one of the fruits that hung low upon the Tree, and raised it to her lips. Its odour filled her with desire of it. She tasted and did eat, and shuddering at its potency that coursed into her veins, she stayed without motion and as if in sleep.

With her long gentle hand she drew back her hair that lay heavy as gold upon her shoulders, and supple as the serpent himself languished in her own beauty. She raised her head and stared with her eyes, exulting and defiant, yet the radiance of the mountain now smote upon her eyes and dazzled her mind not as with light but with darkness. Dread and astonishment came upon her, and in fear even of herself she turned for help to the serpent that had persuaded her there with his false and evil counsel. And behold, she was alone. She was alone and knew herself for-

saken. With the fruit that she had plucked from the forbidden branches she drew back cowering from beneath the Tree; and she fled away.

The darkness of the forest smote cold upon her body as she fled on by the way she had come, stumbling and falling and rising again, seeking she knew not what, but only to escape from the wild tumult of her mind. Her naked limbs bruised, her breath spent, she came into the presence of

Adam her husband who had come forth to seek her. With countenance bleak and strange, she crouched kneeling before him, thrust the fruit into his hand, and said: "See, see, the wonder the serpent hath made known to us! Taste and see!"

Her voice rang falsely on his ear. At sight of her face he trembled and, utterly loth and because he loved her, he took the fruit, and deaf to the voice within him, did eat.

In that moment they knew that they had sinned. Their eyes were opened; they looked out upon the Garden, and all things that were familiar in it were now become estranged and remote from them. Power was in their minds, but of knowledge, not of love. A grief no speech could reveal had veiled its beauty. In fear and horror they gazed on one another. Shame overshadowed them. They saw that they were naked, yet knew not where to turn to hide from their own shame. They plucked off leaves from a fig-tree and sewing them together made themselves aprons.

Smitten with doubt, they turned away each from each, and the love that was between them faded from out of their faces like the dew that vanishes in the heat of the day. Burning, mute, shaken with fear, yet on fire with life, they sat, their minds in torment; then, not daring to raise their horror-stricken eyes to sight, they turned again as if for refuge one to another. And Eve hid her face in Adam's hands, and they wept.

At sound of it a fawn that was browsing in a green hollow beneath the branches of a cedar tree lifted its eyes towards them, and, as if in fear, sped away and fled.

Night drew near; the level rays of the sun barred with shadow the vale in which they sat, and the milk-white flowers at their feet were dyed with its red. The firmament above them was flooded as if with flame, that as they looked ebbed out and was quenched. And the song of a multitude of birds in their green haunts rose to a wild babbling rapture that now was desolation to them to hear, then died away and all was stilled.

And behold the serpent was of their company. "Hail, wise and happy!" he whispered with flickering tongue.

But even as they gazed on him with horror and loathing in their eyes, they heard in the silence the sound of the Lord God walking in the Garden in the cool of the day, in the sweet fresh air that comes with evening. They were sore afraid, and hid themselves from his presence amongst the trees of the Garden. But even as they stood together, seeking in vain for refuge where none could be, there came the voice of the Lord calling to Adam.

"Adam, where art thou?"

And the sound of the voice that had been their life and joy stilled their hearts with terror. They came forth from out of their hiding-place, and Adam bowed his head, for he dared not look upon the Lord God.

He said: "I heard thy voice in the Garden, and I was afraid, because I was naked; and I hid myself."

And the Lord God said: "Who told thee that thou wast naked? Hast thou then eaten of the fruit of the Tree, whereof I commanded thee that thou shouldst not eat?"

Adam bowed his head yet lower, hiding his face, his eyes fixed upon the ground.

"The woman", he said, "whom thou thyself gavest to be with me, she gave me of the Tree, and I did eat."

And the Lord God said unto the woman: "What is this that thou hast done?"

And the woman said, weeping: "The serpent beguiled me—and I did eat."

Then said the Lord God to the serpent: "Because thou hast done this thing, thou art from henceforth accursed among all living things upon the earth. Upon thy belly shalt thou crawl, both thou and thy kind, and dust shalt thou eat all the days of thy life, and all that come after thee. And I will put enmity between thee and the woman, and between thy seed, and all that shall spring out of thee, and her seed. And it shall bruise and crush thee, and thou shalt lie in wait to bruise her heel."

The serpent, the all-subtle one, the sower of mischief, sorrow and malice, looked stonily upon the Lord God, hearing his doom, in evil cold and corrupt. And this Satan went forth from out of his presence, eternal foe of man, though in the loving-kindness of the Lord God there should arise one to defeat his evil and to redeem man's sin, and paradise shall be restored to him again.

When the serpent was gone his way, the Lord God said to the woman: "Because of this that thou hast done, thy griefs shall be many. In sorrow and anguish thou shalt bring forth children. Yet the desire of thine own nature shall bind thee to thy husband. In him shall be thy strength and refuge, and he shall rule over thee."

And unto Adam he said: "Because thou hast hearkened to the voice of thy wife, and hast eaten of the Tree of which I commanded thee, saying, 'Thou shalt not eat of it,' cursed shall be the ground for thy sake and by reason of thy sin. Thorns also and thistles shall it bring forth, and weeds shall cumber thy labour, and thou shalt eat the green herb that springs therefrom. But in toil and in weariness and in the sweat of thy brow shalt thou find thy bread all the days of thy life, until thou lay down thy body in death, and be turned again into the earth whence thou wast taken. For dust thou art and unto dust shalt thou return."

And Adam and Eve, smitten to the soul, fled away from the presence of the Lord God into the night, and returned

into the darkness of their hiding-place in the Garden.

The Lord God was grieved to the heart because of their sin and sorrow, and communing in his wisdom he said within himself: "Behold, this man is become like unto one that is divine, seeing that, though it is not for his own peace, he hath attained the knowledge of good and evil. And now it may be in pride and disobedience he may sin yet again, and put forth his hand and pluck of the fruit of the Tree of Life, and eat and live for ever in shame and grief."

Therefore did the Lord God, though he was never to leave them utterly alone or abandon them, determine to cast Adam and Eve forth from out of the Garden of Eden, and to exile them into a world that could be no more a paradise, and where there could be no peace except that which their love and desire of him could bring them, for solace of their bitter banishment.

In the darkness that is before dawn they awoke where they lay, but into the sorrow where sleep had found them. They arose, and behold, there stood in watch round about them Cherubim of heaven whose eyes were like flames in the light of their countenances, unendurable to their gaze.

Adam and Eve fled from before them, stricken with dread, cold with anguish, and came through chasms to where in the sea-like gold of the risen sun the river of Eden flowed out beyond the Garden, falling in foam with sound of thunder from height to height. And the vast circuit of the earth lay spread out beneath them where they stood, dense with enormous forests, parched with sand, chequered with ice-capped mountains, through whose valleys the four rivers rolled their waters, which are the four great rivers of the world.

Thither they went down out of Eden, and dared not rest, until, looking back, even the verges of the Garden that had been their joy and peace were hidden from them. And night fell, cold and dark, and they were alone.

And at the east of the paradise whence God had cast out Adam, he set Cherubim, angels of heaven, and in their hands were flaming swords, turned every way, to keep and guard the way of the Tree of Life.

# THE FLOOD

# The Flood

Centuries of time went by, and the generations of man continually increased on the earth. They scattered over wider and wider tracts of country, venturing on into regions until then strange and untrodden. There were some who lived a life of continual roving and wandering. They pitched their tents in the wild as fancy led. Others found good pastures and dwelt there, tilling the ground and gathering together flocks of sheep and herds of cattle. Yet others reared up cities, and walled them in and fortified them against their foes. And they set up kings over them, mighty in pride and soldiery and armed with weapons of war.

They learned, too, the skill of many handicrafts and how to work in metals. They fashioned instruments of music, for dancing and feasting.

They made wine out of the grape and were merry. And the daughters of men were fair as the morning. They walked in their beauty like barbaric queens, bedecked with fine raiment and jewels of gold and coloured gems.

In these days men lived to a great age, and amassed knowledge and discovered secret arts and became practised in magic, and were wise in their own eyes.

But though there was no end to the skill and invention and curiosity of their minds, the spirit of life within them languished as if in a prison-house, and was darkened. The knowledge of what is good and what evil was theirs. They were free to make choice between them. They chose evil and not good, and refused the Lord God their love and obedience.

Pitiless and defiant, wherever they went, greed and violence and cruelty went with them, and no man was safe. They not only did evil, but in heart and imagination hated and fought against the good. The memory of the paradise that had been made for man had become less than the substance of a dream. And when, in despair at the defeat of their wild desires, its vision returned to them, they mocked it down and reviled the very thought of it. Angels fallen from grace entered in upon the earth in those days, and there were tyrants and giants in the land, terrible and mighty. Human life had become a mockery and a snare, because of the vileness of the spirit within.

And the Lord God, looking down from the heavens upon the earth which he had created, once radiant with light and peace and innocence, and now a waste of sin and woe, repented him that he had given life to the dust. He was grieved to the heart that man, whom he had made in his own image and of his divine love, had fallen to a state so dark that even the hope and desire of goodness had perished in him. And the Lord God said: "I will do away man, whom I made out of nought, from the face of the earth, and all things that have life; for it repenteth me that I created them."

One alone of all men living found grace in his eyes. He was faithful and blameless. Loving goodness and hating evil, he had withdrawn himself from his fellowmen and lived apart from them; and the Lord God was with him in the silence and secrecy of his heart. The name of this man was Noah, and he had three sons, Shem, Ham and Japheth.

There came a day when the Lord God warned Noah that an end was soon to come to the evil that man had brought upon the earth, and that it should be cleansed of its wickedness and corruption. And he bade Noah build an ark, or ship, directing him in the knowledge and understanding of his mind how in all things it should be made. As the Lord God bade him, so did Noah. He chose out and felled cypress and pine for timber, and with his three sons laboured day by day, until night came down and they went to rest, to fashion and build the ark, though as yet they knew neither its use nor its purpose. In length this ark was to be three hundred cubits—a hundred and fifty human paces from end to end. In breadth it was to be fifty cubits; and in height thirty—of such a height, that is, that the topmost branches of an oak tree would show green above its roof.

When Noah and his sons, having hewn and planed their timber, had laid the central keel and buttressed it and built up the curved ribs of the ark and roofed it with beams, they walled it all in with planks of cypress round about, shaping and leaving in it a narrow window, which skirted the whole circuit of the margin of the roof that covered it in. A great door also was made for its entering-in in the side of the ark, which could be opened and shut at need.

When this had been done and the towering outer walls or shell of the ark were sound and secure in all their joints and angles, they daubed them over with melted pitch or bitumen to make it proof against the weather and to seal up all crevices and crannies there might be between its timbers, so that no water could enter in.

That done, they built up within the ark and beneath its roof, three separate floors or storeys, with cross-pieces and planks, the lowermost in the belly or underpart of the ark, the other midway above it, and the third beneath the long

[ 43 ]

narrow window that had been cut out within the space of eighteen inches from the margin of the roof. They left openings, too, or hatchways, at fitting intervals in each of the three floors or storeys, with a ladder to each by which those within the ark would be able to ascend and descend from one to the other.

These they then divided by walls into rooms or chambers of various shapes and sizes, convenient and proportionate, and all in accordance with the plan and design made by Noah. When these were complete with their doors and passage-ways, they daubed over the whole of the inside of the ark with pitch also.

For many months Noah and his three sons toiled on in the building of the ark, pausing only to eat and for rest and sleep. They chose out only the finest trees and perfect timber for their purpose and fashioned and finished their handiwork with all the skill they could.

But the day came at length when their work was at an end. The last wooden peg had been driven home, the last inch pitched, and all refuse had been cleansed away and removed. And lo! more gigantic in shape and bulk than any monster that had then its being in the depths of the oceans, their great ark, or ship—mastless and rudderless—lay ready. It was made, and in all things complete. Pitch-black and glistening in the splendour of the sun and high upon dry land it towered, in no way fine and delicate, but of immeasurable stoutness and stability, and strong to withstand not only the buffetings of wind and tempest, but to ride in safety upon waters wild as those of the sea.

They stood together in its shadow, looking up and surveying it, and they rejoiced at sight of it and at the thought that their anxious toil was over. That evening they feasted with their wives and their children, and gave thanks to the

Lord God; so that this day should always remain with them in mind and be held in solemn and happy remembrance.

When Noah and his three sons had finished the building of the ark, the word of the Lord God came again to Noah. He was warned that a great flood or deluge was soon to descend upon the earth, blotting out for ever in one swift death the evil and violence and cruelty of men without pity and without remorse.

But with Noah himself the Lord God made a covenant of peace. He promised him that he, with his wife and his sons and all his household, should be saved alive when that day of judgment should come. For this the ark had been made. Of all men living Noah alone had remained just and faithful.

As in the building of the ark, so in all things else that the Lord God bade him, Noah obeyed. And during the weeks that followed he himself and his three sons laboured without ceasing to prepare against the calamity that was soon to overwhelm the earth. For it was not only they themselves who were to find a place of refuge, but Noah had been bidden to assemble together two of every kind of living thing that was on the earth, beasts of the field and of the forest, birds of the air, and whatsoever around them enjoyed the breath of life.

To keep these creatures safe until the day when they should enter with them into the ark, Noah and his three sons made pens and folds, fencing them in so that no wild thing from without should enter, or captive within win free. They found caves also in the hills and rocks for beasts that are by nature wild and solitary in their habits, or secret and timid. When this was done, Noah's three sons went each his own way according as their father had directed them, to entice or snare or drive into the places prepared for them the living creatures they had in mind. From least to greatest they knew their ways and natures, and where to seek them, and how to tame and persuade them to submit themselves into their keeping, both the timorous and delicate and the fierce and strong.

So day by day and week by week they gathered together two of every kind of living thing that roved around them or dwelt beneath the blue of heaven in the sweet winds and rains and dews, throughout the region of valley, plain and mountain, lying in a wide circuit around the place wherein they had built the ark. Mate with mate they brought them in, and fed them and kept them secure and in good liking, lion and lioness, the fox and his vixen, horse and mare, bull and cow, ram and ewe, boar and sow, the wide-browed elephant and his mate, the gazelle and the hare, the coney of the sands, the antelope of the rocks, sheep and goat, the crafty cat, the gnawing rat, and the dark-delighting mouse. All these and countless others they assembled in the resorts that had been prepared for them, making ready for the day of the entering-in. The birds of the air, too, of every kind and feather, shape and song, from the eagle of noonday to the little wren—the gentle pelican, the blue-mooned peacock, the cuckoo and the thrush; all these and every living thing besides—where Noah and his sons had bestowed them, and in quarters best fitting for their ways and natures —awaited the day of the entering-in.

The ark was set in the midst, and busy continually was the whole household of Noah. Twilight descended; and they rested from their labours. The absent ones returned to the camp. The cries and callings of the four-footed creatures, and the birds' shrill sweet evensong ceased beneath the stars in the hush of the plain around them, where darkness enclosed them in. All was still.

And sleep enfolded them, renewing life and strength in

wayworn foot and weary limb. Only the nightingale poured on into the starry dark a song of delight, that yet seemed to echo with grief and exile.

Strangers sometimes came that way, men with their hunting-dogs—men of great stature and faced like the hawk; keen and ferocious. Noah greeted them with civility and offered them food and drink. But when he solemnly warned them of the horror and destruction that were soon to come upon the earth, they merely mocked at him. They surveyed with their hard bright eyes the great clumsy wooden ship that lay casting its vast shadow on the grass beside it in the light of the sun, then turned their heads and stared insolently into his face as if into that of a man without wits, or with a mind ridden by the haggard deceits of insanity.

They spurned his gifts, jeered at his warnings, and went their way, blinded in their folly even to the changes and strange appearances in the heavens and in the scene around them that were revealing themselves before their very eyes.

The weather darkened; winds wailing in the vacancy of space rose up and fell again. Vast flights of birds showed themselves in the skies of daybreak and sunset. There came a restlessness and fearfulness among the wild things of the earth. They were seen prowling in places where they had never ventured before, drawing near to the dwellings of man as if for refuge, and driven away with blows and curses. The radiance even of noonday became sad and sickly, though but little cloud was to be discerned in the firmament. In the midst of night strange lamentations, as if from bodily wanderers, broke the stillness. The pitch-black ark, its timbered roof glistening in the wan light, lay heavily on ground cracked in all directions in the windy heat of the day, for the earth was stark with drought, and the great door in its side gaped wide.

And the word of the Lord God came to Noah, bidding him go into the ark and take into it all the living creatures that were to be saved alive from destruction. So Noah and his three sons made a bridge of timber of a strength that would bear the tread of the mightiest beasts then on earth. This they laid between the door of the ark and firm ground; then each according to its kind, every living creature which they had in keeping and readiness for this day was brought into the ark, and there tethered or chambered in the places set apart for them. Two by two, and mate with mate they brought them in.

The greatest beasts and those whose habit it was to rove by night and sleep by day were given their places in the lowermost storey of the ark, beneath its undermost deck. The shy and delicate were cribbed where the light could shine in on them from the window. To each was its own particular place set apart in the pens and chambers within the hive-like confines of the ark. So too with the winged things, and with the scaled. Behemoth was there, and there, too, the mouse. All things that lived and moved, and had their being on the earth around them, found refuge there. They entered in from the sunlit plain into the gloom of the great ship. They entered into it, as though into a haven, from ills of which they had some faint forewarning, and none languished or pined or fell away in spirit or refused to eat.

Moreover, in the bins and chests and baskets which had been made ready and stood all in order and in place where they would be needed, Noah and his sons had laid up an abundant store of grain and hay and fodder and seed. Of all herbs and plants too, that would retain their virtue and nourishment for many days to come. These were for the food and sustenance of the beasts and the birds and the creeping things.

They hastened now to finish their preparations, for warnings abounded that the dreadful hour drew near. In the midst of his labours one or other of them would hastily lift his eyes to scan the heavens, so grievous were the signs which now showed themselves there and on the earth beneath. And they redoubled their efforts for fear that anything should be left unready and undone.

As for the least of the little things that haunt the air and solitudes and crevices of the earth, they seemed of their own wisdom to have already set up their habitations in the ark. The queen bee and her myriad workers made their cluster there; and the wise ant her nest. Butterflies on their painted wings floated out of the sunbeams into the dusk within, and of the lesser birds some had even built their nests on the ledge that ran beneath the long narrow window made for the coming-in of the light under the ark's dark roof.

When all the animals and birds, the reptiles and creeping things were safely within the ark, then Noah gathered his family together, his wife, his three sons, Shem, Ham and Japheth, and their wives, and their children. The last wild yellow light of evening dyed the heavens when in awe and dread they went up into the ark. And to each was given a sleeping-place in the great inner chamber wherein they were to spend the days that were to come. And when they had one and all crossed over into the ark, the bridge of timber was flung to earth, and the massive door turned upon its staples and was shut.

A cold trumpeting wind had begun to blow, lifting into the air dense clouds of sand and dust. It increased hour by hour, until nothing could be heard from within the ark but the sound of it streaming across the high rounded roof and wailing in every nook and cranny. Lightnings wild and luminous flared in the skies, but at first without sound of thunder. And when the tempest of wind began to lull, there fell the first few drops of rain.

The rain increased in volume until it seemed to those safe in the shelter of the ark as if sky and earth had mingled together in a dreadful confusion. The wells and fountains of the deep were broken, the rock-bound water-courses foundered, and the windows of heaven were opened. The deluge descended upon the ridged roof of the ark in a steady sullen roar and surged against its sides. Hour followed hour and even the huge wooden walls of the great ship trembled beneath the cataracts of the rain. And soon from its long window nought was visible but a world lost in water and lit by lightnings. And at length the ark that till then had lain upon the earth as if no force could so much as stir its enormous keel, was lifted as if by a gentle but mighty hand, swayed, came to rest again, heaved upward, and at length floated upon the waters.

When Noah and his three sons had gone their way to and fro in every part of the great ship, carrying with them the lamps they had moulded out of clay and filled with oil and a wick, and examined it in every part and returned together and reported nothing amiss, they gave thanks to God for their salvation.

And darkness, furious, awful and distraught, drew over the flooded plain, whose encircling mountains were already veiled from view with the wrack and cloud of tempest. Shrill outcries and lamentations were borne faintly in on the blast of the winds, but at last died down and were heard no more, unless from very far away. And the children were laid to rest in the sleeping-places prepared for them.

But during that first night little sleep visited those who watched over them. There were stirrings and sighings and snortings as the beasts they had in charge snuffed the frag-

rance of the waters of the deluge and were disquieted by the din and tumult. They shared a narrow solitude in that chaos of water.

But as the days went by there came peace and tranquillity within the ark, and at length the humans within it grew so accustomed to the endless gushings of the rain upon roof and walls, that they were no longer troubled or dismayed, and the sound of it at last became almost unheeded.

Buoyant yet stable upon the face of the deluge, the ark floated beneath the louring skies whithersoever wind and water led, in a mist so dense no eye could discern where cloud and water met. But those within its walls, and in the safety of God, went about their daily tasks, portioning out the grain and fodder they had stored up within it, and tending the living things they had in their charge, in trust and confidence that they would be delivered at last from the danger and desolation that beset them.

For forty days and forty nights the rains continued without pause or abatement, and so obscure were the skies, that the light of dawn was hardly to be discerned when it began, or the oncoming of darkness when nightfall descended upon the deep.

The hours of sleep were divided into watches, Noah's three sons taking each his turn, so that nothing should go amiss and remain undiscovered, for each made his rounds according to the time set for him, passing from one storey to another and ensuring that all was secure.

There came a day at last when the roar of the deluge began to diminish, and the wind to fall to calm. And the fountains of the deep were sealed, and the rain from heaven was restrained.

There was now quiet on high above the earth. But a deep gloom still prevailed within the ark because of the prodigious canopy of cloud that obscured the whole firmament. All sounds, except the stir and callings within the wooden walls of the ark, were now hushed. And though there was movement in the clouds above, amid a vast sea of light where their fleeces were smitten to silver by the sun, nothing of this could be perceived from the window of the ark. Until one morning in his watch before dawn Shem stood peering out alone across the tumultuous waste of waters. And lo, as he looked he descried afar off a faint yet dazzling strip of silver between earth and heaven on the margin of the deep. His heart leapt within him, for he knew that it was the radiance of the rising of the sun, and that he was looking towards the quarter of the horizon which is the east.

He ran at once with these glad tidings to Noah, and they

awakened Ham and Japheth and their mother and their wives and their children, and all rose up hastily and gathered together at the window and gazed out, their minds filled with a joy beyond all words, their eyes exulting in this first gleam of the veiled radiance of the clouded sun. There they knelt and prayed together, and gave thanks to the Lord God.

Hour by hour the light increased, and the bitter surges of the deluge sank to rest, until at last even the blue of heaven began to show. But all around the ark, as far as sight could reach, there stretched a sea of water, green and placid, though blackened here and there with ghastly wreckage. It sparkled in the sunbeams, so that human eyes unaccustomed to the glare were almost blinded as they watched. And ever and again the mighty mastless vessel heaved on the slow swell that moved across the deep, rose, and dipped again. The ocean of waters seemed to be lulling itself to sleep with long-drawn sighs.

Moreover, not only the light but the heat of the sun now began to steal its way into the confines of the ark. Through a crevice of the window the bees found out an egress and sipped the dew on the roof and the nectar of the few blossoming weeds that had found harbourage there. The birds preened their wings and broke into merry wild-hearted song, whose voices for many days had been still and mute. Their sweet-billed notes rang shrill in the stealing sunshine.

From storey to storey, pen to pen, and chamber to chamber of the ark, the beasts called the joyous news from one to the other, for happy life began to stir again within them; and the desire for freedom, for the woods and pastures, valley and mountain, to move in their blood.

But though to all seeming the rains were now over and gone, no sign of land was anywhere detectable above the waters, nor even, as far as could be discerned, through the mists that veiled the horizon, did any mountain peak as yet uprear its crags. Yet morning, noon and evening the waters which had prevailed upon the earth continued to abate.

And the Lord God remembered Noah, and those who were with him in the ark. He caused a warm and gentle wind to pass over the earth, enveloping the waters. They diminished continually until at length and in all surety there showed afar off a mountain-crest jutting out above the flood into the sapphire skies, as if fashioned of crystal and alabaster.

Then Noah, considering within himself, chose from among the birds in his keeping a raven, and opening the window of the ark, he loosed it out of his hand. With one clap of its wild wings it darted out into freedom, and in the twinkling of an eye both the bird and its image reflected on the glass of the waters had fled away and vanished out of sight, never to return. For it found food in such abundance on which to glut itself in the wreckage of the flood, that it came back to the ark no more.

Noah waited for seven days, then took a dove and released her from the window of the ark. But the dove, that is a tender bird, found no rest for the sole of her foot where she could be content, for still the waters of the deluge covered the face of the earth, and she returned to the ark and fluttered at the window. So Noah put out his hand and drew the dove back into the safety of the ark.

He waited yet another seven days, then set her free again, and behold, as they stood watching at even-fall, she came again to the window of the ark, her snowy breast and plumage dyed with the rose of sunset, her round eyes gleaming. There she alighted; but now she brought with her in her bill a tender young olive leaf that she had plucked off

from its stem, and Noah knew that the waters were indeed
abated and assuaged from the earth.

And when he sent her forth again, she too returned to
him no more.

The ark rested at last in the hollow between the peaks of
Ararat, the high mountains of Armenia, and Noah and his
sons removed its timber roof from off it, and they looked
down upon dry ground. And the Lord God bade Noah
come forth from out of the ark, himself and his wife, his
sons and their wives and children.

"Bring out with thee", said the Lord God, "every living thing that is with thee in the ark, beast and bird and creeping thing, that they may be fruitful upon the earth and multiply."

Then the sons of Noah took of the timber which they had stripped from the ark and made a bridge of wood, and they thrust open the great door and let down their wooden bridge. And Noah with all his household went forth out of the ark under the blue of heaven in the burning sunshine upon the earth again, now wondrously flourishing in the sweet airs of the morning. They lifted their pale faces and breathed deep, and they walked together upon the solid earth; and the cries of the children resounded with delight, echoing against the weed-bearded sides of their great weather-worn ship.

That morning was spent in setting free the host of living things, all in order and each according to its kind, which had shared with them the safety of the ark and which they had fed and tended throughout the days of the flood.

Rejoiced they were to snuff the sweet free air of morning, and a mellay of cries and challengings rose from their throats, as they leapt and fawned and gambolled, shaking their shaggy coats, preening and sleeking themselves and marvelling in the sunlight. It was as if for the time being the peace of Eden had come upon the earth again, for during the many days of their dwelling within the ark they had become at peace one with another and with those who watched over them, and the enmity which the wickedness and cruelty of man had brought upon the earth had lost its sharpness, and for a while fears and doubts of him were stilled.

Then Noah built an altar to the Lord God and made sacrifice to him. And the Lord God blessed Noah and his sons and gave them the earth for their possession, and the lordship over all living things upon it for their use and care. He bade Noah and his sons go out into the world with their wives and children and seek each his own dwelling, so that their children's children should increase upon the earth and live at peace one with another, praising him who had given them life.

And as Noah and his household worshipped before the Lord, a faint mist, high in the noonday firmament, shaped itself across the blue as if it were a veil between heaven and earth, and the rays of the sun smote on the mist, and a great bow of broken light, burning with all the radiant colours that show upon the earth and in the waters and that are reflected in every living thing, flower and insect, beast and plumed bird, spanned the peaks of Ararat, where Noah and his household were gathered together with their possessions about the empty ark. It arched the green world over; and the light of day smote fair upon their upturned faces.

And the Lord God said to Noah: "Behold, I have set my bow in the clouds, and it shall be a token of an everlasting covenant between me and thee and all that come after thee, that never more shall there be a flood to destroy the earth where the life that I have created hath its dwelling. But after the rain shall shine the sun, and this bow that I have set in heaven shall be a sign of the covenant between the Lord God and his living creatures upon the earth, for evermore."

# JOSEPH

# His Dream

After the death of his father Isaac, Jacob, with his whole household, his sons, his servants, his flocks and herds and sheep-dogs, came to sojourn in the green and wooded vale of Hebron which is in Canaan. Here they pitched their tents, and led their flocks afield, for Hebron lies in a country rich in pastures and in clear well-springs of water.

Now of all his eleven sons Jacob loved Joseph the best. Until Benjamin was born, he was the youngest of them all, and he was too the only son of his beautiful mother Rachel, who was very dear to Jacob. Not only for this reason but for the child's own sake also, Joseph was Jacob's best-beloved; and, with no thought of any ill that might come of it, he favoured him in all things, delighted to talk to him, and he gave him many presents.

He made him also a loose tunic coat of many colours, sewn together in delicate needlework in a bright pattern, and with sleeves to the wrists. And Joseph, being in age still little more than a child, delighted in his bright-coloured coat. But when his brothers saw it, they envied and hated him. For in this his father had yet again shown his great love for Joseph and had favoured him above themselves, and they could not speak a friendly or peaceable word to him.

As Joseph grew older, and in all that he was and did showed himself more and more unlike themselves, jealousy gnawed in their hearts like the fretting of a canker-worm. Above everything, they scorned, and even began to fear him, because of his dreams. They too, as they lay with their flocks, wrapped in their goat-skin cloaks beneath the dews and burning stars of the night, had their dreams; but these either vanished on waking or were broken and senseless. But the dreams that came to Joseph in his sleep were not only of a strange reality, but seemed to carry with them a hidden meaning. They were like the crystal shimmering pictures of the air, called *mirage*, seen by wanderers in the desert, the reflections of things afar off—but far off in time not in space.

One late summer evening when he chanced to be with them in the fields, and sat a little apart from them, lost to all around him in the light of the moon—a moon so dazzling clear that even the colours of his coat were faintly distinguishable—they asked him sourly what ailed him.

"He sits out there", said one of them, "mumbling his thoughts like an old sheep too sick to graze." Joseph answered that he had been haunted all day by the memory of a dream. He was but a boy and he told his dream out to them, thinking no evil.

"I dreamed", he said, "it was the time of harvest, and we were reaping together in the fields. It was sunrise, and the corn being cut, we were tying it up into sheaves. Even now I seem to feel the roughness of the binder in my hand, though the place we were in was none I have ever seen in waking. I tied up my sheaf and laid it down, as you did your sheaves. And in my dream the sheaf that I had bound rose up as if of its own motion from the stubble and stood up there in the burning sunshine, and your own sheaves, that lay scattered around it, rose up also. And as I looked, they bowed themselves and made obeisance to my sheaf that was in the midst of them. Now what can be the meaning of such a dream, and why does it stay so continually in my mind?"

His brothers tried in vain to hide their anger.

"Meaning, forsooth!" they said. "Who art thou that we should bow ourselves down before thee, and that thou shouldst have dominion over us? The place for thee is with the women and sucklings in the tents." And they hated him the more.

Joseph was silent and made no answer, but the dream in its strangeness and beauty stayed on in his mind. He knew it must surely have a meaning, if only he could discover it; and when he dreamed again, he told his dream not only to his brothers, but to his father.

"I dreamed," he said, and his face was lit up at memory of it, "and, behold, in my dream it was the dead of night, yet the sun was in the heavens and the moon also. They shone there together, and I could see the stars. There was no wind, and all was still; and I counted the brightest stars, and they were eleven. And as I looked and wondered, it seemed that not only these eleven stars, but the sun and the moon stooped and bowed in their places in heaven before me and made obeisance. Then I awoke."

His brothers listened with louring faces, glancing covertly one at another, but Jacob his father rebuked him.

"Cast such crazy fancies out of thy mind," he said. "And God forbid that it should be even so much as in thy dreams that I and thy mother and thy brethren should come to bow ourselves down before thee and be humbled before thee!" None the less, the dream disquieted him, and there came a day when he remembered it again.

It chanced one evening after this, and when Joseph had passed his seventeenth birthday, that his father called him into his tent. He bade him set out on the morrow and go in search of his brothers, who had led their sheep to new pastures beyond the vale of Hebron, and not far distant from a town called Shechem.

"Go thy way early and seek them out," he said, "for they are among strangers and enemies. Ask them how they fare, and see thyself if it be well with them and with the flocks; and when you have rested, bring me word of them again. And may the Lord watch over you!"

Proud and happy in the trust his father put in him, Joseph rose up at daybreak next morning, kissed him, bade him good-bye, and set out at once. The day was calm and fair. It was springtime, the air was sweet with birds, and on the wayside and in the hollows of the hills hosts of wild flowers shone in their colours in the sun, crocus and anemone and narcissus. And as he went on his way, no omen chilled his heart of what was in store for him, and no foreboding that every step he took was towards a strange country from which in this life he would return home again no more.

He came at length to Shechem, an old walled and beautiful city of Samaria that with its gardens lay in a valley between two mountains, and rang with the music of more than a score of water-springs. But his brothers were no longer there, and loth to return to his father without news of them, he pressed on into country unknown to him, and lost his way.

A stranger met him as he was wandering at random in the wild. He saw how young he was, and that in spite of being anxious and footsore he still held on his way, so he hailed him and inquired whom he was seeking.

"It is my brothers," he said. "They are shepherds, but have gone on from Shechem where I looked to find them, and now I have lost my way. Tell me, I pray thee, what place is this and where it is likely they have gone?"

It chanced that this man had not only seen the shepherds but had overheard them in talk one with another, and he told Joseph they were now in all likelihood with their flocks near Dothan.

"It lies", he said, "on a hillside above its vineyards where there is a plentiful well of water." And he told him how he would find it. He repeated what he had said, "Follow on as I have told thee, and thou canst not miss the way."

He turned and watched until Joseph was out of sight. And Joseph hastened on eagerly, all weariness forgotten. Now on the northern side of Dothan there were hills, their slopes shagged with grey-green groves of olives, but on the side towards the south, it was flat country, so that his brothers, who were sitting there with their flocks and staring idly out across the grassy plain, spied out Joseph while he was still afar off. And they muttered morosely one to another: "Behold, the dreamer cometh!"

As they watched him making his way towards them in a coat of many colours, the hatred that had long smouldered in their hearts broke into flame, and some of them began devising together to murder him.

"He is alone and at our mercy," they said. "And here there is none to heed his cries or tell the tale. Let us kill him, then, and hide his body where it will never be found. Then we can go back with a tale that a wild beast must have attacked and devoured him. And who shall deny it?"

But Reuben, the eldest, overheard them muttering together. "No, no; shed no blood," he said. "If you must be rid of him, take him alive and fling him into that pit yonder. But use no violence, or let any harm come to him."

This he said because he himself intended, when the opportunity came, to set Joseph free, and to bring him back in safety again to his father. The rest of them argued and wrangled, some on this side and some on that, but at length they agreed together not to kill him. When Reuben was sure of it, and that no harm would come to Joseph until he could come back and take him into a place of safety, he left them and went away alone.

Joseph drew near, rejoiced to be at the end of his long journey and to see his brethren sitting in peace together with their flocks. But before he could so much as give them greeting or tell them why he had come, they seized him, stifled his cries, stripped off his coat of many colours, and bound him hand and foot. They carried him off to a deep dried-up pit or water-cistern. Into this pit they flung him down, and having dragged back the heavy stone again that

had lain over the mouth of the pit, they left him there, returned to their camping-place, and sat down to eat.

While they were eating together, some jesting and others silent and uneasy, they heard in the distance shouts and voices borne on the windless air over the flat country. They lifted up their eyes and saw afar off a company of Ishmaelites, merchantmen, with their camels. These fierce swarthy tribesmen were journeying from Gilead which lay beyond the Jordan, a region famed for its balsam and groves of tree laurel, musical with the murmur of wood-doves and songs of birds. They were following the track of the great caravans that would bring them to the sand-dunes on the coast of the Great Sea, and then, on, and at length into Egypt. Their camels, neckleted with chains of metal, their links shaped like the crescent moon, were laden with sweet-smelling spiceries and fragrant gums which they had brought with them to barter or sell to the Egyptian em-balmers and physicians.

When Judah, who had sat silent and aloof, saw these men with camels, he said to his brethren: "See now, here is a way out. If we leave the lad in the pit, he will perish of thirst and we shall be no less guilty of his death than if we had killed him with our own hands. Let us hail these ac-cursed Ishmaelites, and sell him for what he will fetch. That way we shall see some profit in what we do, and we shall be for ever rid of him and his dreams. But not death, I say—for is he not our brother, the son of our father, and of our own flesh and blood?"

To this, though sullenly, they agreed. It was near sunset when, dragging away the heavy well-stone again, his brothers drew Joseph up out of the pit and freed him from the thongs with which they had bound him. He stood half-naked and trembling, faint with the heat of the pit. The sun smote blindingly on his eyes after the pitchy darkness in which he had lain—beaten and bruised and unable to stir hand or foot. He watched, while his brothers bargained with the crafty dark-browed Ishmaelites. They agreed at last to sell him to them for twenty pieces of silver, and divided the money between them. This done, the Ish-maelites knotted the cord that still shackled Joseph's wrists to the saddle of one of their camels, and continued on their way.

When Reuben came back at nightfall to the pit, called, and found it empty, he was smitten with remorse. He rent his clothes—as was the custom with these wandering tribesmen when to their anguish any great grief or disaster befell them—and he returned in despair to the camping-place. There he found his brethren and their flocks, hedged about with branches of thorn as a protection against wild animals.

"The lad is gone," he said, "and I, whither now shall *I* go?" But some of them pretended to be asleep, and none made answer.

Next day they killed a kid and dabbled Joseph's coat in its blood, then turned homewards with their flocks, and came at length to their own place and to their father's tent, and, with the pretence of grief on their faces, stood before him. His first thought was for Joseph, but he looked in vain for him.

Jacob questioned them anxiously. And when he told them how Joseph had been sent out to seek them in the valley of Shechem, they stared one at another, as though in horror and dismay. Then one of them named Simeon took out the torn and blood-bedabbled coat and spread it out before him.

"We knew nothing of what thou sayest until now," he said. "But on our way back from Dothan where we lay, we passed by a thicket of thorn trees in a wild and solitary place, and we found this. It is so bedraggled and drenched with blood that we cannot be sure if it be the coat you gave Joseph. See now, is this thy son's coat, or no?"

Jacob looked and trembled and turned away. "It is my son's coat," he said. "My son, Joseph! An evil beast hath devoured him; Joseph is without doubt rent in pieces. I shall never see his face again!"

He bowed himself in his grief and wept. He rent his clothes, and put on sackcloth like one who goes in mourning for the dead, and withdrew himself from them all, and remained in solitude for many days. His daughters and his sons, grown sick of their own treachery, came to him in hope to comfort him, but he refused to be comforted.

"Beyond the grave," he said, "but not until then, we two shall meet again. And my son Joseph will see how I have mourned for him." And he continued to grieve for Joseph, so great was the love he bore him. Only in Benjamin, who was his youngest son, did Jacob find solace as time went by. He loved and treasured him not only for his own sake but because, now that Joseph was gone, he was the only child left of his mother Rachel, for she had died when he was born.

# In Prison

After many days' journey, in scorching sun by day and starry cold by night, the Ishmaelitish merchantmen, with their camels and spices and other merchandise, came down into Egypt. There all that Joseph saw was new and strange to him. They made their way into the chief city of Egypt and pushed on through the babel of its thronged and narrow streets into the marketplace. Here they unladed their camels. On the morrow they took Joseph into the slave-market, where captives from all countries that bordered the land of Egypt were bought and sold. And Joseph himself was bought by an Egyptian whose name was Potiphar, a man of wealth and one of the king's high officers.

At first sight of his keen open face, though it was now haggard with pain and sleeplessness, Potiphar judged well of Joseph. Unlike most of his slaves, Joseph was not sent to labour in the fields and vineyards under a taskmaster, but was taken into Potiphar's house and became his personal servant.

And the Lord was with Joseph; he kept him in all perils. Whatever Joseph did, he did well. He prospered in the house of his master, the Egyptian. And seeing that in all things he was upright and faithful, Potiphar as the years went by gave Joseph more and more authority in his household, and at last made him steward or overseer over his servants and his slaves, not only those who were within the house, but also over his gardeners and the tenders of his orchards and vineyards. So entire was his trust in Joseph that he had no cares or anxieties apart from his office under Pharaoh the king, and knew nothing of what passed in his household except only what he himself had to eat and drink. In all that Joseph did, he was answerable to Potiphar alone.

Yet in age Joseph was still but a young man. He was of a natural courtesy, and he had an open and beautiful countenance. And Potiphar's wife, who had often cast her eyes on him as he went about his business in the house, began to lie in wait for him and to pine for his company. She was a woman false and vain, and by all the deceits she knew she strove to beguile him, and at last spoke openly of her love. But he hated her, mind and body, and refused to listen.

"I entreat thee", he said, "say no more. My lord has shown me many kindnesses. He has made me chief of all his servants, and so complete is his trust in me that when at evening he returns home, he does not even question me on what has passed in the house during his absence. Everything and everyone in it has been given into my charge except only thee thyself; for thou art his wife. How vile a thing would it be, then, if I were to deceive him and sin against God."

Day followed day, and still the Egyptian's wife continued to pester him, until there came a morning when, they being alone together, lovesick and shameless, she once more besought him. He turned from her with loathing, and fled out of the house. And she knew at last that her deceits were in vain. Her love, never else than false, corrupted instantly into bitter hatred. And having proof that Joseph had been in her company, she set about to revenge herself against him.

She summoned the other chief servants of the household

and lied to them. "See now," she said, "this vile Hebrew whom my lord bought from the slave-traders and set up over you all! Why, he makes mock and insult even of me, the wife of his master. There is nothing safe from him."

That night when her husband was with her she lyingly accused Joseph, and this she did so guilefully, weeping, and as though in shame of having to confess what would anger and trouble him, that Potiphar believed her every word. He was beside himself with rage. He summoned his slaves and bade that Joseph should be bound and instantly cast into prison—the prison where offenders against King Pharaoh himself were kept in captivity. And Potiphar thought of him no more.

There Joseph lay, in a foul dungeon, and was set to such pitiless labour that when night came and the day was done, he was thankful to fling himself down in the darkness and forget his miseries in sleep. Yet in spite of all the hardships that he shared with the rest of the prisoners—driven and beaten and half-starved—he never gave up hope or lost courage. And the Lord was with Joseph in the prison. As time went on, his mere presence there became a solace to the wretchedness of those who languished with him, and the guards or warders spoke well of him, eased his labour and freed him of his fetters.

It thus came about that the governor of the prison having heard nothing but good of Joseph, began himself to show him favour. He discovered that this young Hebrew was not only a man whom he could trust in word and in deed, but that he was of a rare sagacity of mind, wise in counsel, swift in decision, and fearless in acting as he deemed right. At length he set Joseph next in authority under himself, and gave not only his chief captives into his charge but even the control of the prison.

Years passed by, and though Joseph was now no longer wretched in body, and had many things to busy his mind, the freedom he longed for seemed as far away as Canaan itself. Yet he did not repine; nor did he ever despair of his release at last. Whatever the days or the years might bring, he trusted in the Lord, and in that trust his mind was at peace.

Now there came a day when the chief butler and the chief baker of Pharaoh the King of Egypt—the one his cupbearer or high chamberlain and the other his steward—offended against their lord, the king. So hot was his wrath against them that he not only banished them from his presence, but commanded that they should be given into the charge of the governor of the prison, who was captain of the guard, until he himself had considered what punishment they merited.

These two, the chief butler and the chief baker, were men of high standing in the court of Pharaoh. Wherefore the governor of the prison bade Joseph himself attend on them, instructing him to show them the courtesies due to their rank and office, but none the less to be vigilant that they did not escape. Morning and evening Joseph waited upon them, and they found such solace in his company, and came so much to trust in his discretion that they would talk freely with him and confide in him their hopes and fears.

The days of their confinement in the prison had continued for many months when on one and the same night these two, the chief butler and the chief baker, dreamed each of them a dream, then awoke and dreamed no more. Even when daylight was come they could not rid their minds of what had troubled their sleep. And as they sat together in the room that had been set apart for them in the prison-house, they told one another their dreams. They were deeply troubled and perplexed, for their dreams were of a kind that seem to be haunted with a hidden meaning, yet neither of them could discover it or expound it the one to the other.

So it was that when Joseph came in to them in the morning, and greeted them, their voices were low and spiritless, and their faces dejected as if they had some burden on their minds. And though there were few in the prison under him who were never wretched and in despair, he did his utmost to enhearten all he could, not only because this was natural to him, but because he himself was in not much better case than they.

At last, looking upon these two as friend to friend, he questioned them. "Why", he said, "are your faces downcast, and why do you look so sadly this morning?"

The chief butler answered: "This night that is gone we have each of us dreamed a dream. Dreams closely resembling one another that have haunted our minds ever since, yet such we can neither understand nor forget. Were we free men, we could consult some diviner of dreams who would declare them to us and make them clear. But in this prison-house where shall we find anyone who has the least knowledge of the matter?"

"The divination of dreams", said Joseph, "is with God. I too have been a dreamer. Tell me your dreams, I might help you. It grieves me to see you so sad."

Then first the chief butler told Joseph his dream. It was in this wise. "I dreamed", he said, "I saw a vine, greener in its freshness to the sight than any vine my waking eyes have ever beheld. This vine had three branches, and little by little yet all in an instant and even as I watched, they broke into buds which themselves unfolded into blossom, and these having dropped their petals became clusters of green grapes that ripened and swelled before my very eyes. All in a moment the vine that had been winter-bare was heavy with fruit. And behold, the cup of the king, of King Pharaoh, was in my hand, though till then I knew it not. And I plucked a cluster of the grapes and pressed its juices into the cup, and it was wine; and I hastened in from the vineyard into the palace and gave the cup into Pharaoh's hand. Then I awoke, and could sleep no more."

Joseph listened. So intent was he on the words as they were spoken that he himself seemed to be lost in dream; and when the chief butler had fallen silent, and sat eagerly watching his face as he stood before them, he made answer like one deep in reverie.

"This", he said, "is the meaning and interpretation of thy dream. The vine thou sawest was the vine of Time, and the three branches upon it were three days which in life as we live it may come and go like shadows upon water, but which in thy dream budded, flowered, and bore clusters of ripe refreshing grapes all in a moment, and so—to Pharaoh the King. Be no more sad or downcast, but take comfort, for in three days thy troubles shall be over. Pharaoh will remember thee, and will show thee grace and restore thee into his favour, and thou shalt be his cupbearer and minister to him as of old. And oh!" he added, "when it is well with thee, I beseech thee of thy kindness remember me, and make mention of me to Pharaoh, and, if it may be, bring me out of this prison. Canaan is my country; I was sold into slavery when I was but a boy, and snatched away by force from the tents and pastures where I lived as a child, and from a father who loved me. And I have done nothing here that they should have cast me into a dungeon."

The chief butler, in the fullness of his heart, gladly promised Joseph all that he asked of him.

Meanwhile the chief baker had sat intently listening to all that had passed, his eyes in his narrow, hawk-like face fixed upon Joseph. And when he knew that there was nothing but good and fair in the chief butler's dreams, he at once related his own.

"This was my dream," he said. "I was walking—and no one by—in the open under the heavens, and there were three baskets upon my head, one on the top of the other. And I knew—though how I cannot tell—that in the uppermost of the three baskets were fine wheaten loaves of my own making for the king's table, and for the lords of his household. And this was a strange thing, for I am, you must

[ 77 ]

know, by nature exceedingly careful of what is in my charge, and though the loaves were for the table of my lord the uppermost basket was uncovered. Now as I walked, the skies overhead became laden, overcast and dark. Wherefore I went on in haste to do my office, but the birds of the air, spying out these dainties, swooped down in a ravenous fluttering cloud over my head and I was powerless to scare them away. As I say, they came down upon me in a host, scrabbling upon the basket, and devoured everything that was in it. Now tell me, seeing that all is well, why were the heavens above me dark, and why was my topmost basket uncovered?"

On hearing this, Joseph turned away his head in distress and made no answer. The face of the chief baker wanned, but he pressed Joseph to speak; and Joseph was at last persuaded.

"May it be forgiven me," he said, "but this, alas! is the meaning of thy dream. As with the vine and its three branches, so the three baskets on thy head were a symbol of three days. In three days from this, Pharaoh the King will hale thee too out of this prison-house. But not for good. He has discovered some evil, and in his wrath he will hang thee on a tree, and the birds of the air shall eat thy flesh from off thy bones."

All came about as Joseph had foretold. On the third day after, Pharaoh made a feast to all his household, for it was his birthday; and his high officers and the lords and governors of his provinces were bidden to the feast, and there were rejoicings throughout Egypt.

As was his custom, Pharaoh commemorated his birthday by recalling to mind those of his officers and servants who had offended against him. To some he granted amnesty and pardon, and forgave them. And among these was his chief butler. He was recalled into favour and, as in former times, waited upon his lord the king as his cupbearer when he sat at meat.

As for the chief baker, Pharaoh's anger was hard against him, for much was revealed that had been hidden. He too was set free from prison, but to be hanged upon a gibbet. And the birds of the air stripped his bones of their flesh, and another man was appointed in his stead. So all things came to pass as Joseph had divined and foretold. Yet did not the chief butler remember Joseph, but forgot him.

Seeing at length that no help was to come from him, Joseph cast out of memory the longing that had sprung up in his heart that day, like a gourd after rain, and for the two years that followed continued to go about his duties as he was accustomed to in the prison-house.

# He Divines Pharaoh's Dream

B
ut there came a day when Pharaoh the king himself dreamed a dream, and was profoundly troubled in spirit.

It seemed he stood beside a river, and there came up out of its waters seven kine or cows, which fed together at the river's brink. And as his eyes watched them in his dream, they were followed by another seven kine, different in shape and appearance, which, browsing nearer, suddenly fell upon and devoured the seven that he had first seen. And he awoke.

When at length the drowsiness of sleep stole over his senses, he dreamed again. He saw, as it were, flourishing upon one stalk or stem seven full ears of corn. But as he looked and wondered, there sprouted out on the same stem another seven, black and mildewed, which so utterly defaced and destroyed the full ears that nothing of them remained. Again he awoke, shaken and cold with dismay.

Sleep returned to him no more that night. He lay weary and restless, pondering on the two dreams, which unfolded themselves again and again before his waking eyes as vividly as in sleep. But however intently he considered them and compared them one with another, he could draw out of them no semblance of a meaning for the reality of day. Yet he was assured in his heart that these dreams were no mere idle shows of the night, but had been sent to warn him, and held a meaning as yet hidden from him.

Even when the fair beams of morning lit up his great chamber windows and the day had begun, his mind was no less disquieted and dark with foreboding. So he summoned his diviners and magicians—men who were wise in the interpretation of dreams and of omens. With heads shaven, and in their white mantles, they came into his presence, made obeisance, chaunted his praises, and stood awaiting his pleasure.

But when he had told them his dreams, they were one and all at a loss to expound them. And though they debated long together, and each of them did his utmost by every means of magic and sorcery that he knew to discover a meaning, there was none of his diviners that satisfied Pharaoh or in whom he could put his trust. He dismissed them from his presence with displeasure. And when the chief butler, who was waiting upon him, saw in what disquietude of mind the king was, and how even the most cunning of his soothsayers had been unable to interpret his dreams, there sprang up in his mind remembrance of the long heavy weeks that he had shared in captivity in the prison-house with the chief baker, now long dead, and how their cares had ended.

That evening, as Pharaoh sat at table, he asked leave to speak to the king. "Thy servant", he said, "hath this day been reminded of the past and of a promise that he made but that until now he has failed to keep; for which he is greatly to blame. Pharaoh may of his grace remember that some time ago he was offended with his servant, and also with his servant who was at that time the chief baker in Pharaoh's palace. And we were both of us put under ward of the governor of the prison, both myself and the chief baker. One night—after many weary days of banishment from Pharaoh's presence—we dreamed a dream, both I myself and he, and were greatly troubled. For our dreams seemed to have some meaning, though we knew not what it was. Next morning we told one another our dreams, which were much of a likeness one with the other, and we were sorely perplexed by them. And there came in, as was usual, a young man, a Hebrew, the servant of the governor of the prison, who waited upon us. We had spoken with him before, and thought well of him and of his understanding and courtesy. And each in turn we told him—the chief baker and myself—our dreams. And behold, even as he expounded them to us, so everything came to pass. My lord the king, of his mercy, restored me into his favour, and made me his cupbearer again, even as I am to this day. But the chief baker did not find favour in Pharaoh's eyes, and was hanged."

"What manner of man", said Pharaoh, "was this young Hebrew?"

"He was a young man of a rare wisdom and of a beautiful countenance. The governor of the prison-house thought well of him, and it grieves me that I have forgotten him so long."

Then Pharaoh sent messengers to the governor of the prison, and bade him (if this young Hebrew were still alive) deliver him up without delay, and bring him into the presence of the king. Whereupon the governor of the prison sent in haste for Joseph to do the king's bidding, and told him that Pharaoh himself had sent for him. They were by now friends together, servant and master, and he spoke kindly to him, and wished him well, and lent him suitable clothes in which to appear before the king. So Joseph shaved himself, put off his prison clothes, and changed his raiment, and was brought into the vast pillared council hall of the royal palace, and into the presence of Pharaoh himself.

Surrounded by his priests and diviners, his noblemen and officers of state, some among them men of Syria and Ethiopia and of Nubia, chosen from near and far for their sagacity or valour or influence to serve him, Pharaoh was seated upon a dais under a canopy. He was garbed in a robe of fine linen adorned with gold and coloured enamel. His chair of state was of gold. Two serpent heads of gold couched on his temples. Beside him stood his fan-bearers.

When Joseph had been brought in, he made obeisance to

[ 83 ]

Pharaoh, bowing with his face to the ground before him, and stood whe: he was. But Pharaoh bade him draw near, and looking gravely upon him, spoke with him—these two together.

"I have dreamed a dream", he said, "which the spirit within me assures me has a meaning that is of moment—and a meaning moreover of which I should be made speedily aware. But there is none among my priests and diviners who can expound it to me. It has been told to Pharaoh that thou thyself art possessed of a natural understanding of dreams, and a divination to pierce through their strange disguises to what they intend. Is that so?"

And Joseph answered the king: "The interpretation of dreams is with God, and only he of his wisdom can give the insight to divine this dream."

Pharaoh stooped forward a little where he sat. "So be it," he said. And he told Joseph his dream.

"I dreamed", he said, "I stood upon the bank of a great river in flood. And as I stood musing there, looking upon the turbid flowing waters, behold, there came up out of the river seven kine. They came up, I say, out of the river—sleek, well-nourished beasts, and comely. They browsed together in the green sedges in the pastures of the marsh by the brink of the river. And as I looked, yet another seven kine came up from out of the river; but these were beasts lank and deformed, dreadful to look upon and ominous. Indeed I have never seen their like before in the whole land of Egypt. These also stood grazing awhile, and in so doing, drew near to the other seven. And it seemed in my dream—more swiftly even than I can recount it now—that of a sudden the lean lank cows fell upon and utterly devoured the seven that were sleek and comely. Yet could no mortal eye see any change in them. They were none the better for it, but remained as lean and lank as before. At this I awoke, troubled with an inward dread.

"When at length sleep returned to me, I dreamed again. But this dream is hard to tell, it was so swift in vanishing; and it appeared, as it were, all in the empty air. I saw upon one stalk seven ears of corn, full and fair and ripe for harvest, which yet in an instant were clean gone and vanished away, devoured by seven other ears, meagre and mildewed and smitten with the corruption of the burning blast of the east wind. Then I woke and could sleep no more.

"These then are the dreams that I have related to my magicians and diviners of secret things, and not one of them has yet been able to make clear their meaning to me, yet meaning my mind assures me they have."

He ceased speaking, and Joseph stood awhile silent before him, his face rapt and absent, his eyes fixed. Then he raised his head and looked on Pharaoh, and bowed himself before him and made answer:

"The two dreams", he said, "have one meaning, and in both of them God has revealed to Pharaoh what he is about to do. The river the king saw in his dream was the river of Egypt, which, like time, flows on continually, and year after year renews the harvest on which Pharaoh's whole realm and might depend. The seven cows that came up out of its waters were sign and symbol of seven years. So also with the dream of the harvest-field; the meaning of both dreams is the same. The first seven in each dream mean seven full and copious years—years of great plenty. So, too, with the seven lank and famished cows, and the seven ears of corn stricken and blasted with the east wind. These are seven years of famine. By Pharaoh's dreams God intended to reveal to him that a period of abundant harvests is coming to Egypt, and that the whole nation will rejoice in them. But after them will follow seven years of bad harvests, years of woe and dearth. So that not only will the seven good harvests be forgotten in Egypt, but the people will be in want and misery and will cry for bread. It was God's will that this should be revealed to Pharaoh in the dreams of sleep. Therefore Pharaoh dreamed twice, since two warnings are better than one. And what has been forewarned God himself will surely bring to pass."

Pharaoh pondered, his eyes fixed upon the face of Joseph, and he knew in his heart that the interpretation of his dreams which this young Hebrew had given him was the true meaning of them.

In this belief he questioned Joseph: "Verily I believe what thou sayest to be true. When, then, the seven evil years draw near, what hath thy God revealed to thee should Pharaoh do?"

Joseph considered within himself in silence a while. Then he answered Pharaoh that he should choose from among his counsellors a man wise and far-sighted, and to him should authority be given over all Egypt. Let this man, Joseph said also, appoint officers to serve under him, men of trust and repute, each in his own province throughout the land. During the seven years of plenty it should be their duty at the time of harvest to collect under the king's authority and each in his own province, a fifth of all the corn and wheat that had been grown in that province, and to store it in barns or granaries that should be built in the chief cities.

"By this means," said Joseph, "a vast store of grain will be gathered together and kept safe in the granaries, sealed under the seal of Pharaoh the King, and nothing of it during the first seven plentiful years shall be used or wasted. Then when the years of famine come, the doors of the granaries shall be opened, and the people will bring their money and buy food according to their need. Only thus can the disaster of famine be prevented, and the people shall realize the wisdom and foresight of the father of all, Pharaoh the King."

The wisdom of what Joseph had said was simple and clear, and yet showed a marvellous insight into affairs of state in one so young. His face, too, was animated and eager with his thoughts. He spoke like one who repeats what he hears as though it is prompted by a voice within him—one whose only thought is truth, having neither heed nor fear of aught else. Pharaoh fixed his regard on him with great care and intentness. He himself had a mind generous and able to perceive a wisdom that was yet beyond his own divining, as the moon gains her light from the sun.

At last he withdrew his eyes from Joseph and turned to the courtiers and counsellors that were about him. And they too marvelled.

Then said Pharaoh the King: "Where in all my realm shall we find one to excel, nay even to equal this man in wisdom and understanding, and in whom is the spirit of God?"

Then he turned again to Joseph: "I see", he said, "that the God of all is with thee, and there is none in all my realm can give me wiser counsel than thyself. To thee, then, do I entrust the doing and execution of all that thou hast advised. Full authority do I ordain to thee over the whole land of Egypt, to choose out able and trustworthy men to be officers over my provinces, to amass the corn during the years of plenty, to store the grain, and to obey thee in everything at pain of their lives as thou shalt direct. And all my people shall obey thee, according to my decree."

In token of this, Pharaoh took his signet ring from off his finger and put it upon Joseph's finger. And he arrayed

Joseph in a robe of fine linen such as was worn only by the chief lords of Egypt and by the king's counsellors. Over this he hung about Joseph's neck a chain of fine gold. And Pharaoh gave command that a chariot should be prepared for Joseph that in beauty and richness of workmanship should be but second to his own. Thus Pharaoh appointed Joseph lord over all the land of Egypt.

"I am the Pharaoh," he said, "and this is my decree: that not a man shall stir hand or foot in all Egypt without thy consent." Pharaoh, moreover, gave Joseph a name which he himself had chosen, *Zaphnath-paanear*, meaning thereby the saviour of the land, or the revealer of secrets.

From that day onwards, apart from Pharaoh himself, Joseph was first in Egypt in rank and power. He was thirty years of age when he was made Pharaoh's chief counsellor or vizier. When the king in his splendour, attended by his courtiers and high officers and with his guard of horsemen, rode out in state from city to city throughout the land of Egypt, the chariot of Joseph followed next after his own. And a herald or runner went on before his chariot to announce his coming. And the people in the streets and all who waited everywhere to watch and to see him, bowed the knee to Joseph as he passed by, hailing him with acclamations of " *'Abrek! 'Abrek!* Lo, now pay heed. Behold the lord of all!"

By the grace of Pharaoh also, Joseph took to wife Asenath, the daughter of a prince of Egypt named Potipherah, who was priest of the Temple of the Sun in the city of Heliopolis or On.

As he had foretold, the harvests of the seven years that followed were marvellously rich and plenteous. In all things according to his command, the officers or stewards whom he had appointed to serve under him collected a fifth of all the crops in Egypt, and laid it up in many-chambered granaries. These—in cities where there was none already for the feeding of the king's army and his slaves—had been built for this purpose. In every city was a granary wherein was hoarded the grain that was not needed for food in the country surrounding it. The corn thus accumulated throughout Egypt was at last like the sand of the sea for abundance, so that no strict account could be taken of it, for the plenty of it passed all measuring.

In these years two sons were born to Joseph. The first he named Manasseh, a word that means, "Causing to forget", for, as he said to Asenath, the mother of his son, "God hath made me forget the travail that is gone." And his second son he called Ephraim, which means, "Fruitful", for God had made him to grow and to flourish and had blessed him in a strange land wherein first he had had nothing.

But the seven years of plenty came to an end, and they were followed by seven years of extreme dearth and famine. During these years the mighty river of Egypt which in its annual season flooded the country on either side of its banks, leaving behind it when its waters fell away a rich silt or sediment without which the arid sunbaked sands of Egypt would have borne no crops at all, had flowed further inland than in living memory it had ever flowed before. But in the next seven years its waters ran scant and shallow, so that only a narrow ribbon of land on either side of the dwindling river could be sown with seed. Nor was the famine in Egypt alone, but in all the countries surrounding it.

When the people of Egypt had consumed what corn they had themselves saved and laid aside from their good harvests, and were in great need, they appealed to Pharaoh for food. And Pharaoh made proclamation that any in want should come to Joseph, who, as his vizier, had power to ordain all things as seemed best to him.

Then Joseph gave orders to the stewards whom he had appointed in the cities of Egypt that the granaries and storehouses which were stuffed to their roofs with grain, their entries sealed with Pharaoh's seal, should now be opened up, and that corn should be sold to all that came to buy. And as from time to time he decreed, so was the price fixed.

When rumour spread far and wide that while there was famine in all the countries neighbouring on Egypt, there was plenty in Egypt itself, there came strangers and aliens from all parts into Egypt to buy corn. It had become the warehouse of the world. And Pharaoh's treasuries were filled to overflowing with the money that was paid to the stewards of the granaries, both by the Egyptians and by the strangers that came from afar with their caravans, their camels and their asses. There, none was poor and none hungry.

As in all the countries bordering on Egypt, so it was in the land of Canaan, and even in the well-watered and fruitful vale of Hebron, where in their tents dwelt Jacob and his sons. Their harvest had failed again and yet again. The earth was parched up in the heat of the sun. The pastures near and far lay bare and dry. Their flocks and herds were perishing for lack of grass and fodder, and there was an extreme dearth. So great was their need that their store of corn would soon be at an end, and they knew not where to turn for help.

There came a stranger one evening to their tents who reported that there was not only corn in Egypt, but corn in such plenty that it was for sale to all who came, and that he himself was about to set out thither. Those of the sons of

Jacob who heard him, listened eagerly, but said nothing.

The stranger was entertained with what little hospitality they had to offer. And when he had bidden them farewell and gone his way, Jacob turned to his sons and said: "Why do you stand looking darkly and doubtfully one at another? What folly is this? Has not the man told us that there is corn in Egypt, and that we can buy there all we need? Up, and take money with you then, saddle your asses and set out without delay. Make all the speed you can, both in going and returning, that we may live and not die."

They turned from him without another word and began to prepare for their journey. On the morrow the ten brothers set out from Hebron, following the track of the great caravans that go down from Gilead into Egypt, as had the Ishmaelitish merchantmen two and twenty years ago, when for twenty shekels of silver his brothers had sold Joseph into slavery and he had been led off at the coming on of night, never to return.

But Jacob would not let Benjamin go with his brethren, lest peradventure any harm should come to him.

# His Brothers in Egypt

Day by day the great caravan which Joseph's ten brothers had joined with their asses was swollen with strangers of sundry races and tongues and with their beasts of burden. And in the midst of this barbaric concourse they came at last to the chief city of Egypt, where Joseph was now vizier or viceroy, second only in power and lordship to Pharaoh himself.

When with their money they entered the granary to buy corn, the clerks who kept tally of the corn mistrusted them at sight. First, because they were Hebrews, and next, because on being questioned they could give only a confused account of themselves, being unable to make themselves understood in the Egyptian tongue. The clerks brought them to the steward who had control of the granary, and he himself, having interrogated them and doubting what they said in answer, sent them under guard to the great hall of the vizier.

They were brought therefore into the presence of Joseph himself, where he sat surrounded by his officers and by those in attendance upon him. There they waited before him until he was at liberty to hear for what reason they had been brought thither. He raised his eyes at length, and bidding the steward come forward, saw these ten strangers awaiting his pleasure.

At sight of them his heart leapt within him. He knew instantly who they were, and longed to make himself known to them. Only joy was in his heart to see them; but first, he determined to test them and to discover how time had used and changed them. So he sat motionless and made no sign of recognition. They drew near, and bowed themselves before him with their faces to the earth.

And, as if the long years that had gone by had never been, the dreams of his boyhood returned into his mind— the sheaves of corn in the fields of harvest, and the stars in the night sky. But his brothers gazed at him only with awe and misgiving; they were troubled, being strangers in a strange land, and ignorant of why they were regarded with suspicion and mistrust. And they knew him not, for the years had much changed him. He had been but a stripling in his first youth when they had last seen him, bruised and bound and almost naked in the hands of the Ishmaelites. Now he was come to his full manhood, being thirty and nine years old, and he had seen many sorrows and afflictions. Besides which, he sat before them, grave and austere, and raimented in his robes of office, Pharaoh's chain of gold about his neck, his signet ring upon his finger. They knew only that they were in the presence of one who had supreme authority, and that their safety and perhaps their very lives were in his hands.

With countenance unmoved he heard the reasons given by the steward of the granary for their having been brought before him, though all that was said was past their own understanding. Then he called for an interpreter and, through him, addressed them as if they were not only men of no account but under sharp suspicion. He spoke harshly to them.

"Whence come you?" he asked them.

"From the land of Canaan," they answered

"And why?"

"We are come hither to buy food," they said.

But he pretended not to believe them. "Nay," he said, "that, it may be, is a reason simple enough as you think to deceive me. But I give it no credence. What proof of it have you? It is not to buy food that you are come hither, but rumour having reached you that there is dearth in Egypt and that its people are in distress, you are here to spy out the defences of the land. You are enemies of my lord the king. Treason is your aim. You are spies."

They protested, assuring him that this was not so. "Indeed, my lord," they said, "we are no spies, but peaceable men, shepherds. Our grain was all but spent, and our flocks and herds were dwindling daily for lack of pasture. The famine is very grievous in Canaan. And having heard that there was corn in Egypt, we set out with money to buy. But the men of the granary refused to sell to us."

"They did well," said Joseph. "For I perceive by your very looks and demeanour that you are spies—Hebrew spies. To see the nakedness of the land you are come."

"But indeed no, my lord," they pleaded, "for were we spies, we should not be together and in one company. Indeed we are ten brethren of one household, sons of one father, and——"

But Joseph broke in upon them. His countenance had darkened, though they knew not why. " 'Ten,' you say; have you then no other brother? Has this father you speak of no other sons?"

"Yea, my lord," they said, "there is the youngest. But he is very dear to our father and remains with him in Canaan. And there was yet another, but he is no longer with us. Indeed, my lord, thy servants are honest men, and no spies."

But Joseph still professed not to believe them. "Whether

what you say be true or false," he said, "I cannot yet tell. But I will put you to the proof. For by the life of Pharaoh, you shall not escape me until I have assurance that you are the shepherds of Canaan you say you are, and nought else."

Without further word, he gave orders that they should be kept in strict charge until he should have time and occasion to examine them again. They were thrust into prison and lay there three days, being treated not as captives condemned to punishment, but as men under arrest and suspicion. On the third day they were brought before him again.

Joseph told them that he had considered the account they had given of themselves. "Your lives", he said, "are in my hands; and of a surety, if what you tell me prove false, you are in very great peril. But my trust is in God, in whom is truth and justice. You profess to be harmless shepherds of sheep, sons of one father dwelling in Canaan. Hearken, then! I will believe you so far as to keep only one of you as hostage for the rest, until you return again. Begone out of Egypt at once, take with you the corn you came to buy, and go in haste, for if what you have said be true, your father and your wives and children may be in sore straits for want of food. But bear in mind that you do this only on one condition—namely, that without delay you return again into Egypt and to this city, bringing with you the youngest of you, this brother of whom you have spoken. By this alone shall I be assured of your honesty, and by this alone shall you save the life of the one among you who remains in bondage in Egypt. Else he shall surely die."

In low voices they talked anxiously one with another as they stood before him, debating what he had said, and wholly unaware that he knew their language, for this day also he had addressed them only in the Egyptian tongue, and by means of an interpreter who was familiar with the Hebrew.

The long hours of doubt and dread they had spent in the prison-house had brought the past before their minds, and though they had spoken with caution lest they should be overheard, there had been strife between them. For even remorse itself makes enemies of those who have conspired together in evil and treachery. But they had now made their peace one with another. "Assuredly", they were saying, "this judgment has fallen upon us because we are guilty, though not of what this man now charges us with. It is because of our brother Joseph that all these misfortunes have overtaken us. We saw the anguish of his soul when he entreated us to take pity on him, and we refused to listen."

And Reuben could not refrain himself. He reminded them bitterly: "Did I not implore you to spare the child, and not to sin against him and against his father? But you mocked me down and played me false. And now at last has come the day of reckoning—our blood for his."

Listening to their talk, and seeing their trouble and distress, Joseph was grieved for them. He withdrew himself away from them a little to hide his tears; for there were many memories in his mind between that day and this.

When he returned to them again, he gave orders that Simeon should be the one kept back as hostage for the rest. This he did because Simeon was next among them in age to Reuben, the eldest, and Joseph had not known until now that Reuben had interceded with them and saved his life when they had intended to kill him. Then Simeon was bound before their eyes, and a guard of soldiers haled him away to the prison. The rest of them Joseph dismissed from his presence without further speech with them. But meanwhile he had secretly instructed his steward to ensure that

after they had been provided with what corn they required, each one of these Hebrews' money should be hidden in the mouth of his sack. He bade his steward, too, supply them with every thing they might need on their journey back to Canaan. And this was done.

So the nine brothers, their asses laden with corn and all that they needed, set out, and at night came to an inn or camping-place and rested there. When one of them that evening opened his sack to get provender for his ass, he espied to his amazement a bag of money in it—a leathern bag tied up in the mouth of the sack. He ran at once to tell the others of what he had found.

"This bag of money", he said, "must have been hidden in my sack, for it was certainly not there when we saddled our asses this morning. Shekel for shekel it is the price I paid for my corn."

At this their hearts sank within them. They knew not what evil might follow from it, and they were afraid.

When they were come into Canaan and had reached their journey's end, they told their father all that had happened to them while they had been away. "Without reason being given," they said, "we were seized, and taken before the man who is lord under Pharaoh over the whole land of Egypt. In power and honour he is next to Pharaoh himself. He treated us harshly and accused us of being spies. We answered him suingly and assured him that this was not so, that we were honest and peaceable men—ten out of twelve brethren, the sons of one father, and that of the other two, one is no more, and the youngest with you in Canaan. Yet he still refused to believe us. And we were taken away, and for three days lay in a dungeon, knowing not what evil would come on us next."

"How then", said Jacob, "did you escape out of his hands?"

"Why," said they, "when we were brought before him again, he spoke to us less harshly and said that he had decided to put our word to the proof. 'By this,' he said, 'I shall know whether you be honest men or no. One of you shall remain here in strict charge, and the rest of you shall take the corn you need. And now be gone!' he said. 'But take heed to me—for if you do not speedily return, bringing with you this younger brother of whom you have spoken, then shall I know—as I believe—that you have lied to me. And the one of you I hold in charge shall surely die.' Then Simeon was taken, and we made all haste away."

When Jacob heard this, he bitterly reproached them.

"What evil have I done that you bereave me of my children? Joseph is not; Simeon is not; and now you would take Benjamin from me. All these things are against me and I can do nothing."

Reuben grieved for his father and drew near to comfort him. He promised that if Jacob would consent to entrust Benjamin into his charge, he himself would bring him back unharmed and in safety. "And if I keep not my word with thee," he said, "thou mayest kill the two sons I leave behind me. There is nothing dearer to me on earth." But Jacob turned away and made no answer.

And when presently, after unlading their asses, they found, one and all, that the money which they had paid for their corn had been hidden in their sacks, they stared in consternation one at another, and were sick with foreboding.

They told their father of this, imploring him to let them return at once into Egypt. But he refused to listen.

"Nothing you can say will persuade me to let your brother Benjamin go with you. Joseph is dead. He too was but a boy when he went out to seek you in Shechem and came back to me no more. Now Benjamin is the only son left to me of my old age. If I were to consent to his going and any harm were to befall him while he was with you, it would bring down my grey hairs with sorrow to the grave."

The famine increased. The skies were like brass, the earth baked hard as brick, and there came no sign or hope of any relief. They waited on from day to day until the corn they had brought from Egypt was running perilously short and would soon be consumed. Their flocks and herds grew lank and sickly; even their little children were ailing for want of milk and nourishment. And Jacob could refrain himself no longer.

"There is not a day to lose," he said to his sons. "You must go at once and bring us a little food. And I myself will remain here with Benjamin."

And Judah once again, and as tenderly as words could, assured his father that this was impossible. "The man who was lord over Egypt, did solemnly swear and protest to us: 'By the life of Pharaoh', he said, 'unless, when you return, your brother be with you, you shall not see my face again!' If we venture without him, then not one of us, as I believe, will ever come back alive."

Then said Jacob: "Why did you deal so ill with me as to even mention to this man that you had a younger brother?"

"But he questioned us closely again and again," said his sons. "He inquired where we came from, who were our kindred, if our father were still living, if we ourselves were his only sons or had he yet another. How could we else, then, but answer him according to the tenor of his questions; how could we have evaded them? How, too, could we have foreseen that he would snatch at our words and say: 'Return and bring your brother with you'?"

Then Judah pleaded yet once again with his father. "Give the boy into my care," he said. "And let us set out at once. The corn we bought is all but gone, our little ones will soon be crying for food. If we stay now, death stares us one and all in the face. I myself will be surety for him, and if I fail to bring him back to thee safe and sound, be mine the blame for ever. For except we had lingered, we should by now have already gone and come back again."

Then said Jacob: "What must be, must be. Make ready at once and go. But do not venture empty-handed. Take the best of the little we have left and carry it down to this man for a present; a little balsam and some honey and storax, spices, nuts and almonds—whatever we have that is sought after by the Egyptians; and let it be our choicest. Take not only double money with you, lest, as I suspect, in these last months the price of corn may have risen, but take also the money that was hidden in the mouths of your sacks. That, maybe, was only an oversight, but will be proof of your honesty. And Benjamin shall go with you. Delay no more. And may God Almighty be with you and ensure you mercy when you come again into the presence of this man, that Simeon may be restored to you, and that he keep not Benjamin. But if it be God's will that I am to be bereaved of him, then I am bereaved." He wept and withdrew himself out of their sight.

# He Reveals Himself

His sons with all haste prepared for their journey. They loaded their asses with the presents their father had bidden them take with them—honey, spices, balm, almonds—the best they had in store. They took with them also double money—twice the amount they had taken on their first going down into Egypt, and the money also which had been concealed in their sacks.

When everything was ready, Benjamin came out to them from his father, and they set out together. He was young and fearless, and he had his mother's beauty. And he was eager beyond measure to see the great lord of whom he had heard his brothers speak, and the cities and temples and tombs, and all the famed marvels of the land of Egypt, and the splendour of Pharaoh.

In due time they presented themselves before the steward of the granary. He sent word to Joseph that these Hebrews were come again, and that they had brought with them a lad who they said was their youngest brother. When Joseph heard this, his heart welled over with joy and happiness. He summoned his steward, the overseer of his household, as he himself had been under Potiphar: "Take these men to my house", he said, "and see that everything is done to put them at their ease and comfort, for they are to dine with me at noon."

So his steward himself went to the granary as he was bidden. There he found the Hebrews still in custody. He led them away through the streets of the city, reeking with dust and heat, and loud and busy with traffic. On either side of the crowded alleys were the shops of the goldsmiths and the sandal-makers. There, too, the barbers, cook-shops and pastry-cooks, potters and beer-houses. A throng of wayfarers of a score of different races jostled them on every side. Benjamin gazed about him in astonishment—at the Egyptians themselves, painted and bewigged, with their folded cloaks and long walking-canes; at the women tattooed on chin and brow, their hair dyed blue, with their collars of beads and precious gems and their tinkling bracelets. The scene was past comparison beyond anything he had ever dreamed or imagined.

The steward brought them at last, where all was quiet, to a gateway of carved stone, in the shade of a dark green acacia tree. Through this they entered the courtyard of Joseph's house. It was paved with stone, and from it terraces went down, set with pools and conduits of water, serene and glittering in the sun under the deep blue of the Egyptian skies. Lilies, the flower of the lotus, lay in bloom snowy and golden amid their flat green leaves in the water. Ducks of bright plumage floated upon it. It was screened with green trellises of vines.

Beyond, they looked out over Joseph's orchards, apple and pomegranate, palm and fig, in the shade of whose leafy branches were many wild birds, sparrow and wagtail and dove. But for these, and the bell-clear sound of running water and the stir of the servants who came and went, all was still and tranquil, and the air was cool and sweet.

When Joseph's brothers, who stood waiting beside their asses in the courtyard, knew that this was the palace of the great lord himself, they were abashed and filled with mistrust. They murmured one to another: "It is for no good of ours that we have been brought hither. It must be because of the money that was put back secretly into our sacks. It is a device to betray us. We are alone and defenceless. This great lord will accuse us falsely; his servants will fall upon us, and seize all that we have. We are doomed."

While the others thus waited in grievous trouble of mind at what might come of it, two of them went to the entry of the house and asked if they might speak with the steward.

"Sir," they said, when he came to them, "we entreat thee to think no evil of us. We are, as you know, from the land of Canaan, and strangers here, and we have merely journeyed down again into Egypt as we did before, and as we were bidden, to buy corn because of the famine. When we were sent away after our first coming here, we found when we unladed our asses that the money we had brought with us had been restored to us and hidden in our sacks—the money we had actually paid for the corn. Nor have we any inkling of how this came about. But we have brought it back with us, with other money to buy food, and here it is."

Joseph's steward answered them courteously and reassured them: "All is well. There is nothing to fear. Surely it cannot but have been the will of your God, and of the God of your fathers, that this treasure came to be hidden in your sacks? Of my own knowledge you paid the full price for your corn, and I have a record to prove it so."

Then he brought Simeon to them, and himself led them within to where they could refresh themselves and prepare for the coming of Joseph. He gave them water to wash their feet, and their asses were fed and watered. There, with hearts renewed, they made ready the present they had brought with them, the aromatic gums and spices, the honey and pistachio nuts, for they had heard that Joseph would be returning at noon, and that they were to eat with him. They talked eagerly among themselves, marvelling at the splendour and strangeness of Joseph's house, and wondering what was in store for them after the kindness that had been shown to them by the steward.

When Joseph came home, they were taken into his presence; and they bowed themselves and made obeisance. And they presented him with the gifts which they had brought with them from Canaan. And Joseph in thanking them almost betrayed himself in his speech. The old words of delight evoked by a thousand memories sprang into his mind as he saw the familiar plaited baskets and breathed in the fragrance of the spices. But he stayed himself, and through his interpreter asked them of their welfare. "Is your father," he said, "the old man of whom you spoke to me, still alive, and in good health?"

"Thy servant our father", they said, "is still alive and is well."

Looking from one to the other, Joseph's eyes rested at last on the face of his brother Benjamin, his own loved mother's son.

"Is this, then," he said, "the younger brother whom you told me of? You have done well to bring him with you."

He gazed long at Benjamin. "May God", he said, "be gracious unto thee, my son." But the words faltered on his lips, and he turned away in haste, for his heart yearned for Benjamin and he could not keep back his tears. He went into his own chamber alone, and wept there. And when he had grown calmer, he rose and washed his face, and returned to them again, restraining himself.

He signed to his steward that the feast should be served,

and the whole company gathered there sat down to eat. His own place at the feast was set apart by reason of his dignity and lordship in Egypt. His officers and attendants and other guests also sate together apart; for the Egyptians might not eat of the same dish with the Hebrews; it was forbidden by their priests and their religion.

As for his brothers, Joseph himself arranged the order in which they should sit before him, from Reuben, the first-born, according to his birthright, to Benjamin, the young-est, according to his youth. At this they gazed at one another in astonishment, marvelling how he had divined their ages, for he had seated them in order of age without a single mis-take. And now the feast began. The air was sweet with the fragrance of flowers. There were fruits and meats and wines in all abundance, and they drank out of goblets of glass, a thing they had never seen before.

And as was the custom in Egypt, Joseph chose from the dishes set before him, and sent them by the hands of his servants to his brothers—honouring them as his guests. But the dainties he sent to Benjamin were five times as many as to any of the others; and they ate and drank and feasted with Joseph, and were merry.

And while they sate feasting, Joseph spoke with his steward. "Let these men's sacks", he said, "be filled with corn to the utmost their beasts can carry. And in the sack of the youngest of them—whom you see yonder—put in also the money that was paid for his corn, and hide therein my cup—my silver divining cup. But all this in secret! Let not a rumour of it reach their ears." And the steward did as Joseph had bidden him.

As soon as it was light next morning, Joseph's brothers set out on their journey home; and a joyful and merry-hearted company they were. It seemed that everything was now well with them, their troubles over, Benjamin safe, and Simeon restored to them.

But soon after they were gone, and before they had proceeded far beyond the outskirts of the city, Joseph called for his steward. "Up now," he said. "Away, and with all speed! Take a guard of soldiers with thee and follow hard after these Hebrews, and when thou hast overtaken them, bid them stand, and accuse them openly: 'Why have you returned evil for good? My lord's silver cup has been stolen, even the cup which he uses for divination. He knows of a certainty into whose hands it has fallen, and that that thief is one on whom but yesterday he lavished many kindnesses. What wickedness could be viler!' "

The steward did as he was bid. He took a guard of soldiers, and mounting a camel, rode out in hot haste after them, and overtook them in the desert before yet the sun was high in the heavens. When at sound of pursuit the brothers turned and looked back, they instantly fell silent, and their hearts stood still for dread. They drew up immediately and clustered together about him, in horror of what new disaster was now upon them. The steward challenged them harshly. He upbraided them as if they were outcasts beneath contempt, and he repeated everything that Joseph had bidden him. They gazed one at another in confusion; a cold and awful darkness had fallen upon them.

"God forbid", they said, "that we should have been guilty of such a thing, or that my lord should so much as have thought it of us. Did we not ourselves tell you of the money which after our first journey we found in our sacks, and did we not offer it you again only yesterday? And you said: 'All's well, be at peace, for God has ordained it so'. What need have we of silver or gold that we should return evil for good and rob thy lord himself? And now you even accuse us of having stolen his divining cup! Search as you please, and if the goblet be found in the sack of any one of us, then let him die; and the rest of us shall be bondsmen of thy lord from this day onward."

Then said the steward: "Be it as you say; except that only the one of you in whose sack the cup is found shall suffer, for he alone is guilty. The rest being blameless shall go free."

They unloaded their asses, put their sacks on the ground, and loosed the thongs that bound their mouths. Then, beginning with that of the eldest of them, the steward and his guard searched their sacks one by one until at length they came to the sack of the youngest, Benjamin. There the cup was found, and his money beside it.

At sight of it his brothers rent their clothes in woe and despair. Their darkest premonitions had come true. They knew what fate awaited them, that all was lost. But one and all of them refrained from uttering a word of reproach or making the least sign, by frown or gesture, that they blamed Benjamin or misdoubted his innocence.

They tied up their sacks, loaded up their asses again, and turned back in wretchedness towards the city by the way they had come. Though again and again, as Joseph had bidden him, the steward assured them that it was only the thief himself his lord intended to punish, they refused to have any further word with him and made no answer. With Benjamin in their midst, they made haste to return.

Joseph was seated in his hall of audience amid his officers. He raised his eyes and surveyed them. They flung themselves down before him, their faces to the earth. But he hardened his face and addressed them scornfully and as if in anger.

"What deed is this that you have done? Knew you not that I could divine the truth in this matter?"

Then Judah spoke in answer for them all. "What shall we say unto my lord? How shall I speak? Of what use are words to clear ourselves from a charge so black against us, yet one of which we are wholly innocent? That, my lord, is the truth. But doubtless the judgment of God has fallen upon us not for this evil of which we are innocent, but for the wickedness we have done in the past. We are strangers in a strange land, and have none to defend us. We cannot even speak in a tongue that might persuade my lord to listen. We can but cast ourselves upon the mercy of my lord, and if he so will it, let him make bondsmen of us all, so that we suffer together, and not alone."

And Joseph answered: "God forbid that I should do so! It is known to me which among you was found in possession of the cup. He alone is guilty, and he alone shall suffer. As for the rest of you, there is nothing to keep you here; get you gone in peace, then, while you may. Return to your father in Canaan and let me see your faces no more."

Then Judah drew near to him and spoke earnestly with him face to face, telling him everything that was in his heart and keeping nothing back.

"Oh, my lord," he said, "let thy servant, I pray thee, tell out everything that is in his mind. Have patience, and let not thine anger burn against thy servant, for thou art all-powerful, even as Pharaoh himself. When first we came into Egypt—I myself and these men, my brothers—to buy corn, my lord questioned us, who we were and whence we had come, and who our father was, and were we his only sons. And we told my lord: we have a father, who is now an old man. We said that there was one son remaining with him, a child of his old age, dearest to him of us all, and the only son left of his mother, his brother being dead.

"And my lord gave command to his servants: 'Go and return and bring back with you this brother of whom you speak that I may see him with my own eyes.' And we told my lord, the lad cannot leave his father, for if he should, and any harm came to him, his father would die. And my lord said expressly to his servants: 'Unless your youngest brother come down with you into Egypt, and that soon, you shall see my face no more.'

"Well, my lord, when we came up unto thy servant our father, we laid before him all that my lord had said. And the time came when our need being extreme because of the famine, he bade us come again and buy a little food. We answered that we could not do this unless our youngest brother went with us, since without him we should not even be admitted into my lord's presence. And our father said: 'Why did you so much as mention your youngest brother? You knew well how dearly I love him. You knew that he is the only son left to me of his mother who is dead. Long, long ago his brother, young and happy, bade me farewell and set out upon a journey from which he never returned. It may be that he was torn to pieces by wild beasts. And now you would take his younger brother also, knowing well that if any harm befall him, you will bring down my grey hairs in sorrow to the grave.'

"Oh, my lord, my father's life itself is bound up with this lad's safety. If I return without him and he look for him and find him not, surely his grief will be greater than he can bear; and it is we ourselves, his own sons, that shall have brought down this grey-haired old man with sorrow to the grave. And I myself, alas, shall be the most to blame, for I vowed solemnly to my father to take every care of him. 'If', I said, 'I bring him not back unharmed and in safety, then the blame be mine for ever!'

"I beseech thee, then, my lord, have pity. Let the lad go free, and return home with his brothers, and let me be bondsman in his stead. My lord, I could not bear to return without him and see my father's grief."

Joseph heard him in silence to the end; glancing from one to another of his brothers, as they stood in fear and disgrace before him, and letting his eyes rest on Benjamin, who was a little apart from them, not daring to lift his head for shame that he should have been thought guilty of stealing the cup. And when Judah spoke of his father, and there returned into Joseph's mind all that had passed since he had seen him, he could refrain himself no longer.

"Let every man", he said, "withdraw out of my presence, except only these Hebrews."

When Joseph's officers and attendants all were gone and there stood no man with him except his brothers, he came down to them and made himself known to them. And he wept, so that even the Egyptians who lingered on the threshold heard him weeping.

And he said to his brothers: "Come near, I pray you. There is nothing now to fear. For see, I am Joseph—Joseph himself, who long ago you thought was dead. Tell me, I beseech you, is indeed all well with my father? Is he truly yet alive?"

But his brothers were troubled at his presence, gazing at him in dismay, and could make no answer.

Joseph smiled at them: "It is no wonder", he said, "after the many years we have been separated one from another that you should still be in doubt of who I am. But come now, look closely at me, for I am indeed and in truth none other than Joseph, the very Joseph whom you sold to the Ishmaelites and into Egypt. Be no more distressed or angry with yourselves because of that. God sent me on before you so that in this time of need I might preserve your lives, for else you might have perished for want. For two years now there has been famine in Egypt. But five years are yet to come when there will be drought and bitter scarcity, and want and suffering must increase. Take comfort, then; remember only that it was God in his mercy who made me the means of this deliverance and of saving not only yourselves, but your children and your children's children, who will follow us when we are gone. I say, then, it was not you who sent me hither, but God. It is he alone who hath given me power under Pharaoh to act as seems best to me—lord of his house and viceroy of all Egypt. Hasten then and return with all the speed you can to my father. Give him this message in these same words: 'I myself, thy long-lost son, Joseph, am awaiting thee here in Egypt, pining to see thee again, anxious only for thy health and safety.'

"Say that, and tell my father also that you have seen me face to face, even as I am; and that the God of whom he taught me as a child has made me lord and ruler over all the land of Egypt. Entreat him not to delay, but to return with you into Egypt. A place shall be found for him and for you all where you shall live near me and under my protection, you and your wives and your children, your flocks and herds, and all that you have. Through all the evils that are yet to come I myself will provide for him and for you all, and will cherish his last years lest he should come to poverty."

As he stood in their midst, his words followed one upon another out of his inmost heart like water welling from a long-sealed fountain. And his face was lighted with his love.

But still they dared make no sign, or, after so many vicissitudes, trust even their own senses. They gazed and were silent.

"But, no?" he said, smiling. "I see you are still in doubt. Well, then, Benjamin your youngest and my own dear mother's son shall tell you what I say is true, that it is my own mouth that speaks to you, and that I am indeed his brother Joseph."

And he took Benjamin into his arms and fell upon his neck and kissed him, and in love and joy wept upon his shoulder.

Seeing this, the rest of them were at last reassured and believed him. They drew near and he kissed them all in turn.

After that they talked together for a long time in private there, for there was much to hear and much to tell. There were no bounds to their happiness.

# Jacob Comes Down into Egypt

When Joseph's steward and the officers of his household heard what had come about, they too rejoiced. And it was told Pharaoh himself that after many years of separation, Joseph's own brethren had come into Egypt to buy corn, and had at first not recognized him or even so much as dreamed it was he; but that he had now made himself known to them and they were reunited. This pleased Pharaoh well, and he himself spoke with Joseph.

"Tell your brethren", he said, "that it is Pharaoh's will and desire that they return at once into their own country and bring back with them your father and their wives and children. Bid them trouble not with what goods they have. For from henceforth they shall have the best that Egypt affords, they shall live on the fat of the land and shall never again be in want or danger. Let them be supplied with baggage-wagons and with whatever else they may need in their long and arduous journey into Egypt—for themselves, their wives and their little ones and for your father. Thou knowest that in all things thy joys are my joys. Let nothing then be wanting for their comfort and for thine own peace of mind. The best that Egypt has is theirs."

So Joseph gave orders that his brothers should be provided with baggage-wagons as Pharaoh had said, with horses to draw them, and beasts of burden, and all things else and every comfort that his father or their wives and their daughters might need on the journey.

For presents, too, from himself, he gave them one and all changes of raiment, the choicest in Egypt, famous through the ages for the fineness of its linen. But to his brother Benjamin he gave three hundred pieces of silver and five changes of raiment. To his father he sent a present too, such as prince might send to prince—ten he-asses laden with all the riches of Egypt—things of beauty, rare and costly; and ten she-asses, their paniers piled with wheat and fruits and delicacies for his comfort on the journey.

The next morning, when they were assembled together in the courtyard of Joseph's house, and beyond its gates stood ready the baggage-wagons and the asses and the servants that were to go with them, Joseph himself came down out of his house to greet them and to bid them farewell; and his two small sons were with him. He embraced his brothers, and gave them but one word of counsel. "Remember only this," he said, "that between you and me there remains nothing now but love and friendship, so let there be peace between you all. No reproaches, no recriminations, nothing but well and fair until we meet again. I would not that you fall out with one another by the way."

They talked together until the last moment came for their departure. Their cares were over, and as they set out in the clear brightness of the morning a great company of Joseph's household watched them go.

Day after day they continued on their journey, sleeping when dark came on where it was customary for caravans to camp for the night, until, after they had turned inward from the sea, they came without mischance into Canaan. News had already been brought to Jacob from servants whom he had sent out to keep watch for them, that they were drawing near. They came together to his tent, and when he saw that Simeon was with them, and Benjamin himself was clasped again in his arms, he bowed his head in thanks to God for this great mercy.

Hope had all but faded into despair; now he was at peace. But when they told him that his son Joseph was not only still alive but was lord and governor over the whole land of Egypt, he gazed at them trembling. His heart fainted within him; for joy itself may be so sudden sweet as to be beyond credence. He could not believe them. He sat gazing mutely into their faces, and they were filled with remorse.

Even when they repeated to him in Joseph's own words the message he had bidden them bring, his mind was still in confusion. It was not until, supporting his feeble footsteps, they led him out, and with his own eyes he saw the Egyptian wagons, and the horses that had been sent to carry him into Egypt, that he doubted no more. His spirit revived within him.

"It is enough," he said. "Joseph my son is yet alive: I will go and see him before I die."

As Pharaoh the King had expressly decreed, preparations were now speedily made to leave for ever the Vale of Hebron—now parched dry as bone with the long drought —in which they had dwelt peacefully so many years. They gathered together all that remained of their flocks and herds, and loaded their beasts of burden with their tents, their clothes and all the goods they had gotten in the land of Canaan.

On the day appointed, before even break of dawn, their little ones were up and ready; wild with delight and expectation. They mounted up into the Egyptian wagons—

and the mothers with their babies. They marvelled at the horses of Pharaoh and their caparisons of gilded leather. The sun rose; the dew-mists thinned away. The cry of the drivers sounded, and the crack of whip. The horses strained at their traces. With the bright clothes of the children in the wagons, and their smiling faces, it was as though great heaps of nodding flowers were in motion, as in the first of morning the happy multitude began to set forward. The fresh windless air rang with their talk and laughter, with the bleating of sheep, the lowing of cattle and their sheep-dogs' barking; and a great dust rose into the sky, beaten up by hoof and wheel, and gently descended again after they had gone by.

And so they came to Beersheba, the southernmost city of Canaan, which few among them were to see again. There they pitched camp, and rested, and there Jacob offered sacrifices to the Lord and poured out his heart in thankfulness for his great mercy. It was the place where he was born.

That night as he lay asleep there came to him a vision; and in dream he heard a voice calling him: "Jacob! Jacob!" And he knew in his dream that it was the voice of God.

He answered: "Lord, here am I."

And the voice said:

"I am thy God and the God of thy fathers, and I will never forsake thee whithersoever thou goest. Fear not to go down into Egypt. There I will make of thee and of thy sons a great nation. And thy children's children shall return and possess this Canaan that thou lovest. Here thou thyself shalt find thy last resting-place, and thy son Joseph shall lay his hand upon thine eyes and give thee peace in thy long sleep."

And Jacob awoke from his dream, and was comforted.

The next day Judah was sent on ahead of the cavalcade to inquire of Joseph where they should pitch their tents when, their journey over, they had come down by the sea coast into Egypt. And, as Pharaoh had ordained, they went up into the land of Goshen which lay a little northward, between the Lake of the Crocodiles and the great river. It was a region richer in good pasturage than any other in Egypt. As soon as word was brought of their safe arrival, Joseph made ready his chariot, and with his officers and his bodyguard, he rode out in state to welcome his father and to show him honour.

It was evening when he drew near. He alighted from his chariot and approached on foot, and presented himself to his father in the entering-in of his tent where he stood waiting to receive him. Jacob was now bent and feeble with age, but his face lit with rapture at sight of Joseph, as in the radiance of the declining sun he bowed himself low before his father. He put his arms about Joseph's neck and embraced him. And he wept upon his shoulder, and there was a long silence between them. Then he tenderly drew back Joseph's face and gazed into it in joy and love, and he said: "My son, my son! Life hath nothing more to give me. Now let me die; for I have seen thy face again and know that thou art still in the land of the living."

They talked together for many hours alone. Then Joseph bade his father farewell for a season, though they were soon to meet again, and he returned to his own house. He took with him five of his brothers, and presented them to Pharaoh, each of them by name. They bowed themselves and made obeisance, and Pharaoh conversed with them by means of an interpreter, questioning them concerning the condition of the country of Canaan from which they had come, and their lives and their occupations.

They told Pharaoh that the famine was still very grievous in Canaan, that there was little hope of respite, and that had it not been for the corn they had been enabled to buy in Egypt, they would have perished at last of hunger and want. "For we ourselves are shepherds," they said, "and depend on our flocks as our fathers did before us." They spoke with grateful hearts of the land of Goshen; praising it for the richness of its pasturage and its abundance of water for their sheep and their goats.

When they were gone out from the presence of the king, Pharaoh spoke alone with Joseph.

He said: "Let thy brethren remain in the land of Goshen; they shall dwell there in peace and security. It is a region like this Hebron, it seems, of which they tell me, and if there be among them any that have knowledge and skill in the keeping of cattle, let my herds be given into their charge. They shall be made overseers over my herdsmen and be responsible to me for them. And now, tell me, is thy father safe and well after so long a journey?"

And Joseph brought Jacob his father into the presence of Pharaoh. The old man raised his trembling hands in salutation of the king and blessed him. And Pharaoh inquired of him concerning his life and of his long experience in this world. He asked him: "How old art thou?"

And Jacob answered the king: "The days of my pilgrimage on earth are now a hundred and thirty years. Few and evil have they been when I reflect on them. I have not attained, nor shall I attain, to the age of my father and of his father before him. For my life has seen little rest from wandering, and my griefs have been many."

Pharaoh spoke very graciously to the old man and with all the courtesy and reverence due to his grey hairs and to one who had endured so many sorrows.

So, as Pharaoh had decreed, Jacob and his household with all his children and grandchildren settled in the land of Goshen. There they lived in peace. And Joseph watched over them like a father whose one care is the safety and comfort of his little ones. He supplied all their needs, and they wanted for nothing.

But in Egypt—as in Canaan—while still the great river refused its fostering waters, the famine increased in severity, until apart from the grain in the royal granaries, there was no bread in all the land, and only by Joseph's wisdom and forethought were the people saved from perishing in misery and starvation. The money they paid for their corn was amassed in the treasuries of the king, and his wealth was beyond all computation. And when their money had been expended, they were compelled to barter their cattle, their horses, their flocks, and their asses, in exchange merely for bread, so sharp and extreme was the famine.

These gone, they had nothing but the service of their own bodies and the land they owned to offer in payment. Wherefore they sold their land to the king for corn and for seed. And when the granaries of one district were exhausted Joseph removed the people that dwelt there to some other region of Egypt, where there still remained supplies of grain sufficient for them. Even after the years of famine were over, the people continued to lease their lands from the king, and for rent paid into the royal treasury one-fifth of their annual harvest, except only the priests of Egypt who were under the personal protection of Pharaoh, and who were provided with all that they needed out of his royal bounty.

For seventeen years Jacob lived on in the land of Goshen. His sons prospered and had great possessions there. And the family of Israel grew and multiplied. But there came a day when he was so enfeebled with age and sickness that he knew his earthly pilgrimage would soon be at an end, and that he must die.

Message was sent to Joseph that his father was sick unto death. He came in haste to see him, bringing with him his two sons, Ephraim and Manasseh. The women that were waiting upon his father in the tent withdrew. The old man lay upon his bed, as if asleep. In sorrow beyond speech, Joseph knelt down beside him and laid his hand in caress upon the wasted hand of his father. His eyes opened; he gazed into Joseph's face and smiled, as if all his troubles were now ended.

"Thou hast come," he said. "It is enough. There is little

time left to me, my son, but I have one urgent thing to ask of thee. If peradventure I have found grace in thy sight, I entreat thee that in the last thou wilt deal kindly and truly with me, and bury me not in Egypt, where I am a stranger, but carry me again into Canaan, the land of my fathers. There and with them let me lie at rest in the burial place that is prepared for me."

Joseph gazed into the wasted face. "Whatsoever thou mayst ask of me, that in truth will I do."

And Jacob said: "Nay, I entreat thee, let it be a vow between thee and me, my son, for it is matter very near to my heart."

Joseph sware unto him, and his father was greatly comforted. Strength returned into him. He raised himself in his bed and thanked God that he was now at peace.

Then Joseph brought his two sons into the presence of his father. They stood within the entry, tarrying until he should call them near.

But Jacob's eyes were dim and he looked at them without recognition. "Who are these?" he said.

"These are my two sons", said Joseph, "whom thou knowest well. They were given me of God in Egypt, and are come to ask thy blessing."

He led them by the hand and brought them to the bedside, and his father stretched out his hand and laid his right hand on Ephraim's head and his left hand on Manasseh's, and he did this wittingly though he knew that Manasseh was Joseph's firstborn. For in the light of death he foresaw that in years to come the descendants of the younger would exceed those of the elder in greatness and numbers. And he blessed them and embraced them.

He reminded Joseph how the Lord God had appeared to him in a vision in the night when he lay sleeping in the

wilds of Bethel, and how he had made known to him that
those who came after him should inherit the land of Canaan
for an everlasting inheritance.

"Very dear was thy mother Rachel to me, my son, but
when we were journeying from Bethel but a little distance
from Ephrath near Bethlehem, she died at the wayside. I
mourned and wept over her, and there I buried her. How
then could I else but love thee very dearly also, thee and thy
brother Benjamin? So, too, these thy sons, whom thou
lovest, shall be remembered, and they shall partake of the
glories of Israel when it has become a nation and is entered
into the land that God hath promised. For many long and

weary years I had not thought to see thy face again, and now behold God hath not only restored thee to me, but hath given me breath to bless thy two sons also."

And Ephraim and Manasseh bowed themselves before the bed and withdrew. When Joseph was again alone with his father he watched beside him, and between his fitful slumbers they communed together.

"Behold I die," said Jacob, "but God shall be with thee." And Joseph stooped himself, weeping, beside the bed, and kissed his father, and Jacob gave him his last blessing.

Then the rest of his sons came together into his presence and he blessed them one and all, predicting with his last words what the future would bring forth for all that came after them, their children's children for unnumbered generations. For though the shadows of death were darkening over him, his mind was clear and his vision untroubled. With this he bade them a last farewell, and composed himself to die. He drew his feet up into the bed, yielded up his spirit to God who gave it, and was gathered to his people.

When Joseph saw that life was gone, he prostrated himself beside his father, kissed him and wept over him, and remained with him in death, alone, in bitter grief.

Then to the physicians who were in his service, men skilled in the embalming of the dead, he entrusted the body of his father, and they embalmed it with precious salts and spices and swathed it in the finest linen. And not only Jacob's sons and their households mourned for him, but Pharaoh himself, his chief counsellors and his whole court and the Egyptians throughout Egypt, from the highest to the lowest, mourned for him also. Seventy days was the period of Egypt's mourning for this stranger, for the story of how Joseph, Pharaoh's renowned vizier, had as by a wonder been restored to his father and to his brethren long after he had been given up for dead, was known throughout the whole country, from one end of it to the other.

And Joseph made known to Pharaoh that he had solemnly sworn to his father that his body should be buried not in Egypt, since it was a country strange to him, but in the land of Canaan, where he was born, and in the tomb of Isaac his father.

"Give me leave, I pray thee, then," he said, "to absent myself from Egypt a while, that I may keep the vow I made to my father when he was nearing death and may bury him in the place where he himself desired to rest. Then will I return again." And Pharaoh consented.

A very great company went up out of Egypt to Jacob's burial, for not only Joseph himself with his brothers and all their households, except only their little ones, followed his father to the grave, but also the chief officers of Pharaoh's palace, the governors of the cities of Egypt, and the stewards whom Joseph had appointed over the granaries. There went with them also an escort of many chariots and a multitude of horsemen.

When this great concourse had come into Canaan, to the threshing-floor of Atad that was beyond Jordan, the mourners who followed after the gilded coffin containing the embalmed body of Jacob, lifted up their voices and made lament with dirges and wailings. There Joseph and the lords of Egypt that were with him mourned for his father seven days.

When the people of Canaan who dwelt near the Jordan heard this great mourning and lamentation, they marvelled. "Of a surety," they said, one to another, "this must be a day of sore sorrow and bitterness to the Egyptians."

And afterwards, Joseph and his brethren went on alone and the body of their father was laid to rest beside his father

Isaac, in the tomb hewn out of the rock at Machpelah, which Abraham, Isaac's father, had himself purchased and prepared for his own burial-place. Then Joseph and all who had accompanied him into Canaan returned into Egypt.

The funeral pomp and ceremonies of the Egyptians, and the great cavalcade that had gone up with them into Canaan were to his brothers a fresh revelation of Joseph's sovran power in the land. And when they were alone together again, mere shepherds and overseers of cattle, they were seized with misgivings.

The fear had suddenly come upon them that maybe it was only while their father was still alive that Joseph had refrained from requiting them for all the evil they had done against him; that through the years which had gone by he had been merely concealing his hatred of them, biding his time; and that now the day had come when his full vengeance would sweep down upon them.

A messenger was sent; for they feared to see him. By him they made known to Joseph that when their father was lying sick to death they themselves confessed their act of lying treachery against him, after they had sold Joseph to the Ishmaelites.

"And he himself charged us before he died", they said, "to give thee this message. 'Say unto my beloved son Joseph,' he said, 'forgive, I pray thee, the evil which thy brothers did against thee, and all the misery that came of it.' We entreat thee then to heed the words of our father and of thy father, and to forgive us the evils of which we were guilty against the God he worshipped."

Joseph was distressed that they mistrusted him. He at once sent for them all, and they were brought into his presence where he sat alone. They prostrated themselves before him and made obeisance as of old.

"Behold," they said, "we are the servants of the God of thy father. Do with us as seems best to thee."

And Joseph reassured them. It grieved him to the heart to see them humbling themselves before him.

"Put away your fears," he said. "Think you that I stand here in God's stead to judge and punish whom I may? Surely it is not so. For even though in the days that are gone and best forgotten you did me this injury, it was his will that only good should come of it. For by this I was made the means of saving you and your wives and your little ones and many another from death itself. Put away all your cares then, and think no more of them, either now or at any time in the future. Believe only that it is my one hope and desire to protect you and your little ones, and to watch over you, lest being among strangers in a strange land you should come to any harm."

He comforted them and spoke kindly to them, saying all that was in his heart, and they doubted him no more.

So Joseph continued to dwell in Egypt, and they with him. He lived long enough to see around him his son Ephraim's grandchildren, and the children also of Machir, the son of Manasseh. Even when he was a very old man, these little ones would be brought in to see him, for he loved children. And they would sit talking to him upon his knee.

But the day came when he knew that death was approaching. And he sent for his brothers to bid them farewell.

"I am dying", he said, "and these must be my last words to you; bear them, I pray you, in mind. God will surely be ever with you, and in his own season will bring those who come after you up out of Egypt and into the land which he promised to Abraham, to Isaac, and to our father Jacob, even into Canaan. In that day may I myself be remembered, as may God remember you. Vow unto me then that my bones shall be carried up hence and laid to rest beside my father." And they swore it to him.

And Joseph died, being a hundred and ten years old. And his physicians and embalmers embalmed his body and laid it in a coffin, and his coffin was enshrined in a sarcophagus of rich and strange and curious workmanship, and this was given into the charge of his brethren in Goshen. And Pharaoh the king and all his court and the whole land of Egypt sorrowed and mourned for Joseph many days, for of all the king's counsellors none in foresight, divination, power and wisdom, had been greater than he.

# MOSES

# The Ark of Bulrushes

Now Jacob was called Israel. He was the son of Isaac, whose father was Abraham, the servant of God. And these are the names of Jacob's sons that came down with him out of Canaan into Egypt: Reuben, Simeon, Levi, Judah, Issachar, Zebulun, Dan, Naphtali, Gad, Asher and Benjamin. With their households, their wives and their children, seventy souls of Jacob's blood in all, with their servants and herdsmen and handmaids, they came down, and set up their tents in the rich pastures of Goshen, a land east of Egypt, and west of what were then the northern reaches of the Red Sea. And a shallow cultivated strip of land, watered by a canal, stretched out east again of Goshen towards this sea.

There, as long as Joseph lived, and in his loving favour and protection, they dwelt. There they prospered, following the peaceful life of shepherds. And to some of them was deputed the charge of the king's cattle. They were the keepers of Pharaoh's herds.

As time went on, they died, and all their kindred and all that generation. But their children's children who had been born and reared in Egypt, and their descendants also, increased so abundantly that in the centuries that followed they spread abroad throughout the whole region of Goshen. They became a nation. The land was filled with them.

They too continued to prosper. But there came at length

a day when a new king arose in Egypt—a king to whom the name and fame of Joseph was naught. He was a man of a rare personal beauty and renowned for his valour. He reigned for many years, and in power and conquest was one of the mightiest monarchs that ever sat on the throne of Egypt. He led his armies to victory in Syria, in Libya, and in Nubia. He besieged Khetesh, the chief city of the Hittites, on the island in the midst of the river Orontes, and utterly subdued them. He built vast solemn temples to the gods of Egypt, rich in splendour and treasure, himself both priest and king. The avenue of sphinxes, man-headed lions of stone, which he caused to be made, his prodigious pylons or gateways, the granite image of himself towering above thirty cubits in stature from its headdress to its foot, and the records of his victories incised in the stones of his monuments—all these continue for earthly record of him to this day.

But he knew not Joseph. The services that as viceroy Joseph had rendered to Egypt in the seven years when its harvests failed and when by his insight and wisdom he had saved its people from famine and death, had been forgotten. In the eyes of this Pharaoh the Hebrews in Goshen were no longer a favoured people under his special grace. He regarded them with suspicion and distrust.

They occupied territory on the most dangerous frontier of Egypt. He saw how rapidly they grew in power and numbers—a race of alien blood and customs and religion, and, though small in stature, keen and alert in body and mind. And he feared that a day might come when Egypt being at war, they might ally themselves with his enemies and, fighting against him, fling off his domination over them and become a free people. His distrust poisoned his mind against them; and when the campaigns beyond his borders no longer occupied his mind, he took counsel on the matter with his chief statesmen and advisers.

"These Hebrews", he said, "have become a danger and a menace, and if nothing be done to keep them in subjection, they will swarm like flies among us to such a degree that they will become more numerous than the Egyptians themselves. Let us so deal with them, then, as to give them neither the power nor temptation to revolt and to betray us."

He set over them masters of works or overseers, men who would enforce his orders with a high hand. These overseers divided Goshen into districts, and the Hebrews who dwelt in them into droves or gangs. They were each of them responsible for a certain district; and over every gang they appointed a foreman who was himself a Hebrew. They spared no man either on account of his youth or age or infirmity—all must serve the king.

Little by little they increased the labour they exacted from the Hebrews until they had reduced them to a state of cruel bondage from which there was no release. They brought down their lives to a continual hardship, compelling them to toil like beasts of burden, driven on by rod and lash, until, worn to skin and bone, they could work no more, and were flung aside to die.

They cut canals and built dams, by means of which the waters of the great river of Egypt were heaped up to higher levels for the irrigation of the soil. They dug ditches and made conduits, and raised water from one conduit to another by means of buckets fixed to a pole hung upon an axle between two posts—filling and emptying, filling and emptying from morn to eve, to water the Egyptians' crops, to replenish their fish-ponds, and flush the conduits in their gardens and orchards.

In the glare and heat of the sun they laboured all day in

the desert quarries. They hewed and cut and dragged away over wooden rollers or on sleds huge ponderous blocks of marble and granite to serve for the building of Pharaoh's temples to the strange gods of Egypt. For monument and sculpture also—gigantic images and obelisks fretted with hieroglyphs proclaiming the valour, glory and wisdom of the king.

But for the most part these slave-gangs were set to the making of bricks. Some dug out the silt or mud. Others carried water in their water-jars from the tanks or cisterns to moisten it. Yet others kneaded the mud, trampling it with their feet until it was smooth and fit for use, and mixing with it chopped-up straw to bind it together. The more skilled among them then shaped the mud thus prepared by forcing it into great sanded moulds stamped within with the symbol of the king.

The bricks thus shaped, while still soft, were carried off on a framework of wood, slung from a yoke over the shoulders, and were stacked in rows one above the other, with chinks for air between them, and straw to prevent them from sticking together. There they lay until they were baked dry and black in the blazing heat of the sun.

Such were the labours of the Hebrews—the men of Israel—under Pharaoh, which they were compelled to endure without complaint; wageless, hopeless and ill-fed. Yet, the more ruthlessly they were oppressed and afflicted, the more they increased in numbers and the further they spread. The Egyptians came to look on them with loathing and contempt.

Seeing at last that no toil or hardship he had devised could keep them in subjection, Pharaoh decreed that of all the children born to the women of the Hebrews only their daughters should be allowed to live. Their sons, their men-children, were to be snatched away at birth from their mothers' breasts, and flung into the Nile. As he commanded, so it was done. There was lamentation and weeping in Goshen. And for this, beyond all else, the people of Israel feared and hated Pharaoh and his overseers; but were powerless to revolt.

None the less and in spite of this decree there came about the deliverance of Israel; for the Lord raised up a leader among them whose name has been famous throughout the ages and to this day.

There was a woman of the family of Levi whose name was Jochabed. She was a widow when her husband had taken her to wife, and she already had two children, a daughter named Miriam, and a son, but three years old, called Aaron. She was of a lively and fearless spirit, and when a second son was born to her, she hid him away. He was fair in face beyond any child in Israel, strong and comely, and she counted her own life as nothing so long as he was safe. For three whole months she nursed and tended him and kept him hidden, though every passing footfall and his least little cry filled her with terror that her secret might be discovered.

When she could hide him no longer, she began to think within herself what she should do to keep him safe. And there came a bold device into her mind. She went down one evening to the brink of the river, and gathered there a bundle of the long flowery-tufted reeds or bulrushes that grew in its shallows. Of these she made a little ark or coffer or jonket, hollow within and rounded without, and woven close. And she plaited a roof or lid to it, on a hinge.

When the ark had been securely woven together in the fashion of basket-makers, she daubed it over with silt and pitch to make it water-tight, even as long ages before had been the great ark of Noah himself; and she left it to dry.

As soon as it was light the next morning, and while the stars were yet faint in the sky, she rose up, and having fed the child and done all that was needful for his comfort, she lulled him into a deep and quiet sleep again, and kissed him, and put him into the ark and covered him over with the roof of rushes which she had woven to shield him from the heat of the sun. Then, with her daughter Miriam, she stole off down to the river, no-one by, and hid the ark among the nodding water-weeds at its brink. Having made sure that it would float in safety where it lay, she left her small daughter to keep watch over it, and herself returned home. The child then hid herself among the reeds and rushes where she could keep the ark continually in sight.

The birds flitted back to their haunts; only their trillings and the lapping of the water and the sighing and whisper of the reeds broke the hush. The hours sped softly on, and nothing had come to alarm or disturb the child when of a sudden she heard the sound of voices sweet and clear. She peered out of her hiding-place and, scarcely able to breathe, drew swiftly back again.

For, behold, it was the daughter of Pharaoh the King whose voice she had heard, and who with her maidens was come down to the river to bathe. Presently after, still laughing and talking, her maidens withdrew; and, fair themselves as lotus flowers, strayed along by the water-side gathering lilies, while, with none but her own handmaid to attend upon her, this princess, the daughter of Pharaoh, prepared to bathe.

On drawing near to the river in her naked loveliness, she looked and saw there the ark hidden among the reeds, black but glinting in the sun, and rocked gently to and fro

upon the rippled water. She stayed, wondering, and, with the palm of her hand above her eyes, steadfastly watched a while, in doubt of what this strange object could be. Then she bade her handmaid wade into the water and bring it in.

This she did. Lifting up the ark in her arms from out of the water, she carried it to her mistress, and she herself lifted its lid. And there, mantled up softly within, its cheeks flushed with sleep, was a little child, which, as soon as the bright beams of the sun pierced into the narrow darkness wherein it lay, stirred in its slumbers, awoke and wept. The

[ 139 ]

daughter of Pharaoh stooped, and taking the child into her arms, nestled it to her breast, and soothed its fears.

At sound of her gentle voice it looked up into her face and stayed its weeping; and with the tears yet wet upon its cheek, thrust out a hand and smiled. The young princess gazed at it in wonder and delight. She was smitten to the heart by its beauty and helplessness, and was filled with compassion. Glancing covertly about her, she said to her handmaid: "See now, this must be one of the Hebrew women's children. What shall be done to keep it safe—for surely it is in great danger?"

At this, the child's sister, who had been intently watching all that took place, drew near, and bowing herself before the daughter of Pharaoh, asked if she should go and call one of the Hebrew women, to nurse and tend it.

"Do as thou sayest," said the daughter of Pharaoh, "and go quickly, for I know not how long the child has been without food."

Her heart bounding with joy and excitement, the little maid at once ran off to her mother and told her everything that she had seen and heard. They came back together, and the daughter of Pharaoh, after but one look into the woman's face, gave the babe into her keeping.

"Take this child into thy charge," she said, "nurse it most carefully, and see that no harm come to it. If any should ask whose child it is, send word at once to me, and I will protect thee. It shall stay with thee until it is grown a little, and is of an age to be safe with me. And thou shalt have the wages due to thee."

At this the woman—who was indeed the child's own mother—could hardly keep back her tears, for joy. She bowed herself before the daughter of Pharaoh and in all things did as she was bidden. From that day on her care was over. She loved the child ever more dearly, her one sorrow being the thought that he would some day be taken away from her. And the daughter of Pharaoh provided all that was needful for the well-being and comfort of mother and son.

As soon as he was grown to be of an age when he no longer needed her, his mother brought him to the daughter of Pharaoh. She rejoiced to see this lovely child. Slaves were appointed whose only duty it was to wait upon him and to bring him up as if he were by birth and right of the royal house. The princess treated him in all things as if he were her own son, and she called him Moses, which means "Child of the Waters". For—as if some compassionate divinity had hidden him there—had she not found him among the reeds and rushes by the river's brink?

# The Burning Bush

As Moses grew up, he revealed rare gifts of mind and spirit. He was by nature quiet and patient and not easily roused. But, once angered, his heart burned like a furnace, and when he was resolved on a thing no earthly power could turn him aside from it. His dark eyes were set deep beneath clear-cut brows and, unlike the young men of the Egyptians, a short square beard covered his cheek and chin.

What he gave his mind to he mastered; and though he was slow of speech, he was of a spirit that could persist, and press on through all dangers and hindrances. He was a born leader of men and of a will that commands armies. He became learned in all the wisdom of the Egyptians, and while still in his youth was admitted to the college of the priests in On or Heliopolis, the City of the Sun, where the father of Joseph's wife had been High Priest. There, as legend tells, he was known as Asrasif.

But though he was of the high-born company of the priests, he kept himself apart from their mysteries and rites in the vast and solemn temple of Osiris, mightiest of the divinities worshipped by the ancient Egyptians, and judge of the the under-world of their dead. Like Joseph before him, he was faithful to the Lord God of Israel. He prayed to him in solitude under the open heavens, his face towards the east.

Obedient none the less to the severe discipline of the priests, he shared with them in all exercises of the mind— music and geometry and mathematics, and was familiar with the secret knowledge and magic of his own age, and the lore of the starry-minded Chaldeans, the Assyrians, and the Greeks.

He was skilled, too, it is recorded, in the knowledge and strategy of war, and served as an officer in the armies of Egypt when they defeated the invading hordes of the Ethiopians. From childhood he had been accustomed to the graces and manners and luxury of an Egyptian palace, but he knew of what race he was, and that he owed his life and all that he had to his mother's love, and his heart grieved continually over the tribulations of Israel.

When Moses was grown up and in the full years of his manhood, he set out one day, as was his custom, to visit his own people. And he came to where slave-gangs of the Hebrews were at work under their foremen and an Egyptian overseer. By means of wooden rollers laid upon the sand, they were hauling a prodigious stone that had been hewn out of its quarry to the place where it was to be used for building.

The sun blazed down upon the tawny sands of the desert; the air shimmered like molten glass. These Hebrews, haggard and emaciated, stared like brute beasts; the hands of those as yet not broken in to the rope were blistered and bleeding. And as Moses watched them, they stayed a moment to recover their breath, panting with exhaustion, the sweat streaming down from their shaven heads and sun-scorched faces.

But the master of the slave-gang gave them no respite. With curses and lashes he drove them on, treating them with less forbearance than he would even things without life. In pity of their misery Moses could hardly restrain the rage and grief that flamed up in him. He turned swiftly away and strode on.

Throughout the day their cowed and hopeless faces, the looks they had cast him, their weal-scarred shoulders, haunted his mind. He poured out his indignation to his elder brother, Aaron, sharing with him his shame and sorrow at the woes of Israel.

Still in this trouble of soul, he was returning alone a little before nightfall by the way he had come, when a cry of anguish suddenly pierced the quiet, so shrill and piteous that it might be that of a snared beast in the throes of death. He turned aside instantly out of the track. It was no beast that had uttered the cry, but a young Hebrew, one of his own kindred, who was pleading in vain for mercy against the cruelties of an Egyptian that stood over him.

Unseen of either, Moses drew swiftly near. He glanced hither and thither; there was no man in sight. And like an angel of wrath he ran in upon the Egyptian, smote him, and flung him lifeless to the ground. All sounds were hushed in the evening peace. He was alone, trembling and shivering, and cold with dread. He stooped and looked: and stared on in horror of what he had done. At length he hastily scooped out a hole with his hands and hid the body of the Egyptian in the sand.

All that night he lay without sleep and could get no release from the torment of his thoughts. The scene of his wild act of vengeance hung like a picture in the vacancy of the dark, and he was stricken with remorse.

He rose early and went out secretly to the place where he had hidden the body of the Egyptian. And as he drew near in the red glow of the morning, he saw two Hebrews who were bitterly quarrelling. Before he could come to them,

one struck the other down with the staff he carr
was distorted with rage and hatred. Moses ran i
the fallen man from the ground, and staunched

"Why dost thou strike this man?" he rep
other. "What evil has he done? Is he not of our blood, mine
and thine? Surely we at least should be at one together, and
not add to the miseries of Israel?"

The man turned and cursed him. "Who art thou to come
meddling and spying?" he cried. "Who appointed thee a
priest and judge over us? Wouldst thou murder me as thou
didst yesterday murder the Egyptian? Beware of it!"

His voice rang out loud and clear in the bright air. Moses
turned swiftly and hastened away, sick to the soul, and helpless. What he had thought to be a secret had been revealed.
Only a sprinkling of sand covered the body of the Egyptian
from the sight of man. He feared the vengeance of Pharaoh;
his one hope of safety was to flee out of the country while
yet there was time.

When indeed this matter was reported to the king, he was
filled with wrath. He had no love for Moses, who was of the
blood of the Hebrews, not Egyptian, though he had proved
his skill and resource in war. The king saw in him a danger,
and already suspected him of treason. And now that he had
occasion, he sought how he might kill him. But it was too
late. He had already escaped beyond the fortresses on the
frontiers of Egypt, nor did he pause in his flight until he
found himself in a region south of the land of Midian and
eastward of the Red Sea. There in ancient times were the
turquoise and copper mines of the kings of Egypt.

After long wandering Moses came at evening, when the
sun was low, to a well, where there was a grove of acacia
trees. Wearied out in mind and body, but at last out of
danger of pursuit, he sat down to rest. The shade was cool

after the heat of the day, the earth lay at peace beneath the flaming skies of sunset, and a slender crescent moon was in the west.

Now the priest of the Midianites who dwelt near there had seven daughters. And a little while after Moses had come to the well-side, these seven came down with their father's flocks, and began to fill with water the stone troughs that lay beside it, to water their sheep. And as they did so in the wild bright light of the desert skies, they talked merrily together, their sheep and lambs bleating thirstily around them.

They had been there but a little while, however, when fierce and morose herdsmen of the desert also came down with their flocks, and drove their sheep away. Moses at once rose up and defended them against the shepherds, and himself watered the sheep. The damsels thanked him, marvelling who this stranger could be.

When they returned home to their father, Jethro, he asked them, "How is it you are come back so early this evening?"

They told him of all that had happened at the well, and how a stranger, an Egyptian, had not only protected them from the shepherds, but had helped them to draw water and to give drink to their sheep.

"But where is this Egyptian?" said their father. "Why have you let him go? Haste, now, and bring him in, that I myself may thank him and that he may eat with us." They went out gladly and brought Moses in.

Moses supped with them that evening, and talked with Jethro late, and slept in his house. The days went by, and still he stayed on as Jethro's guest. The seven daughters of the priest never wearied of listening as he talked with their father of the wonders of Egypt, its prodigious funeral pyramids reared up by kings of bygone dynasties in the sands of the desert, the solemn temples to its gods, its lore and magic and learning, and the splendours of the City of the Sun. He spoke of the Pharaoh, too, that now sat upon the throne, and of his victories and conquests. And their hearts melted with pity as he recounted the woes of his fellow-countrymen.

At length Jethro persuaded his guest to go no further, but remain with them and become one of his household. Moses was well-content to do so, though at times he was sick for home and pined to return to his own land and to his own people. But he knew that the vengeance of Pharaoh against any who had angered and defied him never faltered or slept, and that to go back was to die.

And Jethro gave Moses his daughter Zipporah in marriage. Two sons were born to him. To his first-born Moses gave the name of Gershom, which means a Stranger, for he himself was a sojourner in a strange land. The other he named Eliezer, which means the Help of God, for in the day of his need God had delivered him from the vengeance of Pharaoh.

The years that Moses spent in the household of his father-in-law in the country of the Midianites—a people who in time to come were to be one of the fiercest enemies of Israel —were serene and happy. He was never to see their like again.

Now in the process of time the king of Egypt died, and his embalmed body with all pomp and ceremony was laid to rest in the innermost chamber of the secret tomb which he had himself caused to be hewn out of the rock in the desolate valley of the dead. And his son reigned in his stead.

This Pharaoh, who was advanced in age when he came to

the throne, had neither the courage nor the sagacity of his father. He was treacherous and boastful, stubborn and crafty. The Hebrews soon had cause to hate and fear him, for he was as pitiless as he was weak. They groaned under burdens too heavy to be borne, and their cry went up to God to deliver them.

And God heard their cries. He remembered the covenant and bond of peace that he had made with Abraham and Isaac and Jacob, and he took compassion upon them. And though they knew it not, the long years of their affliction in Egypt were nearly at an end.

At the approach of summer, when the rains were over and gone, and the sun burned hot in the sky, the grass-land in the region of Midian where lived Jethro the priest began to dry up and wither. And, as was usual at this season, Moses, who had charge of Jethro's flock, led his sheep far back across the wilderness to the lower uplands of the sacred mountain called Horeb, or Sinai. It was a region of vast steeps of naked rock, an inhuman silent solitude; its crags bleached with sun and tempest, its stones burnished by sharp winds and drifts of sand. Few living creatures roved in the gaunt shadow of these prodigious peaks of granite, only the wild goat found a footing there. And flights of birds could be seen on high winging across to Arabia. But Moses had always found happiness and peace in solitude. His own thoughts and reveries sufficed for company at need. Here, the thin mountain turf was green and sweet; and he stayed for many days in these desolate uplands, stark and affrighting even to those whose home was the wilderness; his dogs and sheep his only companionship.

The silence around him stilled mind and heart. Yet he longed for news of those he loved and from whom he had been separated so many years. The wrongs of Israel had

never throughout these years of exile ceased to grieve and trouble him.

One morning early before the dews had dried, he led his flock to fresh pastures, and there he lay down to rest, his staff in his hand, his dogs around him, while his sheep and lambs, each with its own gentle shadow beside it on the sward, grazed peacefully on. And as he sat alone, he fell into a reverie, and his spirit wandered far. Dwindling in distance, the eagle-haunted crags and crests of the mountains towered into the blue waste of noon, while near at hand

[ 149 ]

rose sheer the steeps of Horeb, its summit hidden in cloud. The scream of a bird rang in his ear, and aroused him from his reverie.

And lo, lifting up his eyes, he saw, above and beyond the rock-strewn slope of the valley that mounted up before him, and in a place bare and treeless, a burning bush. The flame of its burning went up from it as from a torch, clear and fervent in the noon-day sun. But though the bush burned on as if with fire, it was not consumed. For the flame was not of earth, but was the glory of an angel of the lord.

Moses gazed at it in wonder, and at length arose, saying within himself: "What marvel is this? I will turn aside and draw near and see this strange sight, why the bush is not burnt."

Leaving his flocks to roam as they willed, he went on up the valley into the solitude of the mountain.

When the Angel of the Lord saw that Moses had turned aside and drew near, he called to him from out of the midst of the burning bush, "Moses, Moses!"

There was no sound else between earth and heaven, and Moses stayed where he stood, his eyes fixed on its miraculous radiance. So still and clear was the voice that it might have called to him from out of the inmost silence of his mind. And he answered the angel: "Here am I."

Then said the angel of the Lord: "Come not hither; but put off thy sandals from off thy feet, for the place whereon thou standest is holy ground. I speak to thee in the name of the Lord God who sent me hither, the God thy father worshipped, yea, the God of Abraham, the God of Isaac, the God of Jacob."

And Moses hid his face, for he was afraid to look upon God. And the voice said: "I have seen the affliction of my people in Egypt and I have heard their wailing by reason of the taskmasters that oppress them. I know their sorrows; and am come down to deliver them and to send thee thyself to Pharaoh the King that thou mayest set my people free and lead them out of Egypt."

The words rang sweet as a clarion in Moses' ears, yet his heart misgave him. "Alas, Lord," he said, "who am I—an outcast and a fugitive condemned to death—that I should confront Pharaoh face to face and bring forth the people of Israel from out of Egypt."

The Lord said: "Be not afraid; I will surely be with thee. All those who sought to kill thee in Egypt are now dead. And for token that it is I, the Lord, who am sending thee thither, the day shall come when thou thyself and all Israel shall serve and worship me upon this sacred mountain."

Moses, still communing with himself, turned his face away and gazed out over the valley where his sheep were placidly browsing and into the distance towards Egypt. And the light of the flame of the burning bush smote on his face, gilding it as if with gold, and the whole earth was still as though in trance.

"But it may be", he said, "when I come before the people and tell them, 'The God of Israel hath sent me, and I come to do his will,' that they will challenge me, and say: 'But who is this God of whom thou speakest: and what is his name?' How then shall I answer them?"

And the Lord God, speaking through the mouth of the angel, answered Moses and said: "I AM THAT I AM: eternal, infinite, the source of all life, all love, all wisdom. And to thee and to my people I will be all that I will reveal myself to be, though as yet thou hast no knowledge of it. Assemble the elders of Israel and proclaim to them: 'Jehovah, the Lord God of your fathers, who was, and is, and ever shall be, hath sent me unto you. I AM hath sent me unto you'. This is my name and it shall be my memorial to all generations. Then say this unto them: 'The Lord God of Israel knows all your sorrows and has seen your distress, and he himself will lead you out and set you free from your bondage in Egypt and bring you up at length into the land that he promised to Abraham, to Isaac and to Jacob, even into Canaan, a good and fruitful land, a land flowing with milk and honey.' And they will listen and pay heed to thee. Then thou and the elders of Israel shall come together into the presence of Pharaoh the king of Egypt, and thou shalt say to him: 'The Lord God of the Hebrews hath revealed himself to us and called us to do his bidding. We entreat thee to let us go three days' journey out of Egypt into the solitude of the wilderness that we may make solemn sacrifice to the Lord our God.'

"But the King of Egypt will refuse to hearken. He is arrogant and stubborn, and no plea or entreaty will move him or cause him to waver. Then shall I stretch forth my hand and I shall smite Egypt with my marvels. Egypt shall be afflicted and all men shall wonder. In that day not only shall this Pharaoh set my people free, but they shall go rejoicing, with their sons and their daughters, and burdened with the riches of Egypt, jewels of silver and jewels of gold, and fine raiment. The proud and haughty of Egypt shall heap gifts upon them and shall urge them to hasten and be gone."

But Moses, still doubting within himself, answered and said: "But even yet it may be that when I appear before the elders of Israel and say the Eternal hath sent me, and declare the sacred name, they may still refuse to believe me, and deny that I come from God. How then shall I give proof of it?"

The voice said: "What is it in thy hand?"

[ 152 ]

He answered: "My shepherd's staff."

Then said the Lord: "Cast it upon the ground."

Moses, as he was bidden, flung down his staff, and behold, as it touched the rock on which it fell, it became a serpent, living and venomous, and Moses started back from it in fear.

Then said the Lord: "Put out thy hand without fear and seize the serpent by the tail."

Moses stooped, and seized the serpent; and its being changed, and lo, it was his shepherd's staff that was again in his hand.

Then said the Lord: "Thrust thy hand into thy bosom."

He did so. And when he plucked it out of his bosom, it had become like the silvery hand of a leper and was white as snow.

Then said the voice: "Cover thy hand again."

And when Moses withdrew his hand, it no longer resembled that of a leper, but was restored to the likeness of the other.

Then said the Lord: "If when thou appear before the elders of Israel, they believe not that thou art come from the Eternal, and refuse to be convinced either by the one sign I have given thee or by the other, and will not listen to thee, then do thou fill a vessel with the water of the river of Egypt and pour it out upon the parched sands on the bank of the river, and the water which thou hast taken out of the river shall become red as blood upon the sand."

Then said Moses: "O Lord God, I beseech thee to have patience with me. I am by nature slow and halting of speech and ever have been. Nor even while thou hast been speaking with me have I been able to say what is in my heart, for I am a man without any skill in the use of words. How then shall I speak before the elders of Israel so that they shall be persuaded and believe in me, and that thou hast sent me?"

And God said to Moses: "Who made the mouth of man? Who causes this man to be dumb and that deaf, and who gives or withholds the sight of man's eyes? Is it not the Lord God, the creator of all? Go then, and think no more how thou shalt say what I have bidden thee say, for I my-self will guide thy tongue and give thee speech."

Moses bowed his head in deep and perplexed thought. He was divided in mind. All his heart's longing was to obey the will of the Lord for the redemption of his people. Yet distrust of himself and of his own powers still held him back. His voice trembled. "So be it, O Lord," he said. "And yet I would that the Lord would send someone to speak for him better able than I am!"

At this, the anger of the angel of the Lord was kindled against Moses. "Hast thou forgotten Aaron thy brother?" he said. "Is he not a Levite and a priest, and hath he no gift of words? Even now he is on his way hither to meet thee, and when he seeth thee, his heart will be filled with joy. Do thou then speak with him, and inspire and direct him in all that he shall say. Thou shalt tell him of the wonders that have been shown to thee this day. I have made thee my prophet before Israel and before the King of Egypt, and Aaron thy brother shall be thy spokesman. In all things thou shalt be his inspiration, as if thou thyself wert of God, and he thy prophet. Take thy staff, and this rod that I give into thy hand. With it thou shalt do miracles and show that I the Eternal am with thee."

The voice ceased and Moses was alone. High overhead the virgin crest of Horeb pierced the sky, its shadow flung dark across the hollow steep on which he stood, as the sun went down into the west. The flame, pure as crystal and of the light of gold, that had dwelt in the midst of the bush yet had touched neither twig nor leaf with fire, no longer shone upon his face and filled his mind with its radiance, for the angel of the Lord had gone his way.

# The Petition to Pharaoh

Moses went down into the valley and gathered together his flock and led them back across the desert to Jethro. He said nothing of what had passed during the days of his absence. His face was changed. The vision he had seen haunted his eyes. He spoke like one who has been very near to death and what lies beyond it, and whose mind is far away. He told Jethro that he wished to leave his service awhile, and to return into Egypt. "Let me go, I pray thee," he said, "so that I may visit my own people again and those near and dear to me in my own country, for I know not even if they are still alive."

Jethro was very gracious to him; the years they had spent together had deepened their affection one for another. He could see that some strange event of which he himself had no knowledge had deeply moved and troubled Moses, and he divined a little of what was in his mind. He asked no questions, but fondly embraced him. "Go in peace," he said, "and may all things be well with thee and with thy brethren from whom thou hast been parted so long."

When they had first met together, Moses had been a stranger, friendless and solitary, his very life in danger. The day was soon to come when he would return into Midian and to Mount Horeb, and they would meet again; but he himself would then no longer be a shepherd of sheep, but the leader and commander of the whole host of Israel.

Having bidden his wife and his two sons farewell, Moses set out on his journey. And while he was passing through the wilderness at the foot of Mount Horeb he met his brother Aaron who was himself come to visit him. He kissed him and great was their happiness. They had much to tell one another; and as they slowly paced along side by side through the parched flats and sandhills of the desert towards Goshen, or sat at evening in the camping-place where they were to sleep, Moses shared with his brother the anxious thoughts that filled his mind. He told him of the wonder of the burning bush and all that the Lord had bidden him do in Egypt, and of the signs and portents that were to be revealed. And they faced together the supreme ordeal that lay before them, giving one another confidence and resolution.

When they came into Goshen, they called together the elders or chief men of Israel, and Aaron revealed to them everything that Moses had told him concerning his communion with the Lord on the sacred mountain of Horeb, and Moses himself showed them the signs and wonders of the Lord. The people believed. The Lord God had seen their sorrow and was compassionate. Their hearts were filled with joy and longing and ardour; they bowed their heads and worshipped.

On a day appointed by Pharaoh, Moses and Aaron and the elders of Israel were brought into the hall of audience in the palace of the king to present their petition. They prostrated themselves before him and made obeisance. And Pharaoh demanded what reason they had for appearing before him.

They answered him: "We come not as suppliants before Pharaoh, but have been sent hither by the Lord, the God of Israel. Our words are his words, and it is his command that we bring to the king. Thus saith the Lord: 'Let my people go out of Egypt that they may make a pilgrimage into the wilderness, and there keep a solemn feast and offer sacrifice to their God'."

As he listened, the face of Pharaoh darkened with scorn and derision. "And who is this God," he said, "that I should regard him? I neither know nor heed him. Nor will I let the Hebrews go."

They answered him: "We entreat thee to have patience and to listen to our petition, seeing that it is not merely we, thy servants, who plead before thee, but the Lord God of the Hebrews who hath made known his will unto us. It is little that we ask: only that our people may be granted a brief respite from their toil in the king's quarries and brick-fields, and may go forth on a three days' pilgrimage into the wilderness, there to sacrifice to their God. Else peradventure some great evil may befall them—pestilence or the sword."

"I say unto thee," said Pharaoh in his wrath, "I neither know this God nor heed him. If God he be, what sign or token canst thou show that he has sent thee? The Gods are mighty, and manifest themselves on earth in marvels beyond man's understanding. You say you are this God's envoys. Give proof of it then, and it may be that Pharaoh himself will do him honour!"

Then in the presence of the king and of his lords and counsellors who were in attendance upon him, Aaron cast down before the throne the rod that was in his hand. And behold, before the eyes of all assembled there, the rod was changed and became a living serpent. They recoiled from it in astonishment and fear. And Aaron stooped and plucked it up from the ground, and it returned to its former shape and semblance, and his rod was again in his hand.

But Pharaoh himself sat unmoved on his throne, a smile

of secret mockery on his high narrow countenance. He
gave command that his wizards or magicians should be
summoned into his presence—men skilled in occult and
secret arts. In the robes of their rites, and each with his
magic wand or rod in his hand, Jannes and Mambres their
leaders, they entered the great hall and made obeisance to
the king. And as Aaron had done, so did they.

They cried their incantations, and cast down their rods
before the throne, and these too of the secret sorcery they
knew became as living serpents. And though Aaron's rod
had the mastery over theirs and swallowed them up, no sign

of wonder or apprehension showed on Pharaoh's face. He turned abruptly and addressed Moses and Aaron by name.

"Now indeed," said he, "can Pharaoh testify how mighty a God has sent you hither! Wondrous in truth are the marvels that he shares with the least of Pharaoh's magicians! But I have heard of you; and nothing good. What insensate folly was this in your minds by which you designed to deceive me? You crave audience of me and avow that some God of the Hebrews—who swarm like pestilent flies in the land—has bidden you go and make merry with him in the wilderness. But what, in the hidden treason of your designs, you are bent on doing is to breed discontent among my work-people, to decoy them away from their labours and pamper them with idleness. Understand then; the Hebrews shall not go; and I warn you to bring no more complaints before me. Look well to it."

That same day Pharaoh sent for the overseers whom he had set over the Hebrews, and commanded that in future not only should the straw that had hitherto been given to them for the making of bricks be withheld, and that the slave-gangs themselves should find where they could what they needed, but that in spite of this the daily tale of bricks required of them should in no degree be reduced.

The overseers and gang-masters made known to the Hebrews that from that day forward, by the king's decree, no more straw would be supplied to them as heretofore out of the royal granaries: and that in future they must find what straw they needed as best they could.

Now the only substitute available was the stubble that had been left in the fields after the gathering in of the harvest. Of long straw they could get none. Then day by day they wearied themselves in the idle and waste labour of grubbing up this stubble-straw; and the tale of bricks, which each gang was compelled to make, fell short of what was required of them.

And as day by day the overseers and their clerks, on checking the brick-piles, found the quantity of new-made bricks to be far less than was customary, they sent for the Hebrew foremen of the slave-gangs and beat them, threatening that a worse punishment was in store for them if the tale of bricks should fall short on the morrow. Enraged by this injustice, the Hebrew foremen met together and in a mob made their way into the city to appeal to Pharaoh. Herded together in the stifling heat by the armed guards who had been sent out to meet them, they were admitted no further than into the outer precincts of the palace, while two of them were led in before the king.

"We come to Pharaoh", they said, "to plead for justice. Why are his servants so vilely treated? The overseers goad us on and rage against us: 'Make brick, make brick!' But how shall bricks be made without straw? And why are we pitilessly beaten if a full day's tale of bricks fall short of what it should when half thy servants' time from dawn till dark must be spent in scrabbling stubble out of the fields? The blame is not ours but Pharaoh's and his overseers', who deal unjustly with his servants."

Then said Pharaoh: "Return thanks to what gods you have if, ere night come, you hang not by the neck to the loftiest gallows in Egypt. It is not because you have too much but too little to do that you come flocking out of Goshen in a rebellious rabble to make complaint. You are idle: you are idle! This also is why I am pestered with men of your race, puffed up with pride and folly, and asserting that some God requires your sacrifices in the sands of the desert. Begone from out of the city and trouble Pharaoh no more, lest the full vengeance of his wrath fall upon you, and that soon!"

And he decreed that the daily labour of the Hebrews should not be reduced by a single brick. The foremen of the slave-gangs were driven like sheep to the slaughter from out of the city. Their appeal to Pharaoh had left them in worse straits than before. They were indeed in evil case; on the one side an implacable tyrant and his overseers; and on the other the resentment of the Israelites who, worn-out with this double toil, worked under them and for whom they were answerable.

As they went on their way, disputing together and racked with the rough usage they had received, they encountered Moses and Aaron. Eager for news of what had passed, they had come out to meet them. The mob raged with fury at sight of them.

"Be God our witness of the evil you have brought on us," they shouted against them, "and may he judge between us and reward you as you deserve! You have poisoned the mind of Pharaoh against us, and made us to stink in the nostrils of all Egypt. And now because of your meddlings he will not rest until he has destroyed us altogether."

Moses turned away and left them, their menaces and reproaches ringing in his ears. As soon as he was alone, in anguish of soul he poured out all that was in his heart to the Lord. All that he had attempted had come to nothing. Pharaoh had not only contemptuously rejected his petition, but had avenged himself on the Israelites and embittered them against himself.

"O Lord God," he cried in his misery, "why hast thou chosen me, and yet hast forsaken me? All that I do is in vain."

And as he prayed, his mind became more serene. And the

Lord comforted Moses in the solitude of his communion with him.

"I am Jehovah the Lord God," he said, "who appeared unto Abraham and Isaac and Jacob; I am the Almighty whom they themselves worshipped. But they knew me only in part and could conceive of me only as their own hearts revealed to them. They knew not that I am the Eternal, who was and is and ever shall be. Yet it was I the Lord who established my covenant with them, that I would give the land of Canaan—the land wherein they themselves sojourned—to their children's children. Speak again to my people. Bid them have faith and be not cast down. The Eternal will be their salvation, and will redeem them from all their grief and woe.

"But if heartsick and impatient and made desperate by the cruelties they endure, they reject thee, and refuse to listen to thee, then do thou thyself return again to Pharaoh, and in all things as I bid thee, do. Stubborn with pride is the heart of Pharaoh, and his eyes are darkened. But my wonders shall be revealed, and a day shall come when thou thyself shalt be as a god to him, and he will humble himself before thee and plead with thee to intercede with the Lord of Hosts on his behalf, lest he himself be destroyed."

# The Plagues of Egypt

At the season of the annual inundation, when the waters of the Nile sweep down in flood from the mountains of Abyssinia, Pharaoh, attended by his courtiers, his priests and officers, proceeded in state from his palace to take part in a festival which, as in years gone by, was to be held upon the river. On his progress thither through the throngs which had come forth to acclaim him, and before he had embarked into the silken-sailed vessel that had been prepared for the ceremony and was moored beside the quay, Moses and Aaron confronted the king by the riverside, and yet again entreated him to grant the petition they had made on behalf of the Israelites. And again he refused to listen to them.

Then in sight of Pharaoh and of the great company assembled there, Moses lifted up his rod and smote the swirling waters. And behold, even as they watched, from shore to shore the whole surface of the flooding river began to run red as blood.

But though many were dismayed at this marvel, it moved Pharaoh not one whit. This also was within the knowledge of his wizards and magicians, and he paid no heed to it. When the ceremony was over, he returned to his palace. Nor did he show any sign of relenting when report was made to him that a wonder unknown in living memory had brought horror on the whole city.

For now the river not only continued to flow blood-red, but the fish in it perished. Its tide was laden with their puffed-up carcases, floating, belly upwards, as the flood-water swept from the mountains down to the sea. The river stank; and not the river alone. The water of the canals also that had been cut out for the irrigation of the fields glistened in the light of sunset, red as blood. Even in the reservoirs of the Egyptians, in their tanks and cisterns, in the very pots and jars they used in their houses—there was water red as blood. As it staled it putrefied and became foul and corrupt. Neither man nor beast dared taste of it. And the Egyptians were compelled to dig round about the river for water fit to drink, and to sink wells.

So it continued for seven days. And when the seven days were at an end Moses came again into the presence of Pharaoh. He warned him that unless he consented to do as the Lord God of Israel had ordained, the creeping things of the earth would bear witness against him and be a cause of shuddering and dread to the whole realm of Egypt. But Pharaoh stubbornly refused to pay heed to him, and dismissed him with contempt.

And even as Moses had foretold, there began to breed in the corrupt and blood-red waters of the river an unprecedented plague of frogs. The mud-shallows amidst the beds of reeds and rushes and the fringes of the water were soon astir and alive with them. They crawled up in an innumerable host from out of the swamps. They spread in myriads over the low-lying lands on either bank of the river, and swarmed everywhere, creeping and hopping not only into the orchards and gardens, fresh and lovely with their leafy trees and flowers, and into the lilied pools and conduits, but into the innermost rooms of the houses of the Egyptians, their bedchambers and their beds, their cooking stoves or ovens, and even into the bowls in which they kneaded their dough for the making of bread. Squat and noisome, there was no cranny or crevice free from them.

Clammy and cold as the mire from which they came, they climbed up, in the dead of night, upon the Egyptians' bodies as they lay asleep, and leapt about the clods in myriads as they worked in the fields. The air resounded with their croaking. Swarms of these harmless, bright-coloured creatures had been seen in Egypt in previous years, to be soon devoured by the waterfowl or to return into the Nile. But there is horror to man in nature's multitudes, and now, leaping and creeping, or staring and inert, they swarmed in every dwelling, even in the houses of the wealthiest nobles and the private chambers of Pharaoh and his queen.

The Egyptians were filled with loathing of the frogs. Why had their gods brought such a visitation upon them? If magic could bring such a pest, why could it not be conjured away? But the priests and sorcerers could do nothing. At length Pharaoh himself sent for the chiefs of the Hebrews and commanded Moses to intercede with his God.

"Think not", he said, "it is beyond the power and knowledge of my magicians to breed frogs. That is simple of proof. But to rid Egypt swiftly, and as with a gesture, of the plague of them that now afflicts the land—that were in truth a wonder. Entreat thy God, then, to remove this vexation from the land, seeing that it is a cause of distress to my people and an affront even to me myself. Then shall I know that he is indeed a mighty God, and that it is fitting the Hebrews should be given grace from their labour in order that they may do him honour."

Moses stayed a moment before he made answer to the king.

"What is thy servant", he said at last, "compared with Pharaoh, lord of all! Thou thyself shalt have this glory over me, and shalt decide at what hour I am to entreat the God of the Hebrews on thy behalf."

Pharaoh gazed at him stonily but concealed his anger. "Why, then, let it be to-morrow, and ere the sun set," he answered. And this he said to try Moses, for he had no belief in his mind that the plague was other than a visitation of nature.

Then said Moses: "So be it. To-morrow I will make my prayer, and the frogs shall be destroyed, and from that day onward none shall be found alive anywhere in Egypt, except only in the waters of the river. By this shalt thou know that there is in power none like unto the Lord our God; and that when he commands, the mightiest must obey."

The plague of frogs ceased. They perished suddenly in their myriads in the fields and orchards, in the gardens and the houses, and wheresoever they had crept for harbourage. Alive they had been pest enough, dead they were a foulness. The Egyptians, to be rid of their carcases, raked them together and piled them up in heaps that rotted in the sun. The air was filled with their stench.

But when it was reported to Pharaoh that as if by a marvel the land had been suddenly freed of this plague, and that to him had been accorded the renown of it, his mood changed. As lightly as he had given his word, so he dismissed all thought of it from his mind.

And Moses stretched out his hand, and with his rod he smote the dust of Egypt, as he had smitten the flooding waters of the Nile. And lo, in the brooding heat of the sun, from the sod-caked shallows of the river there issued a venomous swarm of gnats. They rose, droning, like clouds of fine dust into the air, their wings shimmering glass-like, the sound of them faint and shrill as a harp-string. Athirst for blood, they pestered man and beast both day and night, so that none could get peace or rest from them.

When Pharaoh summoned his wizards and bade them with their magic incantations breed life out of the dust, though in fear of his vengeance they made no answer at that time, they knew that all their enchantments would be in vain. This wonder was beyond their magic, and they themselves were dismayed and gave Pharaoh warning. "We entreat Pharaoh to beware," they said. "These vile Hebrews have knowledge to bring about mysteries of which we ourselves are ignorant. What now is all about us, haunting the very air we breathe, is no magic, but a cause of grave disquiet. We see in it the finger of God."

Yet such was Pharaoh's pride and self-will that he refused to listen to their counsel. In his vengeful malice against the Hebrews his heart was hardened, and the dews of the mercy of heaven were withdrawn from him because of his stubborn opposition to the will of God that he knew and feared yet refused to obey. He denied further audience to the Hebrews. And when Moses intercepted and confronted him as in his two-horsed chariot he proceeded with his courtiers on his way to the river, and warned him that unless he relented, worse evils would assuredly follow, he invoked the curses of his gods upon him and, his countenance distorted with rage, drove furiously on.

But repentance followed hard upon his folly. The wind veered, and began to blow softly yet persistently from out of the south—parching and sultry. And borne in on the stream of it there flitted in upon Egypt legions of dog-flies. Hovering in the air or crawling upon the ground, they crept into every byre and stable and pen and dwelling-house, and were a torment and a curse to all within their walls. The children wailed for pain and weariness. Man's business was brought almost to a standstill. Nor does the dog-fly betray its onset with the twangling of its wings. It settles in silence, stabs with its sharp weapon into the living flesh, and the pang of it is a warning that comes too late.

Yet though throughout the length and breadth of Egypt there was no escape from this blood-sucking pest of dog-flies, the land of Goshen where dwelt the people of Israel was wholly free from them. The Hebrews groaned under persecutors as pitiless in human shape, but of dog-flies there was none.

The ravages of these flies among the Egyptians became

at last beyond endurance, and Pharaoh sent in haste into Goshen for Moses and Aaron. They made obeisance to him where he sate in splendour in the midst of his court upon the royal dais, under its canopy of gold and blue and scarlet. But he was compelled to raise his voice to make himself audible above the droning of the dog-flies. He spoke harshly, his face enflamed, his voice hoarse with rage and chagrin.

"Up, and delay not, but get you gone," he said. "Your petition is granted. Return at once from whence you came. Prepare to make your feast in Goshen and there sacrifice to your God. Three days' grace, and three days' grace only, shall be given you, and my overseers and taskmasters shall be withdrawn meanwhile."

He appeared to speak in haste and as if without fore-thought, yet his words were as crafty as his intention. And Moses was not deceived.

"Our petition to the king", he made answer, "was that he should give grace to the Hebrews to make a three days' pilgrimage into the wilderness, to hold a solemn feast there, and there only, to the one true God. Beasts, then, in plenty we shall need for sacrifice, oxen and bullocks. But as Pharaoh knows well, these are held sacred to their gods by the Egyptians, and it would be a needless cause of offence to them if we remain in Goshen and sacrifice there. There would be riot and tumult. The people would rise up and stone the Hebrews, and bloodshed would follow. Nay, O king, it is into the wilderness that the children of Israel must go, and not less than three days' journey, for such is the will of God."

Pharaoh sat motionless, his lean cheek resting on his hand, his face set in a sullen frown. There was silence in the great hall, but for the whispering stir of the dog-flies.

"So be it," he said at last. "There is wisdom in your appeal to me; and it is true there might be this danger. The least sign of riot or rebellion is hateful to me and would meet with instant retribution. Let then the Hebrews go their way well beyond the confines of Egypt into the desert. But not too far: too far, I say. And now delay no longer, but intercede between me and the Lord thy God."

"Thou hast spoken," said Moses. "I go now to entreat the Lord to free Pharaoh and his people from the visitation that he has brought upon them. But let not Pharaoh vaunt himself over me if the Lord be merciful; and let him not in mockery deceive me yet again, and yet again withdraw the consent that he has now given that my people shall go in peace and sacrifice to their God."

God answered Moses' entreaty, and the dog-flies ceased in Egypt. And yet, once again, Pharaoh the King was false to his own word, hardened his heart, and returned to his obstinacy as of old.

And retribution speedily followed. There came a dreadful murrain or pestilence that spread through Egypt, attacking the cattle, the horses, the oxen, the sheep, and even the camels of the traders that were in the land at that season, so that multitudes of them languished and died of its ravages. Yet of the flocks and herds that belonged to the people of Israel in Goshen none was harmed, and not a single one perished.

Word of this being brought to Pharaoh, he himself made inquiry of his overseers. They reported that the cattle of the Hebrews had wholly escaped the pestilence, that it raged only in Egypt. Nevertheless, he disregarded it. And while the murrain was still in the land, Moses and Aaron went out and met Pharaoh in the way as he was returning into his palace. And when he refused to listen to them, Moses was consumed with anger at this fresh insult to the Lord. He snatched up two handfuls of soot or ashes from out of a kiln, used in the baking of pots and glasswork, that stood near, and before the very eyes of the king tossed them on high and sprinkled them towards heaven.

"Lo, now: watch thou and wait!"

The ashes were scattered; a light wind carried the dust of them hither, thither, and dispersed it far and wide. And behold, there broke out on the bodies of man and beast foul boils and swelling blains, inflaming the skin. Nor did the courtiers and noblemen of Pharaoh's household escape this malady, nor even his priests and magicians.

For when one morning early, after days of weary waiting, Moses once more demanded an audience of the king, not one of the magicians was present. They were disgraced and in deep despondency, and their very faces were so disfigured by reason of the boils upon them, that they were ashamed to show themselves and be humbled before him.

Yet again Moses warned Pharaoh of what would ensue if he continued to ignore and defy the will of God. He foretold that on the morrow there would descend such a storm of hail on Egypt as had never been witnessed since the foundation of the kingdom. Pharaoh himself affected to be unmoved, and answered him disdainfully. But many of his counsellors and officers of state who were present, having taken to heart the wonders that had already been revealed, had come to fear the Hebrews and the God they worshipped. They gave orders secretly to their servants that from daybreak till nightfall on the morrow not one of their herdsmen was to drive his cattle afield. Let him keep them safe in shed, and himself indoors.

Pharaoh slept uneasily that night, fell into a fitful slumber a little before dawn, but awoke again early and rose from his bed to look out from his window at the skies of morning. A scene of splendour and ill-boding met his gaze. Mounting into the vacancy of the heavens and borne upon a wind counter to that which breathed fitfully then died down and rose again on the earth, vast leaden clouds, domed and turreted and utterly dwarfing in their majesty even the temples and palaces of the city, were lit with the silvery radiance of the rising sun.

They towered higher and higher until the whole firmament was concealed, and the light died. And it was as though morning were retreating into the glooms of night. And as Pharaoh watched, out of the hush and stagnancy of the heavens a tempest of wind suddenly swept across the city, and the livid dark was riven by a burst of flame, dazzling his eyes, so that he clapped his hands over them to shut out the glare. For a few moments he stood blinded and motionless, while the very stones of his palace trembled beneath him at the crash of thunder.

And after the thunder came a storm of hail. It whitened instantly as if with hoarfrost the whole valley lying on either side the looping waters of the great river. Throughout the confines of Egypt the steady tumult of its falling could be heard even above the reverberations of the thunder, and the fire of the lightning ran along upon the earth, now hoary with hailstones of ice. The men and the cattle that had escaped the pestilence and that were exposed to this tempest of hail fled in panic for shelter, smitten as they ran by its sharp-edged shards of ice. Within a few minutes from its first onset the crops of ripening barley were utterly ruined, and the blue-flowering flax was beaten to the ground and laid low. The fields of wheat and of spelt that were as yet only in the green blade alone escaped. Never had the like of it been seen before in Egypt.

In the midst of the tempest Pharaoh sent in hot haste for Moses. He sat pale and trembling, his voice scarcely audible in the din of the thunder and the hail, while the lightnings glimmering overhead filled the great chamber with their wild blue light. And he confessed that he had sinned.

"The God of Israel is a God of righteousness," he said. "I and my people are in the wrong. Entreat this God to still these mighty thunderings and to stay this hail. They oppress my very soul. I will let the Hebrews go and you shall stay no longer."

And Moses answered the king: "As soon as I am gone out from the presence of Pharaoh and have departed out of the city, I will lift my hands in supplication to the Lord, and the thunders shall cease in heaven and there shall be no more hail. Thou hast vaunted thyself in thy pride, and he has been merciful. With but one deadly pestilence he might have smitten Egypt and swept away both thee and thy people like chaff before the wind from off the face of the earth. The soul of Pharaoh is in the hands of God. Thou hast been preserved only that thou mayest acknowledge his power and be the cause of his honour and glory throughout the world. But that day is not yet. Thou hast professed to be penitent, but the words of thy mouth are one thing and the heart within thee another. And I know well that in thy secret mind and in the minds of thy priests and counsellors there is no true fear of God."

Moses turned and left him. The hail abated and the lightnings and the thunderings ceased. The sun shone out again in splendour, but on an Egypt ravaged with storm, its fields of harvest sodden and desolate. And when Pharaoh saw that all again seemed well and fair, he flattered himself that by his cunning pretences he had once more outwitted the leaders of the Hebrews. None the less he was shaken in spirit. He not only hated Moses but feared him, and was disquieted with dread of the divine power he still defied but could no longer challenge or refute.

# Egypt is Afraid

Days and weeks passed by, yet reports continued to reach the king of the havoc that had been caused by the tempest and the pestilence and by the disasters that had gone before. His realm was seething with discontent. Rumours that Jehovah, the God of the Hebrews, was the cause of their troubles had filled the people with fear and dark forebodings. The whole traffic and commerce of the country was almost at a standstill and its market places were deserted and empty of merchandise. Moreover, report of the fatalities that had fallen upon Egypt had already spread far beyond its confines and among kings and nations ever awaiting an opportunity to assail her when she showed signs of weakness or was divided against herself. In the midst of these cares and anxieties, Moses appeared yet again in the presence of Pharaoh. He was received in one of the lesser rooms of the palace and but a few of the king's most confidential advisers were in attendance upon him.

"Thou hast seen. Thou hast heard," said Moses. "Thou knowest the evils that have come upon Egypt. At the mere nod of thy head my people could go free to worship their God. Yet again, and yet again, hast thou withdrawn the solemn word spoken with thine own mouth. Take warning, O king, while still there is time. Heed now, though it be late, the will of God that I have made known to thee, lest his judgment fall upon thee yet more heavily and thou cry unto him, but in vain, in despair and remorse. For I say unto thee, if still thou art obdurate, after the tempest shall come the locusts. They shall descend upon Egypt and shall devour every green thing growing that has escaped the hail. Their destruction shall be such as none alive has witnessed since the day that he was born!"

When he had withdrawn from the presence of the king, his nobles and counsellors began to murmur among themselves. They had the welfare of Egypt at heart. And though few of them were yet convinced that the calamities which had befallen the country were due to the intervention of a God they neither knew nor reverenced, they had themselves seen the bitter humiliation of Pharaoh's priests and magicians. They had learned also that this detested leader of the Hebrews was a man to whom all their abstruse and secret learning was an open book; that his deed assuredly followed his word; and that he was possessed of powers against which Pharaoh's craft and obstinacy might serve him for a while but which would at last overwhelm him in defeat.

They spoke openly. "How long", they said to Pharaoh, "shall this man be allowed to entice us on from one destruction to another? The whole country has been laid waste by him and is rank with discontent. Pharaoh's enemies exult at news of it. And now this traitor threatens us with yet another plague that will destroy the little that remains to us of our fruit, our crops, our very bread. Famine will surely follow. Our foes will descend on us and the glories and conquests even of the king, thy father, be wiped clean away. These Hebrews ask nothing more than a brief respite from their labours that they may sacrifice to their God. We beseech thee then to placate them and to let them go. The hand of Pharaoh is mighty: he can afford to relax it a little that at his own chosen moment he may clench it the more irresistibly."

But there were others of his counsellors who believed that the appeal made by Moses was merely a device, and that as soon as the Hebrews were released from the discipline and control of their overseers and taskmasters, his design was to lead them in open rebellion against the lordship of Egypt. Pharaoh wavered between the one faction and the other. In spite of what had gone before, he paid little regard to Moses' threat, for locusts were seldom seen in Egypt and seemed to him of small account. But he thought to gain his own ends by compromise and craft. He sent again for Moses and Aaron and those of the elders of Israel who were with them.

"It must by now", said Pharaoh when they were come before him, "have been made plain to you that menaces are powerless to move me. It has never been my desire to refuse whatever may be just and right. In stubborn folly you thought to defy me, and clemency alone has prevented my vengeance from falling not only on you yourselves but on your people. They shall make their pilgrimage; they shall keep their feast in the desert. But first let me know which among them shall be chosen to go, and which of them shall remain in Goshen?"

And Moses answered the king: "We will go with our young and with our old, with our sons and our daughters, with our flocks and our herds. Thus will we go. From greatest to least of us, O King—halt and blind and helpless, the babe at its mother's breast and the old man trembling on the brink of the grave—not one shall remain behind. Israel is one; and the Lord God Jehovah hath bidden Israel to his feast."

Pharaoh turned with a gesture of scorn to the nobles and counsellors who had opposed him. "See now," he cried, "what overweening insolence is this!"

Then he once more confronted Moses. "In sooth," he said, "thy God must be a mighty god if I ever consent to let thy children go. Thine own words have betrayed thee. From first to last thou hast been contriving this secret treason against me, intending when once thy people, these Hebrews, have withdrawn beyond my borders that they shall never return. Mark well: I will have none of it. If you would serve your God, go; but your grown men only; for that and that alone was your petition. I have spoken; trouble me no more!" And he commanded his servants to drive the Hebrews out of his presence.

Then Moses stretched out his rod over the land of Egypt; and a dry and parching wind began to rise from out of the east. It blew, laden with the arid heat of the vast wastes of the wilderness of Arabia and the desert of Syria that is beyond Canaan. And it continued without ceasing all that day and all that night. And behold, on the morrow at daybreak, the locusts came up with the wind.

Drifting in from the sands of the wilderness in which they were engendered, they advanced host upon host, in league-long clouds so dense from their vanguard to their rear that their sun-shimmering wings spread a shade over Egypt and veiled the face of day. The whizzing of their multitudes above the earth awoke even those that slept, and struck terror into all that heard.

Horn and gong sounded the alarm. Men ran this way and that in terror, their beasts in panic. And when about the middle of the morning the wind fell to calm, this living cloud came wafting down like flakes innumerable of drifting snow. Where they settled, there they stayed, their wings close folded, until the earth was mantled in a moving pall and was black with them. They were strown so close where there was any plenty of food that an upper layer of them, eyed and ravenous, straddled over the one beneath; and above that, others. For though the grass-hopper or cricket, which is of the kin of the locusts, is happy company enough to man as he shrills on his blade of grass in the summer sun, or chirps in the warm dark, the ravages of an army of locusts are a loss beyond computation in these countries of the east.

In the stagnant calm that had followed, the murmur of their voracious chirpings and gnawings shook the air. And the locusts devoured every green leaf from off the branches and every sprouting blade of wheat or remnant of barley that the tempest had spared, and the fruit also that was swelling upon the trees. There remained nothing green and verdant on either side the Nile.

Never before in Egypt had there been seen the like of these hosts of locusts for numbers and destruction, and never shall the like be seen again. The people were in despair. They had begun to take heart after the devastation caused by the tempest of hail and lightning; and now the little that had been saved was lost to them for ever. Famine and starvation lay in wait for them; and they saw in this no natural evil but the hand of God. And though in a frenzy of haste they dug deep pits and trenches, and kindled high fires and flame and smoke, the locusts were destroyed in such myriads that their own bodies put out the fires and filled the pits. And still in their multitudes they came marching on. As well hope to repel the flood-tide of the sea.

Hour followed hour of that disastrous day, and messengers from all parts of Egypt were dispatched with urgent reports to Pharaoh from the governors of his provinces and

the overseers of his granaries. Even those mounted on
horseback were compelled to turn aside to avoid the clotting
swarm of locusts that were trampled by thousands under
their horses' hoofs. And Pharaoh saw clearly the danger
that threatened him if this pest were not speedily removed.
He was dismayed; and in his fear he forgot his pride. Without consulting his counsellors and statesmen, he sent urgently for Moses and Aaron, and confessed that he had
sinned. He sued them to forgive the affront of which in his
haste he had been guilty when at their last audience with
him they had been driven by his servants from out of his
presence.

"I do entreat thee", he implored Moses, "to mediate between me and the Lord Jehovah yet once again, that he remove this atrocious plague from Egypt. It is unendurable
to me. That done, I will decide how what thou askest may
best be achieved."

They left him, and he withdrew himself, his mind in torment, and waited for what the day might bring forth. The
Lord God heard Moses' prayer. There came a wind from
the west, streaming between earth and sky, and the locusts
were drawn up in its flood of air and swept like dust from
off the floor, and perished in the watery waste of the Red
Sea. The fringes of its foam upon the sands of the shore
were black with them.

And when Pharaoh was assured that this new danger, like
the plagues that had preceded it, was at an end, even yet
again his mind and mood abruptly changed. He hardened
his heart and returned to his stubborn connivings.

In my own chosen time, he thought within himself, I will
consider and will decide this matter. These rebellious
Hebrews must be taught that neither they nor their God
can compel me to take action against my will. Let them

wait until I choose to be gracious. He showed no sign of keeping the solemn protestations he had made to Moses, and did nothing.

Nor did Moses himself as in days gone by appear again before Pharaoh. He too made no sign. He waited in patience —knowing too well this stubborn and feeble king to believe he would keep faith with him.

In due season the will of God was revealed to him. There came a day when he stretched out his rod not over the waters or the dust of Egypt but towards heaven. And at his word the violent and burning wind called Hamsin that springs up from out of the south, from the waste of Libya, began to blow, lifting with its blasts the sand and dust of the desert in billows so dense and lofty that the sun's radiance in mid-heaven, from a brilliant orange, dwindled to a circle red as blood and fainter than that of the moon, and then vanished.

There arose also dense emanations of vapour from out of the ground and the low lands of the river, and all Egypt lay canopied in a hot and unnatural night, in a darkness which may be felt. Finer than crystals of snow the sand borne in on the wind silted through every crevice and cranny and mingled with the Egyptians' victuals, and with their wine and drink. At the distance of a few paces man's shape was blotted out; all sense of direction was lost, so that none dared venture out of doors or stir in the streets. Even within the houses the heated air stifled throat and lungs, and the inmates went groping and stumbling, with nought but their feeble lamps to pierce the gloom. For three days continually they saw not one another, neither rose any from his place to go abroad.

But in the land of Goshen the sun as usual rose and set, and there shone clear the natural light of day.

Towards the close of the third day Pharaoh sent for Moses. After long and fevered debate with his advisers, he was wearied out. Divided in policy, they were at their wits' end; the wiser among them urging him to be rid of the Hebrews for good and all, and to defy the will of God no longer; the rest, obstinate and futile as himself, counselling him to temporize. As was his usual practice, he gave way in a little and trusted to his subtlety.

The lights that had been brought to illumine the great chamber of audience flared dimly in the thick and heated air, scarcely piercing its hollow vault of gloom. And Moses when he was brought into the presence of the king drew nearer to the throne than hitherto. He made obeisance, rose and stood mute. The wafting of the fan-bearers stirred on his cheek. He fixed his eyes through the murk upon Pharaoh's countenance as the king addressed him.

"I have yet again", said Pharaoh, "remembered me the pledge I gave you, and have considered your petition. And this is my decree. The Hebrews shall be allowed to leave Egypt and make their pilgrimage into the desert to serve their God; and as a further concession, their little ones shall go with them. Three whole days' grace shall be given them, then shall they return. None shall remain behind in Goshen during those three days, except only your flocks and your herds. Of them you will have no need."

And Moses answered the king: no longer as does a suitor pleading for a monarch's favours, but as one who makes terms with the vanquished.

"Pharaoh in his wisdom is pleased to make sport of his suppliant," he said. "For how shall Israel make solemn sacrifice to the Lord if our sheep and our cattle remain in Goshen? They too shall go with us, and not a hoof be left behind. For not until we come to the place that the Lord has appointed shall we ourselves know what he will require of us. Ay, and thou thyself must give us beasts, the choicest of thine own herds, for the feast that Israel shall make in the wilderness, and these of his mercy shall be accepted of thee as a peace-offering to the Lord our God."

Pharaoh rose from his throne, blinded to reason, his face transfigured with fury.

"Must and shall," he cried, "are these thy threats! Get thee gone; and take heed to thyself! Enter my presence no more. For on the day thou seest my face again thou shalt surely die."

Then said Moses: "So be it. Thou hast spoken well. I will see thy face again no more. Nay, not until thou thyself send for me in irremediable terror and despair. But I have a word for thee before I go. Hearken to it!

"Thus saith the Lord. Again and again we have made our humble petition to thee, according to his word, and thou hast scorned and defied him. Thou hast been warned, and not once but many times have the justice and might of the God of Israel been revealed to thee. Yet when thou didst show any shadow of relenting and didst plead for mercy, his mercy was vouchsafed to thee. But now, this is the end.

"There comes a midnight, and that soon, when the God of Israel will manifest himself yet once again; and thy heart shall melt in thee like water, for the anguish that is come upon thee. But thou shalt relent too late. In that night the angel of death shall wing his way from one end of Egypt to the other, from the mountains even to the sea, and when all the land is hushed in sleep he will smite the first-born of every household in Egypt from the highest to the lowest. From the prince himself, thy eldest son, even to the first-born of the slave woman who grinds corn at the mill—none shall escape. There shall go up to heaven that night such a cry of lamentation throughout all the land of Egypt as has never been heard before, and shall never be heard again.

"But in Israel shall be peace and safety. Nor shall one of the least of her children come to harm. So serene shall be that night in Goshen that not even a dog shall lift its tongue and howl in menace of woe against the moon. And by this thou shalt know that the Lord hath set his seal upon his chosen, and made a severance between the Egyptians and Israel. Yea, and one word more. In that day the proudest nobles and counsellors that stand about thy throne shall come in grief and horror of mind and prostrate themselves before me and make obeisance, even to me, entreating Israel to be gone and to return to Egypt no more. Then, and not until then, will I lead God's people forth."

Moses turned away from before the throne, and in the gloom of the vast gilded hall no voice answered him, nor was any attempt made to stay or molest him. And he went out from Pharaoh hot with anger.

# The Feast of the Passover

He returned to Goshen. He knew that the long conflict of mind and will with Pharaoh was at an end. In the presence of his nobles and counsellors he had not only defied him face to face, but had forewarned him of a calamity with which the judgments that had already befallen Egypt would be as dust in the balance, and which would pierce the king himself to his very heart.

No further parleyings with Pharaoh were now conceivable. They were only once to meet again. And though not even the most headstrong and violent of the king's advisers might dare counsel the king to arraign or destroy Moses openly, there were other methods of ridding Egypt of its enemies. Moses knew well that from this day forward his life would be in unceasing danger. But he gave no thought to it.

Since he had returned from his quiet and serene existence as a shepherd with Jethro the priest of Midian, he had known no release from care. Each day that passed had brought its own ordeal. But his diffidence and self-distrust had left him. He was filled with a great weariness, but his spirit was unshaken. He had come back to his own people after many years' absence; and few had remembered him. Fewer still among the chief men of Israel had not in the long struggle wavered in their trust in him as their leader.

But now, though to all intents he might seem as yet to have failed in his mission, not only was his name a thing of dread in Egypt, but he was beloved and renowned among his own people, and he was hailed throughout Israel as the herald sent from the Eternal to free them from their woes.

When doubt assailed him, he had spent long hours of meditation in solitude on the fringes of the desert. In that silence, broken only by the night-cries of beast and bird, he had watched the stars wheel onward to their setting, and in a voiceless communion of heart and soul he had learned all that the Lord God would require of him. He cast all thought of himself from out of his mind, and laboured fearlessly on in ardour for Israel. And he knew that the day of deliverance was at hand.

He called together the elders. They met by stealth and after nightfall, and Moses laid before them all that had passed during his last audience with the king. He warned them that in his fury Pharaoh might decree inhuman reprisals against the Hebrews to avenge the humiliation he had endured in the presence of his courtiers. He might endeavour by every crafty means he could devise to incite them to open revolt. But they must endure in patience whatever the day might bring forth. They must be strong and resolute; they must trust in the Lord God of Israel.

Egypt's pride was soon to be broken; for what had now been demanded of the king was no longer a mere three days' truce from their quarries and brick-yards, but a release for evermore. They were about to set out on a journey from whence there would be no turning back. Jehovah would scatter his enemies, and Israel would go free. Canaan, the land of promise, their predestined home—this must be the vision continually before their eyes. The whole world should hear that they were no longer a captive and helpless

race enslaved by a tyrant, but a nation free among nations, the chosen people of God.

Many of those who listened were old men wasted with age and weariness. From childhood their days had been spent in a cowed and hopeless servitude. The lash had been their wages; sleep their only refuge from misery; and death their one assurance of release. Yet they had lived on and suffered and endured.

Others among them were in the flower of their strength and manhood, lean, scarred and ravaged with toil, hollow of cheek, but fierce-eyed, fanatical and on fire with hatred of their oppressors. And they too sat motionless and intent.

[ 189 ]

One and all, they had listened in silence, and, except for the fleeting looks upon their faces and the light that burned in their eyes, had showed no sign of what was passing in their minds.

But in the pause that followed, there rose up from among them a murmur, a sigh, of joy and longing beyond all speech. The radiance of a hope no longer faint and far had broken in upon them as if with the light of the risen sun. Tears coursed down their cheeks, furrowed with woe and despair. They bowed their heads and worshipped.

But there were still many things to be considered, and many questions to be answered. They debated earnestly together and far into the night, and when at length the assembly broke up, and they went out silently into the darkness every man to his own place, their plans for the days that followed had been prepared. They had made a solemn vow to obey in everything the will of the Lord God, as Moses had revealed it. In sure and certain hope of their deliverance, and at the hour appointed, the host of Israel was to be in readiness, and none should remain behind.

By evening of the next day every man in Israel knew that the day of deliverance was soon to dawn and how he himself was to prepare for it. Yet these glad tidings had been spread abroad with such caution and secrecy that not a rumour of them reached the ears of the Egyptian overseers or the masters of the gangs.

Now, until this time, the beginning of the Hebrew year had been in the first month of harvest. But henceforward, as Moses had proclaimed to the elders, it was to fall in the earliest month of spring. The night on which he had called them together was that of the vernal new moon. It had been ordained therefore, for an everlasting memorial of the year now before them, that this was to be accounted their New Year's Day.

Moreover, it had long been the custom in Israel to keep sacred the day when the moon of springtime shines like snow in the heavens, and to share together in a feast, as happy as their wretched state would admit, in honour of the Lord. Two weeks—and two weeks only—were yet to run before the first new moon of Israel's New Year would come to its fulness, and the feast they were then to share in joy and solemnity would far excel any that had ever gone before. It was to be prepared for therefore with scrupulous care, since the Lord God himself had appointed it for a remembrance to all Israel.

The days passed heavily by. Midnight followed midnight. The sun rose and sank to his setting in skies continually windless and serene. The horned crescent of the moon appeared in the dying light of evening, and increased in the lustre it borrowed from the sun. So perfect a calm reigned in the heavens over Egypt, after the horrors of storm and tempest, whirlwind and darkness, that Pharaoh and the counsellors who concurred with his policy began to console themselves with the belief that all trouble with the abhorred Hebrews was now at an end.

On the night after Moses had last appeared before him the king had striven in vain to compose himself to sleep. The imprecation that Moses had uttered against him rang on in his ears, like the knelling of a bell, and in spite of an outward indifference, he had been so much moved by it that he had given command to his most trusted servants to keep unceasing watch over the prince, his firstborn.

But as dawn succeeded dawn, and his son was restored to him again safe and well, and no evil omen had shown itself to those who had kept watch within and without his chamber, his spirit revived in him. He began to upbraid himself, and even to mock a little at his fears. Though never within memory had Egypt suffered so grievously, though the state of his realm and people was a cause for grave disquiet, how could it be proved beyond doubt, he questioned within himself, that this was due to divine retribution? And even if it were so, it seemed that the God of the Hebrews had wearied of his demands.

He smiled, the dark eyes in his lean cavernous face fixed in reverie, as he pondered how best to contrive the death of their insolent leaders, to defame even their memory in the eyes of their own people, and to quell without mercy but at not too great a cost—for the life even of a slave had its price —any disorder or revolt that might follow.

But though Pharaoh could thus deceive himself, the apprehensions of the wiser of his counsellors were not so easily allayed. Though, too, at threat of instant vengeance the king himself had given command that no word of what had passed during the last audience he had granted to Moses should be whispered abroad, rumour of it had spread far and wide, and had filled the people with terror of an impending doom.

The Hebrews were now feared as much as in former times they had been hated and despised, and those of the Egyptians who lived in touch with them, and the dwellers in the Egyptian city of Psapt that was in Goshen, sought by every means in their power to placate them with gifts and bribes. Nothing that the Hebrews asked of them, and they asked freely as Moses himself had bidden them, was refused. They accepted these things not as an indulgence but as a right, wages long owing for the evils they had suffered and their centuries of toil.

As ordained by Pharaoh, his overseers and taskmasters

had cruelly increased the labour and the torments of the Hebrew gangs that worked under them, until they were almost beyond human endurance. But the old sullenness and apathy had vanished. Some divine secret hope seemed now to make their sufferings of no account. They toiled on as if all resentment had been clean forgotten.

An ancient song of Canaan, wild and plaintive and sweet, had spread from mouth to mouth. To the Egyptians it was meaningless, and yet as they hearkened, a hidden menace jarred its strains. It haunted them and they feared the sound of it. But when even speech was forbidden between slave and slave, by the light on their faces they seemed to be still singing in their hearts. A hush of dread and expectancy was over the land.

On the tenth evening of the new Hebrew year so brightly shone a great gibbous moon that the light of day waned without interval of darkness into the light of night. On this day, as Moses had commanded through the elders, every householder in Israel had set apart from among his few sheep or goats a lamb or a kid of one year old, the best he had, the first-born of its mother, and without any defect or blemish. This too was a sacred symbol, for ever afterwards the first-born among Israel were to be accounted sacred to the Lord.

This first-born lamb was intended for the feast that was to be partaken of by himself and his whole household four days afterwards, the feast day appointed by the Lord. And if any household, owing to the fewness of its members or its children, were too small to need a lamb for its own use only, it was to share one with its neighbour.

That day, longed for beyond all telling, dawned at length. The Hebrews set out as usual from their quarters to the brickyards, the quarries and the great temple that was then in building. It was a day of furious heat, airless and ominous. The overseers of the gangs, fearful of laying before Pharaoh misgivings so vague that they could find no proof of them, were nevertheless convinced that the Hebrews were secretly plotting against them, and barbarously drove them on. Many swooned with exhaustion by the way, and died, untended, where they fell. But no cruelty devised either by hatred or terror could now extort from the Hebrews a single rebellious word or action: not even so much as a groan of pain or of weariness.

At length the sultry hours drew towards evening, and the gangs were dismissed from their toil. For the last time the hewers of stone laid aside their picks and their mallets, and the makers of bricks their water-skins, their shovels and moulds; and all turned homeward. The gangmasters and overseers withdrew to their own quarters; and the quarries and works, where never more was any son of Israel to be seen at slavish toil again, lay idle in the wild colours of the declining sun.

At the brief hour that comes between sunset and the dark every householder in Goshen took the lamb that he had set apart and slaughtered it for the feast. Then he dipped into its blood a bunch of hyssop or marjoram—a wild, sweet, aromatic herb that grew freely on the walls of almost every dwelling in Goshen—and he sprinkled the blood on the door of his house, on its posts and on its lintel. The doom foretold to Moses by Jehovah was at hand. The angel of death, whose face is veiled, would be abroad in Egypt that night, and no human dwelling would be spared from his visitation except only those thus sprinkled, its door shut and made fast. From this moment until the hour appointed by Moses, no man in Goshen ventured abroad; none went out and none came in.

When night fell, a profound quietude lay over the settlements of the Hebrews. The dewy moon-bright air was chill and sweet with springing grass and flower. No light gleamed out from any window of the mean black hovels walled with sun-baked mud. Every door was shut—its posts and lintel stained dark with blood.

But within those walls was a continual stir and business. The whole long day had been spent by the woman of the household in preparing for the night. Nothing she treasured or might need was to be left behind, except only what was too heavy or cumbersome to be carried away. When the lamb had been skinned and dressed and made ready, she set it down to roast at the fire, whose ruddy glow illumined the narrow walls.

Flat cakes and biscuits without yeast or leaven (for nothing that had any taint of corruption was to have any part in the feast) had already been kneaded and now were baking. Bitter herbs—wild lettuce, endive and nettle—for symbol of the long sufferings of Israel, had been gathered and cleansed for a salad. She did all that she had to do with the utmost care, having provided as far as possible only as much food as would be eaten that night, for no remnant of this sacred meal was to be left over until the following morning. Whatever remained unconsumed was to be burnt in the fire.

An hour before midnight, all was ready. The children of the house, who had been sent early to bed, were woken from sleep, and everyone within it, even the little ones but lately out of arms, gathered together to partake of the feast. In years gone by this moon-bright harvest festival had been held with rejoicings. They had sat down to eat, drink and be merry at leisure, and had for the time being almost forgotten their misery. There had been no need then for haste or secrecy.

[ 195 ]

But this—both the first breaking of their fast this four-teenth night of Spring, and their last anxious supper in the land of their captivity—was no ordinary feast. It was the most solemn hour in the long history of their race—a token that from that day forward Israel had dedicated its first-born to the service of God. Since by his mercy, on this dis-astrous night for Egypt, the angel of death was to spare and pass over the people of all Israel, the feast was to be called the *Feast of the Passover of the Lord*. And his divine influ-ence would be shed on all who took part in it, worn-out in body, deadened in soul, and brutalized though many of them were.

They ate standing, the men of the household with their girdles about their loins, their sandals on their feet, and staff in hand; the women and children in whatever clothes could be provided that would shield them against the cold of the night air in the darkness of the desert. Few words were spoken. Their hearts were too full for speech. They longed for, yet dreaded the ordeal that lay before them. These hovels, mean and squalid though they were, had been their homes. They were to see them no more. They pined for the tents of the wanderer, but they were to ven-ture out into the dread unknown and on a pilgrimage from which there could be no turning back. Who could foresee what dangers and what foes were waiting for them in the drear wastes of the wilderness—the resort, as they had heard, of monstrous beasts and evil demons, with hollow voice and secret music, luring to destruction the unwary and the lost?

Yet there were few among them who did not steadfastly believe in the wisdom and genius of their great leader, or doubted that he had been divinely chosen to set them free. But Pharaoh was mighty and merciless. Death or maiming or torture was the punishment he meted out to his enemies who defied him. How many of their own harmless babes had the Nile swallowed up in its infested waters! And as they looked at their children gathered round them, an icy horror shook them at the thought of the judgment of God soon to be revealed against Egypt, which even the tyrant king himself could not escape.

Astonished at being roused from sleep at so late an hour and at sharing in a supper that seemed as strange and marvellous as a dream, the younger children in hushed voices questioned their father about what they did, and why they were going out in the middle of the night, and where they were going to.

He gathered them around him. It was a feast, he told them, which even they themselves had been expressly bidden to share in by the Lord God. He spoke to them of Canaan also, a little land lying between wilderness and sea, only fifteen days' slow burdened journeying from north to south, only ten from east to west, yet a land wondrously rich in vineyard and orchard, mountain, valley, pasture and well-springs, its vales marvellously fair and sweet with flowers at this season of the year. A land flowing with milk and honey, their earthly paradise, the haven where they longed to be.

There, in the vale of Hebron, before he had been sold to the Ishmaelites, Joseph himself had lived as a child with Jacob his father who loved him. This was the land that, long time gone, had been promised of God not only to Jacob but to his father Isaac also, and to Abraham before him, who had worshipped him in faith and hope.

And now, after all these years of Israel's woes and slavery, they themselves, children with all their lives before them, were about to set out on a journey to a place of peace and refuge for which those who were at rest in their graves had pined in vain with a heartsick longing. In time to come when they had grown up to be men and women, and when, with each returning Spring they kept again this solemn feast, their own children also would question them as they themselves had questioned him.

By then, it might be, the doings of this strange night would be no more than a faint, far memory in their minds. Let them strive then with all their might to keep it clear and vividly in remembrance, so that in their turn they should be able to tell their children all this feast had meant to them, and the wonders that had gone before, and would yet be revealed. Let it be to them for a lifelong token in their hearts; let them bind its remembrance like a frontlet between their brows.

The children listened, their eyes shining, their hearts wildly beating. They promised their father to do all that he had bidden them do, and to keep all that he had said in remembrance.

So, throughout Goshen this, the first feast of the Passover, was being kept; and all Israel was awake and ready.

# The Flight from Egypt

The moon rode high in the heavens above Egypt, smiting with its silver the wide waters of the Nile, and glazing as if with hoar-frost the walls of her temples and palaces and the slabbed sides of her prodigious pyramids. There slept the kings who centuries before had built them as their last resting-place, trusting, though vainly, that their mummied bodies in the long darkness between this world and the next would never be disturbed.

Ink-black shadow chequered the streets, the idle quarries, and the brickyards that all day long had been astir like a swarming nest of ants. Except for the watchmen in her frontier forts and desert camps, and the sentries who kept guard over the palace and armouries of Pharaoh, the whole realm of Egypt lay hushed in sleep. In his own royal city the howl of a dog, the footfall of some homeless prowler or of one abroad in trouble or on an urgent errand, and the far yell of wolf or hyæna, prowling on the outskirts of the wilderness, were the only sounds that broke the silence.

Few stars blazed in the windless heavens, except those that, rising or setting, hung low on the earth's horizon. They were quenched in the glare of moonlight that flooded the skies. At the approach of midnight, the whole land of Egypt, transfigured with loveliness, lay dazed as if entranced. But the avenging angel had gone his way; and

the silence was not only the silence of sleep but of death.

At midnight cockcrow, lamps began suddenly to shine and flit in the dusky moonlit gloom within the dwellings of the Egyptians and to gleam from their windows. Doors were flung open. Cries of grief and horror pierced the hush, and were echoed on from house to house, from court to court. The wide high streets where stood temple and palace and the mansions of the wealthy, and every narrow by-way were suddenly thronged with a multitude of people, demented with anguish, seeking help and finding none.

Tidings of the woeful calamity that had befallen them

spread on from mouth to mouth. And with every moment, terror not only of the known but of the unknown pierced some poor human breast.

Stark and shivering with dread, the attendants whom Pharaoh had appointed to keep watch over his first-born entered his chamber and roused him from sleep. He started up out of his dreams as if at the touch of a spectre. Prostrating themselves before him, with tears and groans, they told him that the son he loved lay stricken and lifeless upon his bed. He gazed at them, his high-boned narrow face wan and lank and vacant, as if, though he had heard the words they uttered, his mind were incapable of understanding them.

He questioned them, and shook as if with the palsy when he realized the full meaning of the news they brought him. And he rose up in the night, he and all his servants and all the Egyptians, and there was a great cry in Egypt, for there was not a house without its dead.

His statesmen and his counsellors were sent for. All was confusion. They came into his presence, misery on their faces and grief in their hearts.

In the depth of night messengers were dispatched to Goshen urgently summoning Moses and Aaron. They were brought at once into the presence of the king, the women and servants of the palace who met them on their way fleeing in terror at sight of them.

The palace was loud with their wailings and the lamentations of the mourners. The bright moon shone in upon its gilded stones, and the nobles, assembled there in attendance on the king, after one glance at these Hebrews, averted their eyes. Pharaoh himself came down from his dais and advanced as if to meet them in the midst.

But a few paces from them he stayed, his face stricken

with woe, mutely scrutinizing them, and advanced no nearer. He spoke like a man almost bereft of his senses.

"I have summoned you hither," he said, "only that I may speak with you face to face. Pay heed to me now as you hope to be heeded of God. Tarry not for the morning but gather together all the people of Israel and lead them out of Egypt. Let them leave nothing that is theirs behind them, neither their children nor their flocks nor their herds, nor anything they own or need.

"Go," he said, "and serve the Lord your God, even as you have said it is required of you." He turned, stooping, then raised his haggard face and looked earnestly on Moses. "As for thee," he said, "I entreat thee to give me thy blessing in the mercy of thy God, for the bitterness of death is come upon me."

He commanded that all things that might be required should be given to the elders without stint, and that Moses himself should be obeyed in everything as he might direct. Word was instantly sent to every household in Israel. And all were in readiness.

They divided what they had to carry away with them between those who could bear it best. Their beasts of burden were already fed and watered, saddled and laden. They took the raw dough they had prepared for baking, they wrapped up their kneading-bowls in the woollen mantles they wore upon their shoulders, and which would serve them as a covering by night. They gathered their children together, and with their asses, their flocks and their herds, assembled in companies, each man in the place that had been appointed him beforehand, under his own chief or elder.

Though the moon gave light in abundance, torches flared; the night was thronged with their host. And the Egyptians—those who dwelt round about Goshen and in its chief city—far from attempting to stay or hinder them in their flight, urged them on. They left their dead, and with terror knocking at their hearts, adjured the Hebrews to intercede between them and the vengeance of Jehovah. Throughout their lives these Hebrews had been reviled and scorned and hated. Now the Egyptians loaded them with gifts and whatever might prove of service to them. They bribed them with their most precious possessions—jewels of silver and jewels of gold, vessels and fine raiment, their ear-rings, amulets, bracelets, and golden fillets. Their one desire was only to persuade and to incite them to be gone. "Else," they cried one to another, "we be all dead men!"

At break of dawn on the fifteenth day of the first month and in the springtime of this their first new year appointed by Moses, the whole host of Israel, men, women and chil-dren, in their thousands, and in their clans and tribes, began their march. They went up armed and with a high hand out of Egypt. And a multitude went with them—Egyptians who had intermarried with them, and prisoners taken in the frontier wars who had shared in the labours of the slave gangs. The earth shook with their tramping, and the cold air of daybreak was filled with the bleating and bellowing of their flocks and cattle and the sound of their chantings as they marched on.

Thus was fulfilled the vision which comforted Jacob when he dreamed that night long gone at Beersheba on his jour-ney into Egypt. So Joseph himself had foreseen and fore-told in the hour that comes before death. Nor was the solemn oath that had been sworn to him forgotten. All these years his bones—Pharaoh's ring upon his finger, the necklet of gold on his breast—had lain close-swathed and embalmed in spices in the painted and gilded coffin that had been pre-pared for him by the most skilful of the embalmers in the

service of the king, his master. The bearers chosen by
Moses himself lifted it from its abiding-place in Goshen and
bore it away, to keep it in safe charge until they should
come at length into Canaan, the land of his desire. There to
lay it to rest for ever in Shechem, in the tomb that had belonged to his father Jacob.

They pressed on—an exceeding great multitude—by
way of the long, narrow, cultivated strip of land that lay
eastward of Goshen; from Rameses on to Succoth or
Pithom, the great cities which the Hebrews themselves had
built during their long bondage in Egypt. Thus they followed the canal of fresh water between the Nile and the sea
which had been made by the Pharaoh who ruled Egypt
when Moses was a child. It was a full four days' journey.
Each nightfall they pitched their camp, and with every dawn
prepared to continue on their way. They made what speed
they could, but were compelled to keep pace with their
flocks and herds, and were encumbered with heavy burdens.

And the angel of the Lord went before them, by day in a
pillar of cloud to show them the way, and by dark in a pillar
of fire to give them light. Thus was the angel of the Lord
continually their beacon, by day and by night, in cloud or
fire.

From Succoth they pressed on to Etham, which lay on
the borders of the wilderness of that name. There again they
pitched their camp and rested.

The direction in which they were now marching would
bring them, if persisted in, to the coast of the Great Sea.
Here was the ancient highway followed by the caravans
between Egypt and Gaza, and by the armies of Pharaoh,
and it was guarded by fortresses and strongholds against the
attacks of marauders.

And the word of the Lord came to Moses, bidding him turn back from Etham, lest the men of Israel, unused as yet to war, might fear to go forward. Next morning, therefore, when they had eaten and made ready, they turned southward towards the wilderness or desert that lies to the east between Egypt and the Red Sea. And Moses led them by way of Pi-hahiroth where was the sanctuary of Osiris, the Sun-god of Egypt, and which lay on the coast between Migdol and the sea towards Baal-zephon—a tower sacred to the tribes that dwelt near by. There, over against the shores of the leaden sea, they pitched their camp.

Throughout their march from day to day they had been closely watched. Spies had followed them, mingling with the throng, and had reported their every movement to Pharaoh and whatever else could be discovered of their secret plans. And when word was brought to him that the Hebrews had assuredly fled out of Egypt, with intent to free themselves for ever from his yoke, and that the whole host of them was now moving south towards the sea, then that evil genius in his mind which had led him on from one disaster to another, whispered within him that surely now he had them at his mercy.

Hatred of Moses blinded him to all else. Jehovah had done his worst; he feared him not. He put away his grief for his dead son, and thirsted only for revenge.

He summoned his chief officers and laid before them the reports that had been brought to him by his spies. "See now," he said, "these Hebrews, in their ignorant folly, are encamped near the watch-tower of Migdol, their aim, it is clear, being to follow the nearer shore of the sea which will entangle them in at length between its tides and the mountains. Surely this god they worship has abandoned them. We have them in our power, and may be avenged on them once and for all for the evil they have brought upon Egypt. They shall drink bitterly of the might of Pharaoh and shall cry, 'Woe! woe on us, for the day that we were born!' "

Those of his counsellors who were as stubborn and stiff-necked as himself acclaimed his decision. And he made ready his chariot, and he mustered his army, and set it in array—his helmed footmen with lance and shield, his archers with their bows and hatchets, his horses and his chariots; his whole power and strength. And he made ready to march.

But first, for vanguard of his army he dispatched six hundred of his chariots with their charioteers and bowmen, bidding the captain in command of them spare neither horse nor man until he had come in sight of the Hebrews, and had brought them to bay. These, then, pressed on in hot pursuit, leaving Pharaoh himself with his main army to follow after them. And all that day they drew steadily nearer, while still the Israelites were encamped near the sea strand.

Towards evening, scouts of the Israelites who had been sent out by Moses to keep watch beyond the camp and to give warning if danger threatened, distinguished afar off across the sands of the desert the faint clouds of dust raised by Pharaoh's pursuing chariots, the vanguard of his army. And a heavy rumour of sound was borne on the air towards them like distant thunder. They stood transfixed, intent and listening.

But their ears had not deceived them. It seemed the distant tramplings even loudened as they hearkened, and the dust cloud of the chariots showed no changes as do the vapours of evening. They turned instantly and fled back into the camp, for lo, Egypt was marching after them, and they were sore afraid.

# The Crossing of the Red Sea

Their report ran like wildfire from one end of the camp to the other, and it was seized with panic terror. These men of Israel, born into slavery and forced their whole lives long to toil for a tyrant, were unused to any discipline except that of the lash and the goad. They had no knowledge or experience of warfare. They were hampered with their flocks and herds already spent by forced marches, and were burdened with a vast hoard of baggage. Only the open spaces of the wilderness lay around them, even to the sea, and there was nowhere any place of defence for their women and children. When they knew that the dreaded armies of Pharaoh were in pursuit of them, their hearts melted like water. And in their despair they cried to the Lord.

But there were some among them who had been compelled to accept Moses as their leader against their will, men by nature rebellious, malcontents. They forced their way into the presence of Moses and reproached him bitterly for the mortal danger into which he had brought them.

"Was it", they reproached him, "because there were no graves for us in Egypt that thou hast enticed us out to die in the wilderness? Why hast thou so dealt with us, compelling us to flee out of Goshen; ay, and our helpless women and children? There at least our lives were safe. When thou didst first return to Goshen and began to incite us to revolt against the king, did we not again and again adjure thee to leave us alone that we might continue our labours in peace and security? Were we the only slaves in Egypt? Is Pharaoh to be cheated of what is his? Far better to live in the vilest bondage under the Egyptians than to die here in misery and our bones bleach in the sands of the wilderness!"

Moses faced them without wavering. Nor did he answer them in anger, nor reproach them for their faint-heartedness.

Far more clearly than they, he knew the supreme danger that now threatened them, and the massacre and horror that would follow if he swerved for an instant from his authority over them. He needed time to consider: but he remained steadfast and unmoved.

"Fear not," he adjured them, "but stand fast. Every man in readiness and unafraid. And you shall see the salvation of the Lord. It shall be revealed to you this very day. Believe only in Jehovah, the Lord God himself, whose wonders you have seen in Egypt. He has seen fit that this Pharaoh should harden his heart even yet again, to pursue after Israel. Blind and stubborn, this proud king believes in his folly that Jehovah hath forsaken us, and that we know not which way to escape, being shut in between the desert and the sea. Watch and wait! For it is Pharaoh himself who shall be taken in a snare, and the Lord shall have glory over him, and all Egypt shall know that he is the Almighty. For I vow unto you that these warriors of Pharaoh, the dust of whose chariots beclouds the skies, you shall see again no more for ever. Jehovah himself shall fight for you, if only you have faith and hold your peace."

He went out alone from among them, and continued on his way until he came down to the margin of the sea whose full flood-tide now lapped its sands. The waste of waters stretched out before him; and there in solitude, his face to-wards the distant land of Canaan, that he himself was to see but never tread, he prayed, wrestling in agony of soul for the safety of Israel. The sweat stood on his face as he bowed himself in entreaty before the Lord.

But peace at length calmed heart and mind; he was com-forted and rose up. It was the hour of the setting of the sun, and even the eastern verges of the horizon to which he raised his eyes were inflamed with its last beams. The whole ample canopy of the heavens was lit with wondrous light and colour, ever changing, melting, its fires mounting, to fade and die with night. He lifted up his hands over the sea in enraptured salutation of the Eternal whom he wor-shipped. Then in the swift cold oncoming of the dark he returned back into the camp.

The pillar of cloud, that had gone on before the host of Israel, had removed and now stood kindled between the starry skies and the wrath behind them. Between the huge straggling host of the Israelites and the pursuing vanguard of the armies of Pharaoh, there settled a region of dense gloom—illumined, like the smoke of a burning mountain, by the sombre pillar of fire that was the abiding-place of the angel of the Lord.

Perplexed, and apprehensive of what this unearthly ap-parition in the heavens might portend, the captain in com-mand of the chariots sent out scouts to reconnoitre. They faded from view in the mounded obscurity of the desert, but only one of them returned to him alive, wounded and terrified, and with nought but his tongue-stump wherewith to speak. Pharaoh's urgent orders in mind, the captain of the vanguard hesitated, but at length, after consultation with his officers, and confident that he had the Hebrews in his power, since their flight was now cut off by the sea, he determined to advance no further in the darkness, but to attack at dawn. His men and his horses were hard spent and needed a brief respite. All that long night the Egyptians drew no nearer.

But with sunset a wind from between east and north had begun to rise, trumpeting mournfully between earth and sky. In the cold of the dark it steadily increased in force and at last grew exceeding strong. It roared under the night, burdened with whispering sand, beneath a sky wildly brilliant with stars, and, in the small hours, lit with the beams of a waning moon.

Sleep came but fitfully to those huddled together about their watch-fires. The women lay in terror of the tumult, clasping their little ones to their breasts, soothing their cries. Yet this was the wind of their great mercy, for in its vehemency it drove back the tumultuous fast-ebbing tide of the sea towards the south-west until its very bed was exposed beneath the stars, and where had been water was now land.

Thus the wind continued to blow in the cloudless dusk of the now dwindling moonlight, and in the watch that comes before morning the whole host was aroused. Even the children who were old enough to walk and who had been slumbering peacefully, lapped warm against the cold, were awakened. And behold, when they looked out towards where at sunset had been the tumbling billows of the sea, there lay before them a mile-wide ford stretching across from shore to shore. The whole hidden desolate channel of the sea lay exposed, and beckoned them on.

The watch-fires of Israel had burned low, and were now heaped high with fuel, to deceive what spies might be lurking behind them. Strict orders had been given that all voices and sounds be hushed. In silence the men drew together in their ranks and companies, and at about the beginning of the last watch of the night they began to move forward. Leading on their timid flocks and their herds and their beasts of burden, they descended the gently sloping sands that had margined the flood-tide the night before, and advanced on to the wind-swept floor of the sea, its salty boulder-strown sands faintly glimmering in the moonlight and the wan of day.

Thus the whole multitude of Israel, with their women and their children in their midst, pressed onward. But for the occasional bleating and lowing of their beasts, the wailing of an infant and the plashing of foot and hoof in the oozy sands and shallow pools of brine between the rocks, they marched in a profound silence, marvelling as they went, and filled with a wild elation between joy and fear at this miracle of the Lord.

And when the main body of them had reached the eastern shore, then the rearguard who had kept watch on the western shore, followed after them with all dispatch. And in the first crystal of daybreak the pillar of cloud was seen to be in front of them in the wilderness beyond the sea. There they halted.

Roving tribesmen of the desert a little before dawn came to the commander of the chariots of Egypt to report this wonder. Utterly amazed and dismayed at news of it, he summoned his officers. The peril of Pharaoh's wrath was on their heads, they dared not pause or consider. The trumpets sounded; the charioteers and bowmen leapt to their stations; the horses were harnessed; the advance began. So translucent were now the eastern skies that even at this distance they could see afar off the faintly gleaming ensign or standard of Moses beyond the farther shore.

The sight filled them with fury. Urging on their horses with lash and cry, they pressed forward in their battalions at their utmost speed. Their iron rumblings shook the air. Else all was still; for the wind that had filled their ears with its hollow trumpetings throughout the night had fallen to calm.

And as the foremost chariots drew near to the seashore, the sun rose, dazzling clear in the stilled air of the morning. It showed for an instant its full orb of splendour above a louring accumulation of cloud that lay on the horizon in the south-eastern quarter of the heavens.

But only for a moment, for the clouds mounted swiftly up after it into the skies, borne on by lofty winds, and now far below them a hot breeze of the desert began to stir, whipping the sand into scurrying whirls and puffs, that swept up like the dancing of phantoms, then fell to earth again.

Having come to hightide-mark on the sea-shore, the charioteers made no pause, but drove on furiously into the bed of the sea, following the pitted track from shore to shore left by the multitude of Israel. But the silt was sodden, the advance slow, and they strove in vain to keep rank and order. Daylight now had dimmed, for clouds were massed on high and obscured the zenith. The morning was black with storm.

And the angel of the Lord looked down from out of the pillar of cloud upon the chariots of the Egyptians. And the angel of the Lord in his splendour troubled and discomfited the Egyptians. Lightnings rent the gloom, and the thunder thundered, with torrents of rain. And when they were come into the midst of the bed of the sea, the wheels of their clogging chariots sank deep into the soft sand, so that they drave heavily. The horses, flecked with foam and affrighted, reared, plunged and stumbled; some bared their teeth and whinnied; and many of the pins that held wheel to axle were snapped asunder, and the wheels fell away. And now,

however wildly the leading charioteers, with their stooping
bowmen, lashed and shouted, they made but little progress;
and they were dazed and confused by the tumult of the
storm.

And some among them, who feared the power of Moses
and the wrath of God, were suddenly seized with terror and
turned back in their tracks, crying "Away! Back! Away!
The Gods are against us! Jehovah fights against us!"

But still those in the rear continued to press on. And in
this mellay they struggled one against another in fury and
consternation in the midst of the bed of the sea, their hearts

pierced with dread of they knew not what danger, their one desire being to regain dry land and flee back away into Egypt. But still their captains urged them on.

Then Moses in the presence of Israel stretched forth his hand toward the sea. And behold there sounded out of the distance—above the din and tumult of the rain and thunder, and the shouts of the charioteers—the roar of water. In a liquid wall of crystal its lightning-lit torrent swept surging back into its customary channel. The Egyptians heard; they turned faces haggard with fear, and knew in their souls the doom that was upon them. But too late; snowy with foam the sea, in its course and strength, swept down upon them in one vast billow, and returned into its bed. Its waves met over them, and submerged them in the deeps, and not one of them remained alive.

Thus the Lord God saved Israel that day from the vengeance of Pharaoh and the armies of Egypt; and the corpses of the charioteers were flung up by the tide of the sea before their eyes, and the sea-shore was strown with their dead. And all Israel was filled with awe and wonder. They believed in their inmost hearts in the Lord, and in his faithful servant Moses, and rejoiced with an exceeding great joy.

In the peace that followed the storm Moses and Aaron and the elders of Israel gathered the people together in a solemn assembly.

And Miriam, the prophetess, took a timbrel in her hand, and the women of Israel went out after her with dancing and music, and sang to the Lord a song of joy and triumph and thanksgiving. And these were the words of the song they sang that day, while the people with their voices in their thousands on the shores of the sea took up the strains of it in mighty unison; and the firmament rang again:

# THE CROSSING OF THE RED SEA

*I will sing unto the Lord, for he hath triumphed gloriously;*
*The horse and the rider hath he thrown into the sea.*
*The Lord is my strength, of him shall be my song.*
*Sing unto the Lord who alone is our salvation.*
*He is my God, to him will I give thanks,*
*The God of our fathers, and I will exalt him.*

> *Mighty he in battles,*
> *Jehovah is his name!*

*The chariots of Pharaoh hath he cast into the sea,*
*His captains and their hosts he hath whelmed in its waters.*

> *They lie drowned in its deeps,*
> *They sank like a stone.*


*Thy right hand, Lord Jehovah, is glorious in power,*
*Terrible in its might, confounding thy foes.*
*In the splendour of thy majesty thou didst shatter them that*
  *challenged thee,*
*As fire amid the stubble ran the flame of thy wrath.*
*Blast of thy nostrils, came the wind from out the south.*
*It gathered up the waters till they stood upon an heap,*
*And the floods were congealed in the heart of the sea.*
*Cried the foe in his pride, "I will chase and overtake,*
*Rich shall be the spoil I will seize and divide.*
*My soul shall be sated with destruction and plunder,*
*With unscabbarded sword I will glut my desire."*
*Thou didst blow with thy wind, and the wild wave covered them;*
*Their clanging chariots gurgling sank like lead into the deep.*
*O Lord Jehovah, what gods can be compared to thee?*
*Glorious and supreme, who is like unto thee?*
*Wondrous in holiness, and fearful in all mysteries,*
*Lo, now thy foes are foundered in the sea.*
*Compassionate in mercy, thou didst lead forth thy people.*
*'Tis thou in thy compassion who hast saved them and redeemed.*

*The nations of the earth they hear, they are afraid.*
*Pangs of fierce woe have seized the princes of Philistia;*
*The proud dukes of Edom are dumb with amaze;*
*The mighty men of Moab they shudder as they hearken;*
*The hearts of all Canaan melt away in fear.*
*Terror and astonishment have seized upon their chieftains,*
*Confounded with thy wonders, they sit stark as is a stone.*
*They shall watch, O Lord Jehovah thy people pass through*
*them.*
*Thy people march on—thy redeemed and thy chosen.*
*Thou shalt bring them in and plant them in the mount of thine*
*inheritance,*
*The place thyself hadst made to be to thee a dwelling;*
*The Sanctuary, O Lord, established by thy hands.*

*There the Lord shall reign for ever and for ever,*
*In the glory of his Kingdom, and world without end!*

# THE
# WILDERNESS

# The Death of Moses

Thus came Israel out of Egypt; and the armies of Pharaoh were to trouble them no more. But his hand was mighty and this blow to his pride bitter to bear. They made no delay therefore and set forward on their great pilgrimage. Even when there was nothing to impede or harass them, the movement of such a multitude was very tardy since the whole host was compelled to keep pace with the children and weaklings, their flocks and herds. They had but few beasts of transport and were heavily burdened, and the day's advance from one night's encampment to the next was a distance seldom more than five miles.

Their course at first lay through the desert of Shur or Etham, a region of shifting sands along the eastern shore of the uppermost reaches of the Red Sea, where there is little green pasture and well-springs of water are few. Beyond this desert lay the wilderness of Zin. Here they turned eastward and came to Rephidim where they defeated the tribesmen of Amalek who had raided and pestered them on their way, and strove to prevent them from reaching the sweet waters of Paran.

They then advanced, ever ascending, towards the mountains of Sinai, through a country well-watered and fertile with groves of palm trees and acacias, and thickets of thorn and willow, the feathery tamarisk and the bright-leafed myrrh.

And when Jethro, the priest of Midian, heard that the Israelites were encamped at Sinai, forthwith he set out with his daughter Zipporah and her two sons to welcome Moses. And Moses went out to receive his father-in-law, and bowed himself before him and kissed him, and they rejoiced to meet again. And Moses brought his wife and his sons and Jethro to his tent, and there he told him of all that had passed since their last farewell. And Jethro rejoiced for all the goodness which the Lord had done to Israel. "Now I know", he said, "that the God you worship is greater than the Gods of Egypt and all gods beside." And he himself offered up sacrifice, and they feasted together, Moses and Aaron and the chief men of Israel.

By Jethro's wise counsel, seeing that the labour of government and the dispensing of justice was too great a burden to be borne by one commander, Moses chose out the ablest men of Israel and made them leaders over the people, rulers of thousands, rulers of hundreds, and of fifties and of tens. And he made many laws and ordinances for the guidance of the people and decreed the penalties and punishments of any who should offend against them. In all small matters the rulers he had chosen sat in judgment over the people. Only causes of great moment and difficulty were brought before Moses himself.

The day came when Jethro must return to his own people, and he went his way. But the host of Israel remained encamped among the mountains of Sinai, amidst gigantic precipices of granite and porphyry. And in their presence, though they were forbidden to draw near beyond the bounds set for them, Moses ascended the sacred mountain called Horeb, on whose slopes, when he sat keeping Jethro's sheep, he had seen the bush that had burned with flame yet was not consumed—the glory of the angel of the Lord.

Alone upon its summit he communed with God, and the
utmost heights of the mountain were hidden in a veil of
flaming splendour, and the mountain quaked, with thunderings and lightnings. There Moses remained in communion with the Lord forty days and forty nights, and
there tablets of stone, inscribed with commandments for the
obedience of Israel, were committed to his charge.

And because he tarried there so long, the people were
afraid and began to murmur, believing that he had forsaken
them and would return no more. They abandoned their

faith in the Lord Jehovah. Even in the shadow of the mountain they gathered together the gold ear-rings worn by their wives and sons and daughters. And following the rites of the Egyptians who in the form of an ox worshipped a god named Ptah, Aaron himself set up the image of a golden calf. And on the morrow after it was made, they rose up early and offered sacrifice before it and prostrated themselves; and when they had made sacrifice, they sat down to feast, and rose up to dance and to chaunt wild songs before this golden calf, trusting in that for their salvation. . . .

Nevertheless it was during their wanderings in the wilderness that a great tent or pavilion was fashioned to be the Tabernacle of the Lord and an enduring memorial to Israel wherein they might make atonement for their souls. And all the people brought precious vessels and offerings for its service, the chiefs of the tribes their gems, their gold and silver and brass, and all who had much, according to their means. Fine linen, dyed blue and purple and scarlet, silk, fleeces of rams and skins, oil for the lights and spices for sweet incense: all these were brought to Moses for the sacred adornment of the tabernacle; and even the poorest among them gave not less than half a silver shekel.

Within the tabernacle stood the altar of sacrifice; and in an inner chamber, veiled with embroidered curtains and named the Holy of Holies, was laid up the Ark of the Covenant between the Lord and his people Israel. This was a chest or coffer of acacia wood overlaid with gold, and within it were the tablets of stone and other precious objects. It was the most sacred symbol in Israel.

The whole tribe of Levi was devoted to the service of the Lord; and Aaron, who was himself a Levite, was at this time High Priest, and his sons Nadab, Abihu, Eleazar and Ithamar, were priests who ministered under him. They had made solemn vows, and had been anointed and consecrated and in their charge was the tabernacle and all that was within it. There they burned incense before the altar, and watched over the Ark of the Covenant, and fed with oil the seven-lamped golden candle-stick that burned in the holy place. And there they made sacrifice.

When in its simple beauty and splendour the tabernacle was completed, the elders of Israel met together in solemn assembly. And the glory of the Lord descended upon it, filling it as with a cloud with his radiance. It was an assurance to Israel of his presence there. When the cloud was lifted from over the tabernacle, they continued their march; but when the cloud rested upon it they camped in the place where at that time they chanced to be, and remained encamped until the cloud was lifted. For this great pavilion with its embroidered veils and curtains was so constructed that these and its poles, its altar and the Ark of the Covenant, could be removed and borne on with them on their pilgrimage.

On the twentieth day of the second month of the second year after their escape from Egypt, the people of Israel left Horeb behind them and journeyed on through the mountainous gorges of the great and terrible wilderness of Paran until they entered the lowlands of Kadesh in the wilderness of Zin.

They were now nearing the southern borders of Canaan. Like a vision of paradise, hope and longing for it had been continually in their minds, the blessed goal of their long travail and afflictions. It was a country that no man among them had ever seen with his own eyes, and it was as yet strange to them and undiscovered. Twelve men were therefore chosen, one from each of the tribes, for a perilous venture. They were given orders to make their way across its frontier by stealth, and to spy out the land, whether it were good or bad, wooded or barren; what manner of people dwelt in it, their kings and chieftains, their cities and strongholds, the numbers of their armed men, their might and wealth.

After forty days' absence the spies returned into the camp at Kadesh, burdened with fresh figs and pomegranates which they had plucked from the trees, and a vine branch with a cluster of luscious grapes upon it so heavy that it had to be carried between two of them, slung upon a staff.

They appeared before an assembly of the chief men of Israel and made their report. They told how wondrously rich in corn and pasture was the land they had seen, its groves of olives, its vineyards and fig trees and its abundance of milk and honey, for they had ventured on into the vale where Jacob had dwelt awhile when Joseph was a boy. But they reported also of the walled cities they had watched or entered, and the strong natural defences of the land, the power of its kings and the people over which they ruled and their men of war. And last, they told of the Anakim, a race of giants, men of prodigious strength and stature, that dwelt in the region of Hebron.

Of the twelve spies only two, Caleb and Joshua, the son of Nun, incited the assembly to march forward at once to invade the land, trusting in God to give them the victory. The other ten, daunted and discouraged by what they had seen, enlarged only on the mortal perils of such an enterprise, and filled the assembly with such terror of what lay before them that they rose up and cried out against Moses, "Would to God we had perished in Egypt! Would to God we had laid down our lives in the wilderness! To advance further is only utter destruction—an evil death to us all and perpetual bondage for our women and children."

When Caleb strove to reason with them and to enkindle them with his own valour, they threatened to stone him where he stood. They plotted together to depose Moses, and to elect in his stead a commander who would lead them back into Goshen by the way they had come, choosing rather a life safe and secure but in miserable slavery under Pharaoh, than to risk their all for so rich an inheritance in sure trust that God would be with them.

So it had been continually. Even though in their dire need miraculous waters had flowed from the rock, and, when other food had failed them, they had been nourished as if from heaven by manna, the gift of providence in the wilderness—manna that was white as coriander seed and tasted like waters made of honey, and that must be gathered early in the cool of the morning ere the heat of the sun should corrupt it—yet in spite of these divine mercies and the wonders that had been revealed to them in Egypt, at every threat of danger or difficulty, dearth or pestilence, they had murmured against him or broken out into open revolt against their leaders. And the punishment of God had been heavy upon them.

And yet again; now, even though the Land of Promise was within but a few days' march of them, they lost all hope and faith. Fainthearted and irresolute, they were never of the same mind from one day to another. And the hordes of the Amalekites and the Canaanites descended upon them, defeated them in battle, and chased them back into the wilderness of Zin. There they abode many long years.

Thence at length Israel journeyed to Mount Hor, where, in the presence of Eleazar and Moses, Aaron the High Priest died and was buried. Thence, they pressed on, southward, through the valley of Elath that lay at the uppermost reaches of the eastern branch of the Red Sea, the Gulf of

Aquaba. And there they came to the ancient highway of the caravans journeying between Mecca and Damascus. Skirting east of Edom, because its king refused them passage through his territory, they entered the land of the Moabites, with whom at the time they dealt peaceably, for they were the descendants of Lot, the nephew of Abraham. And they entered the mountainous region of Nebo, sheer ramparts of naked rock, the colours of their peaks and gorges ever changing in the splendour of the sun as it changes its station in the skies from dawn till eve. And not far distant hence, the waters of the river Jordan flowed into the sea.

So at length they were come again to the very borders of Canaan. And Moses knew that his end was near. He spoke for the last time before the congregation of the elders. He uttered prophecy and gave them his counsel; and he blessed the people. Then he surrendered up the sceptre of Israel to Joshua and charged him to be strong, faithful and of good courage, since to him had been given the glory of leading Israel into the land which had been promised them of old.

When this was done, he himself, weary with age and feebleness but of an indomitable will, went up alone to the heights of Mount Pisgah. There in solitude he gazed out westward, beyond the turquoise-blue waters of the Salt Sea and the river Jordan, over the sand-coloured plain of Jericho, the city of palm trees, towards Canaan, whose wooded mountains and valleys lay spread out beneath him, in the last beams of evening, and to the utmost shores of the Great Sea. He knew that it was not the will of God that he himself should set foot within its borders. So, but in agony of mind, he had stood alone, gazing out over the waters of another sea, while the chariots of Egypt were approaching the rabble of his defenceless followers, and only a miracle could save them from the vengeance of Pharaoh. Now he was at peace in the assurance that all was well with Israel, their pilgrimage at an end. His soul was refreshed with this vision of the future, and he longed to take his rest.

There in solitude he died, the Lord God his comfort; and he was buried in a valley of Moab, though no man knows the sepulchre where he was laid.

# The Fall of Jericho

For forty years the Israelites had wandered and sojourned in the wilderness, in its wastes of scorching sun by day, and bitter cold by night, and they had seen hard warfare. They had defeated Sihon, king of the Amorites, bearded men and hardy, and had slain him with all his host. They had invaded the land of Og, the King of Bashan, a monarch of mighty stature who ruled over sixty cities fenced with walls and with gates and bars, and whose throne was of wrought iron; and they had vanquished Balak and the five princes of Moab who had allied themselves with the tribesmen of Midian.

They burned their cities and destroyed their strongholds and captured a very great booty, with many thousands of sheep and oxen and asses. But hardships had been heavy upon them, and death had wasted them.

Of the grown men among them who had been upwards of twenty years of age when they crossed the Red Sea in their flight from Egypt, not one now remained alive. Many of them had been faithless or rebellious. They had died by the way, or had been slain in battle. But the youngest children, who with dream-ridden eyes had shared with their mothers and fathers in the first solemn midnight Feast of the Passover a whole lifetime ago, were now in the full vigour of manhood. And their own sons had grown up to be young men hardy and fearless. They too had suffered but had endured.

And Israel, though but a race of desert tribesmen, ill-armed and few in numbers by comparison with the great nations around them, from being little better than a cowed and unruly mob of fugitives, had become a doughty, resolute and disciplined people, fierce of spirit, implacable in battle, and under captains bold and valiant and skilled in war. They were now moreover a race united and at one; their hearts aflame with ardour for the one true God they worshipped, even though they could follow his will but stumblingly, and were aware of him but darkly and in part.

All Israel mourned for Moses thirty days, and when the days of their great mourning were over, they marched on from the mountainous region of Nebo and encamped about seven miles north-east of the mouth of the Jordan where it pours its waters into the Salt Sea. It is a region sere and sombre, and sunken lowest of any land on earth beneath the level of the oceans.

But about two days' march beyond and westward of it stood the rich city of Jericho. Strongly fortified, it reared its massive walls amidst the plain, between the river and the mountains of Canaan. And on its downfall hung the conquest of all that lay beyond.

That day Joshua sent out two men, spies, with orders to make their way by stealth into the city and glean what knowledge they could of its power in men and arms and engines of war, and the strength of its defences. They disguised themselves, crossed over the Jordan by one of its fords, and pressed on across the burning plain until, after the heat of the day, they neared the bright oasis in the desert in which at the foot of its hills the city lay. Here were gardens wildly green and sweet to eyes parched with the weary sands of the wilderness. Groves of palms and cypresses, and bowers of green orange trees in bloom—there too,

hedges of budded thorn and aromatic tamarisk, gourd and cucumber and fig, and plenteous vineyards. A stream of marvellous clear water gushed forth from its well-spring in the hills, to brim pools darting with fish, and the moat about the walls—thence to spend itself in a hundred channels, refreshing the gardens in the plain. And many birds made music by the waterside, for it was the hour of their evensong.

The two spies rested here, in hiding. Never even in their dreams had they looked out upon a country so fair. Verily Eden itself might once have been found here. Here then they lay until the sun had set behind the mountains, and the light of day had swiftly ebbed out of the heavens. And a little before nightfall they rose up and made their entry into the city by its eastern gate.

Already dark was down, and since the streets of the city would soon be deserted and any chance wayfarer might arouse suspicion, they knocked at the door of a house that seemed to be open to travellers, to seek lodging for the night. A woman named Rahab dwelt alone in this house, and she herself opened to them. Scanning their faces in the light of the lamp she carried, she admitted them, asked their business, and made them welcome. She set bread and wine before them and left them to refresh themselves.

But though they knew it not, the chief watchman at the gate had seen them enter the city, and mistrusting them for the spies they were, had had them followed to the woman's house. When it was reported to the king of Jericho that two Hebrews were concealed in the city, he was greatly wroth. He commanded that they should be seized instantly and brought before him, and that his torturers should be in waiting.

There came anon, then, a guard of soldiers to Rahab's house and beat upon the door. Spying out on them from a window, she guessed on what errand they were come. She ran in haste to the two spies where they sat supping together, and warned them of their danger. "Follow me now, at once," she bade them, "and with all caution, for there is not a moment to lose." And she herself ran on before them and led them up on to the flat roof of her house, which was built upon the city wall and overlooked the plain beyond it. There she hid them, heaping over them bundles of flax which had been laid out in order, to be dried in the sun for the weaving of linen. She bade them lie close until she came again, and not so much as stir or whisper.

Then she ran down and opened to the guard; and when they questioned and threatened her, she told them that the two men they were seeking had indeed come to the house and had entreated lodging for the night. But as she knew not whence they had come or who they were, she had denied them, and had herself watched and seen them go out of the city a little before dark, while there was yet time and the gates were not shut.

"Whither they went then I cannot say," she said. "But they were spent and on foot and cannot have gone far. Pursue after them quickly and you will certainly overtake them."

The soldiers left her, and set off as they thought in hot chase of the spies towards the fords of the Jordan, with intent to cut them off before they could cross over, though by now it was dark and the moon had set. And the gates of the city were shut after them.

When all sound of them was stilled, Rahab shut to her door and barred it and returned to the spies on the roof. She called to them softly and they crept out of their hiding-place. And she told them why she had given them shelter and had not betrayed them to their enemies. Even at first sight of them, she said, she had pierced through the disguise they wore, and knew them to be spies and Hebrews. For dwelling as she did near the gateway of the city, which was continually thronged with travellers and strangers, she had long since heard the rumour of the approach of the hosts of Israel. She had heard moreover how the Lord God they worshipped had driven back the waters of the Red Sea for their salvation, confounding the hosts of Pharaoh; and what fate had overtaken the kings of the Amorites, Og and Sihon, when they had set themselves in array against them.

"Of a truth," she said, "as soon as we of the city heard

these things our hearts melted within us. The king and all his captains are sick with apprehension. Why else should his soldiers have come knocking here to seize two helpless strangers unless it be for fear of him that sent you? I am myself a sinful woman and of little account, yet I assuredly know and believe that the Lord God who wrought these marvels is the true God that reigns in heaven above and over all things on the earth beneath it, and that the walls and towers of Jericho are less than nought against them that believe in him and do his will."

She stayed, gazing into their faces in the thin sprinkled light of the stars that burned wildly in the skies above them, her eyes darkly luminous, her countenance pale and rapt with the eager motions of her mind and the ardour of her heart. "Wherefore then," she continued earnestly, "I beseech you to vow unto me by the living God that since I have showed you kindness, you also will show kindness to those whom I love, and will save the lives of my father and my mother, my brothers and sisters, in the day of evil, and deliver us from death. What power had I? What if the commander of the armies of Israel had sent out a thousand spies into the city and all had been taken and done to death—what would that have availed against your God, Jehovah? Seeing then that I have kept faith with you, I pray you keep faith with me also."

Then said the two spies: "Our lives for thine—if thou utter no word of why we came here or whither we go. We swear it unto thee. As in our need thou hast dealt truly and kindly with us, so in the day that Jehovah shall give us the victory will we deal kindly with thee."

She was comforted. And she stooped and peered down over the wall of the city to see if aught were stirring. The air was sweet with the mingled fragrance of the spring, and in the hush of night the voice of the water coursing in its channels rang clear and changeable. She turned to them eagerly, yet as though in the peace and silence, sorrowful thoughts had found entry into her mind.

"Come, now," she said. "All is quiet and there is none to overlook us." And she brought them down from the roof into a chamber below, and to a window that hung over the city wall, for her whole house was built high out on the great width of the wall. And she took a strong cord woven of scarlet and bound it fast to the beam of the window, while the two spies stood back watching her and intently listening. And while they waited, their eyes took in all that lay around them in the small light of her lamp, her loom, her hanks of bright-dyed yarn, and the cloth she had woven.

When all was ready for their departure, they spoke earnestly with her, so that everything should be clear between them, and nothing should miscarry when the day of reckoning came.

"It was close on nightfall", they said, "when we entered the city, and we looked but scantly about us. The streets are strange to us, and we know not where thy people dwell. When we are gone, visit them secretly, then, and bind them by oath to breathe not a word of anything thou shalt say to them. And when the city is besieged and the day of the assault is come, see that they all meet together in this house and that not one of them be absent. For assuredly in the heat and terror of battle there will be no help or hope for any found at large in the streets against the vengeance of Israel. Do this then, and let no man else hear of it. And when all thy family are come together, bind this scarlet cord in the window for a signal, so that we and our captains shall see it there, and shall know which house is thine. Thus only shall you all be saved. But if any that are with you venture out of the doors of this house into the streets, then he goes at his own risk; and we ourselves shall be guiltless of his blood."

She vowed solemnly unto them: "Be it all according as you have said, and may the God of Israel remember me! And now," she added, "delay not a moment longer, but get you gone into the mountains and stay in hiding there at least three days. By then the men who are in pursuit of you will be wearied out and will have given up hope of finding you. Then shall you return by night by the ford, and none will molest you."

So she sent them away in safety. And they climbed down by the cord from the window that hung over the wall of the city, and fled under cover of night into the mountains. There they lay close, venturing out only after dark for food, until three days were gone by and they were out of danger of discovery. The third night they crossed the Jordan and returned into the camp at Shittim. And they reported themselves to Joshua.

"Truly," they said, "the Lord hath delivered this country into our hands. The King of Jericho and all his officers and the people that dwell in the city are faint with dread because of Israel."

They told him also of the oath they had made to the woman who had saved them from falling into the power of the King. Joshua bade them bear it continually in mind, and ensure that it was kept to the letter. He commended the two men, and was well-content with what they told him.

On the morrow the Israelites raised their camp at Shittim and marched towards the Jordan. They pitched their tents on the eastern shore of the river and remained there three days. Now it was the season of the year when the Jordan is deep in flood and overflows all its banks. It stretched out before them like a shallow sea, but deep and tumultuous in mid-stream. And there seemed to be no means whereby so great a host could cross from one side to the other, for the fords were now drowned in water, and boats they had none. But Joshua, their commander, was a man of supreme energy of mind and of a high courage. And the Lord was with him.

On the third day he sent his officers through the camp, among the people. They proclaimed that on the morrow, by the grace of God, Israel would resume the march, cross the Jordan and enter Canaan; and that they were one and all to sanctify themselves in preparation for this great day; for the Lord would do wonders. At these tidings all marvelled, and there was quiet in the camp from that hour onwards.

By sunrise on the morrow, as their Captain, Joshua, had commanded, the people had broken up their camp and were now assembled in their clans and companies and were ready. And the priests bearing the Ark of the Covenant advanced in solitude from out of the camp and continued on their way until they came to the shallow flood-waters that lay shining between them and the Jordan's usual channel. And behold, as the naked soles of the feet of the priests bearing the Ark were dipped in the brim of the water, a wondrous miracle was revealed to all that gazed. For the river that yesterday had run, swirling in flood and burdened with wreckage, in the deep gorge of the Jordan, was now dammed; its waters being heaped up near the city called Adam, above twenty miles from where Israel had been encamped.

And the priests, without pause, chanting their hymns of praise, went on down into the channel until among its boulders they were in the midst of the river's bed. There they stayed, the staves of the Ark resting on their shoulders, its gold wondrous in the sunrise. And when they had taken up their station there, the trumpets sounded. And the whole host of Israel—the men of war, the common people, the women and children, the camp-followers—went down after them with their flocks and their herds, their beasts of burden and all that they had. As they filed past the priests—none drawing near them—and looked on the Ark with its cherubim of gold, they lifted up their voices in wild acclamation, in sure trust that while this sacred emblem of Jehovah was safe in a place so full of peril, so too were they.

Hours passed by while the vast multitude of Israel moved slowly on, threading its serpentine way across the gorge. When all were safely gone their way, none hurt or injured, and not even a single lamb lost, the priests followed after them, till all were on dry land.

Then Joshua commanded that twelve picked, sturdy men, one from each of the tribes, should return into the river-bed, and bring up upon their shoulders thence twelve very hard and heavy boulders from the place where the priests had stood who bore the Ark. These Joshua set up in a circle at Gilgal, for a trophy and memorial to all that came after of the wonder that had been seen that day, so that their children's children to unnumbered generations should be continually reminded of how by the grace of God, after issuing from the wastes of the desert, they had crossed that great river, the Jordan, in safety and dry-shod.

And Israel continued the march that day and went up into the plains of Jericho, and because of this marvel the people were moved with awe and wonder and looked with fear upon Joshua even as they had feared Moses before him.

The haze-blue mountains of Moab now left behind them, they encamped in Gilgal many days and there fulfilled the rites of their religion as they were bidden by the priests. There, too, on the fourteenth day of the first month of the new year, they kept the Feast of the Passover and offered up solemn sacrifice. It was the night of the vernal full moon, as it had been in Goshen, and though in this desolate region of Gilgal little verdure is to be seen but that of the prickling briar and the thorn, and spring-time shows but thin and sparsely, yet the early flowers of the year were now in blossom, and the birds and beasts rejoiced in its sweetness. Throughout the forty years since the first Feast of the Passover had been held in Egypt never had there been such joy in Israel. It seemed almost beyond belief that the woes and hardships and the hopes so long deferred of their pilgrimage were over, and that the very soil on which they stood was the land of their desire. Here at Gilgal the host rested, while the men of war prepared to go forward to the siege of Jericho.

On the morrow after the feast, the women of Israel baked unleavened cakes of flour ground from the old corn of the last year's harvest. From that day onward the manna which had been their food in the wilderness ceased and they lived henceforward on the fruits and produce of Canaan.

Now it came to pass one day about éventide, that Joshua, having with his chief officers gone through the camp and assured himself that all was well and in order, and a strong watch posted, withdrew himself alone. He went on across the plain until, in the half light under the hills beyond it, the sombre bastions and walls of Jericho loomed into view, the last faint hues of sunset streaking the western skies. Apart from a few wild nocturnal creatures which had scurried into shelter at sound of his approach, no living thing had crossed his path.

The shades of night gathered swiftly around him as, vigilant and alone, he gazed out over the flat plain towards the mighty stronghold. The day of Israel's ordeal was at hand. And on him alone, their Captain chosen by God, its fortunes now hung. His dark clear eyes became fixed in reverie; his mind in labour with his thoughts. And as he stood musing there, the thrill as of a great peril suddenly troubled his heart. He turned abruptly, his hand on his sword-hilt, and looked. And behold, he was no longer alone, for at a few paces distant there stood as it were a man, his sword drawn in his hand. Yet his look was not like that of mortal. There dwelt a light upon his brows that was not of earth or of its skies now fading in the west; his countenance was serene and glorious. And Joshua in awe and wonder drew near and accosted him.

"Art thou", he said, "for Israel, or comest thou out armed to fight for our adversaries?"

And he said: "Nay, but as prince and captain of the host of the Lord God am I come."

Joshua doubted no more. He fell on his face to the earth, and made obeisance and worshipped. "Answer me, I beseech thee!" he cried. "What sayeth my Lord unto his servant?"

And the prince of the Lord of Hosts said to Joshua: "Loose now thy sandals from off thy feet, for the place whereon thou standest is holy."

And Joshua did so; and with all the strength of his mind he paid heed to the words the stranger uttered. Then he went his way and returned through the darkness into the camp.

Rahab had spoken truly. Rumour of the approach of Israel and of the victories they had won over the lands east-

ward of the Jordan had spread far and wide among the
kings and chieftains and the people of Canaan. The name of
Jehovah who had abased the gods of Egypt was a thing of
dread to them. When then report was brought to the King
of Jericho that even while the waters of the Jordan were in
flood they had been gathered and heaped up as in a wall to
give Israel passage, and that the whole host was now encamped at Gilgal, he was stricken with a deadly terror.
There was no spirit left in him, for fear and dread of Israel.
He dared not sally out to meet them.

And those that dwelt on the outskirts of the city withdrew into its shelter, bringing with them whatsoever corn
and food and treasure they possessed and could carry away
in haste. Its walls and battlements were manned, and the
whole city was straitly shut up. None came out and none
went in. Before even an enemy had showed at its gates,
Jericho lay as if besieged.

And at Joshua's own time the army of Israel, men of
valour, forty thousand strong, marched out from Gilgal
and drew near to the city and encamped there. And the
King of Jericho and his captains awaited the assault.

But day followed day, and still there showed no sign of
when or how it would be delivered. Spies that were sent out
under cover of darkness never returned; false alarms set the
city in sudden violent uproar; and open revolt was beaten
down with a cruel hand.

And in the midst of this suspense there came a day when
the watchmen on Jericho's topmost turrets, as they peered
out over the plain in the cheating dusk of daybreak stood
aghast. A strange and terrifying spectacle met their eyes.

There debouched from out of the camp of Israel upon
the plain rank upon rank of its men-at-arms, by their troops
and their companies, each under its own captain, and in a

great silence. Wending their way well beyond bow-shot from the walls of the city they advanced in close order, as if to encompass the whole circuit of the city. And when the men-at-arms were passed on, there followed in a space seven raimented priests bearing seven trumpets of rams' horns set in silver that were wont to be sounded on days of festival and jubilee in the tabernacle. After them, borne by four other priests upon its staves, there came an object that filled them with disquiet and boding, though they had no knowledge of its use or meaning. It was the Ark of the Covenant

[ 241 ]

of the Lord. And in the rearward of the Ark, yet other thousands of armed men in close defile followed in its train.

Thus in the midst of the host went the Ark of the Lord, the priests preceding it, and, as they walked, blowing with their mouths into their clamorous trumpets of rams' horns. Else Israel marched in silence. Not a man of them spoke to his neighbour, nor made they any sound with their voices, though the clarions of the silver trumpets rang echoing clear and solemn against the walls.

The horror and mystery of the spectacle struck with a deadly cold the hearts of the king and his captains and the defenders of the city as they looked down and watched from their prodigious walls. They had never seen its like before. No wild onset of assailants shouting shrill battle-cry, no twangling storms of arrows hailing upon the walls, nor crash of battering ram. Nought but this voiceless multitude of gaunt and fearless tribesmen, sun-scorched and lean with long travail in the thirsty wilds of the desert, marching on and on in a hush broken only by the shuffle of their footsteps in the sands and the sudden horrific rending of the air by blasts of the silver trumpets of their priests. And after the priests, this gold-slabbed coffer—its bearers clad in strange embroidered vestments—awful emblem of Jehovah, the unseen and unimaginable foe. This and this only. For when the city had thus been compassed once about, the army of Israel withdrew into its camp.

Thus at daybreak for six days one after another the whole host of the army of Israel made the circuit of Jericho; and to those who manned its walls, wearied out with the last watch of night, it was as though the city were an island girt about and encircled with a slow-moving river, not of waters but of men. They were besieged with fear, fear of these enemies without and of the fate awaiting them, and fear of the horror of the mystery in their imaginations.

The seventh day dawned, clear and cloudless in the spring of the year, and yet again the city was encompassed round about as it had been hitherto, but in the mien of those who made the circuit of the city there had come a change. They trod as if exultant, and speechless with joy. And when this day the full circuiting was completed there rang from out of the trumpets of the priests a shrilling clarion, wilder and longer than any that had sounded yet. And when the echo of this clangour ceased, the whole host of Israel suddenly shouted together with a great and mighty shout. And lo, when the sound of the trumpets and of this mighty shout had ceased, it came to pass that the walls of Jericho were broken and fell down flat, its gates were flung open, and the army of Israel went in, every man straight before him. They took the city by storm, burned it with fire, and destroyed all that were within it, except only the woman Rahab, her father and mother and her household, as had been sworn to her by the spies.

From conquest on to conquest under Joshua the armies of Israel marched on. In the first few years that followed the fall of Jericho, of the kings and chieftains whom he met in battle and who warred either in their own might in defence of their cities, or banded themselves together in alliance under one among them greater than they, he vanquished thirty-one.

But centuries were yet to pass before the nations in Canaan were finally subdued. And though the land was divided by Joshua between the tribes each within its own boundaries, according to its strength and numbers, they were not only repeatedly at war with their enemies, but in strife one with another. The day was yet far distant when

Israel was to be established as a kingdom under the domination of one king, mighty and glorious; his seat Jerusalem, the Zion of the Lord.

# SAMSON

# The Angel

South-westward of Canaan lay the territory that had
been divided by Joshua between the tribes of Dan
and of Judah. The country given to Judah was
bounded on the east by the bitter waters of the Salt
or Dead Sea. There, eastward of Jericho, lay desert barren
and desolate. Northward, with its high ridges and deep
gorges, ran the border-line of Judah from the Jordan to the
Great Sea, the cities of Gilgal, Jerusalem and Bethlehem
lying a little beyond and northward of it, in the territory of
Benjamin. This for the most part was a mountainous district, well watered and fruitful, its lowlands or foothills rich
with cornfields, olive-yards and good pasturage. Further-
most to the south of Judah lay Beersheba, with its flat,
grassy and well-watered plateau, and beyond its river that
flowed into the Great Sea was the territory of Simeon.

But though in the days of Joshua the chief cities that lay
in the great plain westward of Judah to the sand-duned
shore of the Great Sea had been captured for Israel, they
had been lost again. Here under the dominion of their
princes dwelt the Philistines, a nation rich and powerful,
skilled and fierce in war, lords of the islands, traders and
seamen, who had come from afar, and after settling in
Egypt, made frequent raids on the southern coasts of
Canaan, and had finally invaded and subdued it. They had
established themselves between Mount Baalah in the north

and the city of Gerar in the south; and in the course of time had advanced into the territory of Dan, and into central Canaan. And they held it in subjection for many years.

In face and feature they resembled the ancient Greeks, with straight noses, high, narrow brows and thin-lipped mouths. The gods they worshipped with cruel rites were Baal and Dagon, and Ishtar or Ashtoreth also, the Moon Goddess. Their troops wore pleated caps upon their heads, strapped beneath the chin, with a cuirass of leather, and kilts to their knees. And they were armed with a small round two-handled shield, a spear, and a short broadsword of bronze.

For many years the territories of Dan and Judah and the southern parts of Canaan remained in subjection to the five fierce and crafty princes of Philistia, and paid tribute to them as their overlords. The southern tribes were not only divided among themselves but again and again had proved faithless to the one true God, had forsaken his worship and followed after the gods of the heathen nations around them. They forgot Israel's miraculous deliverance of old time, and the wonders that had been revealed to them in their long sojourning in the wilderness, and how the Lord had brought them at length into the land that he had promised for their inheritance to Abraham and Isaac and Jacob.

Yet did he never forsake his chosen people, and when in their anguish they repented of the evil they had done, he again and again raised up deliverers, leaders able and far-sighted in action and enterprise. These men were called Judges in Israel; and of these judges none was more feared and hated by the Philistines than Samson. And this is his story.

There lived in Zorah, a shady village in the hills on the borders of Philistia, a man of the name of Manoah. He was a Danite, but unlike many of his fellow-tribesmen he had kept true to his faith and was a man of a devout heart. He was no longer young, and his one sorrow was that he was childless. This was a grief even more bitter to his wife whom he loved—that they had no son to live after them when they were gone, and to be brought up in the fear and love of God.

Now one day this woman was alone in her house, and though her fingers were busy with what she was doing, her mind fell into a reverie. So intent did she become on the gentle longing thoughts that haunted her daydream that when, as if at an inward call, she looked up and saw a stranger standing beside her, she had no knowledge of how he had come, nor even if he had spoken.

But at one swift upward glance into his countenance she knew him to be a prophet or messenger of God. In truth, this was no man, but an angel.

And the angel said to the woman: "Take comfort and grieve no more because thou art childless. I am come hither to tell thee that a son shall be born to thee—a son who from the day of his birth shall be set apart in the service of the Lord."

The woman bowed herself before the angel. So great was her astonishment at his presence there, and her happiness at what he had said, that she could make no answer in words. And the angel revealed to her that for token that this son was not like other children but that he had been consecrated to the Lord, the hair of his head should not be shorn, as was the custom in Israel, but allowed to grow freely and naturally. "And be thou thyself", said the angel, "heedful in all that thou doest. Drink no wine, eat only food that is pure and wholesome, and remember well all that I have said unto thee. For thy son is the gift of God, and he shall begin the deliverance of Israel from its enemies the Philistines."

The woman bowed herself again before him, but when she raised her head, behold, the angel had left her as he had come, and she was alone. Whereupon she rose up and went off in haste to find her husband, trembling and overjoyed, and she told him all that had happened.

"As at this very hour I was sitting alone," she said, "my thoughts far away from all around me, I turned my head and looked, and lo, there stood before me a man of God, the like of whom I have never seen before. For his look was like the look of an angel. And it filled me with such awe and wonder that I could find no words even to enquire of him whence he had come, nor did he tell me his name.

"But this he said, and my heart leapt within me to hear it —he did solemnly assure me that our prayers—your prayers and mine—have been answered, and that I shall have a son. And more than that even; our son is to be consecrated to God from the day of his birth. And he bade me also, Manoah, take great heed in all that I do and in what I drink and eat, since our son will not be as other children but is given to us of God and will do wonders for Israel."

Manoah rejoiced with her, but was troubled within himself. And he prayed that night that this prophet or man of God should return and visit them again, so that he himself might see him and learn from him all that they should do.

The Lord answered his prayer. And the angel came again to the woman. It was morning, and before the sun was high in the heavens. Seated beneath a solitary oak at a little distance from the house, she was working with her needle, and was alone. Her heart was filled with joy and expectation, and when she saw him she hastened out to meet him and entreated him to remain where he was until she could bring her husband. And she herself went in search of him.

She found Manoah with his workers in the fields.

"Come instantly," she said, "for the man of God is here, and is even now waiting for thee in the shade of the oak."

Without pausing, she ran on in front of her husband, and Manoah followed after her. When he came to where the angel was standing beneath the wide-spread branches of the tree, he enquired of him courteously, "Art thou the man who spoke with this woman?" And the angel answered him, "Yes."

Manoah questioned him concerning all that had been in

his mind. "I pray thee, tell me," he said, "when thy words come true which thou hast spoken concerning the son that is to be born to this woman, what are the vows that he shall make? What shall I teach him? How is he to be trained and brought up so that in nothing I do amiss, but ensure that he shall remain faithful in the service of the Lord?"

The angel answered Manoah: "Let the woman give heed to what I have already told her. In everything that I have bidden her, let her obey."

Then Manoah said to the angel: "Wilt thou not tarry with us a while, and rest thyself, until we have made ready a meal, to strengthen and refresh thee?"

But the angel answered: "Even though I remain here a little, urge me not to take food with thee, for that cannot be. If thou wouldst offer sacrifice, thou must offer it to the Lord."

"Tell me, then, only thy name," said Manoah, "so that when what thou hast foretold to this woman come true, we may always keep thee in remembrance and do thee honour."

"Why inquirest thou of me my name," said the angel, "seeing that it is secret, and above man's understanding?"

Then Manoah, marvelling in his mind what manner of man this was, chose out from his herd a kid for sacrifice. He took the kid to a great stone or rock that jutted up out of the green grass not far distant from the oak tree, and laid dry sticks on the stone, and placed the body of the kid upon the sticks, and he kindled them with fire, for a sacrifice and thanksgiving to the Lord.

And as Manoah and his wife, kneeling together a few paces from the rock, watched the flames ascending into the clear morning sunshine, the stranger himself drew near to the rock, and lo, the flames seemed to beat down upon him, and the radiance of his countenance was more intense than their eyes could bear. They bowed themselves to the ground, and the angel rose up and ascended from them in the flames of the sacrifice and vanished into the heavens.

Manoah sprang hastily to his feet, his mind filled with astonishment and dread, and he knew now that this stranger was no man but an angel. He turned trembling to his wife: "What shall we do?" he said. "God's judgment will fall upon us. We have seen his angel face to face and shall surely die."

But his wife, whose heart and mind were so welling over with joy and thankfulness that there was no room for fear, eagerly reasoned with him. "It was in truth", she said, "an angel of the Lord, and now I see that deep within me I knew it from the moment I looked into his face and his eyes dwelt upon mine. But of a truth there is nothing to fear. If God had intended to destroy us, he would not have accepted this sacrifice; nor would he have let us remain here and witness all that we have seen; nor would the angel have foretold all that he did foretell."

At this Manoah was comforted, and they rejoiced together and were at peace. The angel never afterwards appeared again to him or to the woman. And when, as he had foretold, her son was born, she named him Samson, which means, Radiant as the Sun.

In everything that the angel had bidden his mother so was Samson brought up. Neither as a child, nor when he had grown up into boyhood, was there any that could compare with him in beauty and grace and strength in the country round about Zorah, either among his own people or among the Philistines.

He was swifter of foot than a wild animal, impulsive and fearless, yet he seemed not to be aware of his strength, nor had he any vanity, for his face was lit up as a lantern is by the flame within it; and his hair which from his birth had never been clipped or shorn surrounded his face like dark strands of gold. When he was past his first childhood, his mother plaited it and bound it behind his head in seven braids, to keep it untangled and from falling into his eyes.

In all things he obeyed the vows that had been made on his behalf before he was born. He was the never-ending delight of his mother's heart, and Manoah watched over him, and while he was still young restrained him and as far as possible kept him at home. But he was of a rash, wilful and tempestuous nature, as quick to take offence as to forgive, and bent on having his own way.

As he grew up towards manhood, he went in freedom everywhere, learning the ways and habits of the birds and beasts of the steeps and ravines among the mountains, and the craft of the hunter, fearing nought. And he chose companions not only from among his own kinsmen and the boys of the village whose white houses nestled on the mountain side, but ventured also down into the plain and into the company of the Philistines. He mastered their ways and minds, fickle and crafty; though in his heart he despised them.

# The Riddle

While Samson was still a young man, he went down one morning, as he was wont to do, into a fortress town of the Philistines called Timnath, which lay a few miles beyond the valley south of Zorah, and west of Bethshemesh. At the entry of the town as he went on his way, he met a young woman who was the daughter of one of the chief men of Timnath. Samson turned his eyes, and glancing into her dark narrow countenance was entranced by her beauty. His fair face paled, his lovesick heart stood still.

From that hour onward he could think of nothing else. She haunted him, as may a dream; and when he returned home he spoke to his father and mother of this young woman, vowing that he would have no peace or quiet until they consented to let him win her for his wife.

But Manoah and his mother were distressed to hear it. They pleaded with him. "Is there no young woman gracious and beautiful enough among thy kinsfolk or among our own people that thou shouldst without a moment's thought choose for thyself a wife from among these heathen Philistines?"

But Samson refused to listen to them, so wildly burned his love for this young Philistine woman. "Nothing you can say or do", he repeated, "will move me by a hair's breadth from my purpose. Why are you then continually reproaching me, reasoning against what is not of my mind but is eating out my very soul? If you have any love left for me, go down to Timnath and do whatever is needful to persuade her father to let me take her to wife. I can neither sleep nor eat for thinking of her. I love her, and there is none to compare with her."

But in spite of his entreaties Manoah and his mother could not persuade themselves to consent to do as he wished. It was utterly against their hope and faith and desire. They were grieved by his wilfulness and obstinacy, but said no more. They did not know that the Lord had willed it so; nor did they foresee what would be the outcome of it—the blazing up of a lifelong feud between Samson and the hated oppressors of Israel, and the beginning of Israel's deliverance.

Now one morning Samson was again on his way down from Zorah into the valley beneath, and bound for Timnath. As he hastened on, leaping and scrambling down through the wild and rocky gorge of the mountain, now in shafting sunshine, now in shade, he approached a place where the vineyards of the Philistines were spread out over the lower terraces of the hillside, their branches green with their young clusters of grapes. He heard a confused, low droning of bees, and turned aside by a narrow defile through a thicket where flowers grew starry and sweet and burdened the air with their fragrance.

As he stood there, spying about him in search of the hive wherein these wild bees had stored their honey, his heart suddenly stilled within him at some faint call of danger. And of a sudden before he could move hand or foot a fierce and roaring young whelp of a lion sprang out on his path from its covert in the thicket. Its roar ran echoing from crag to crag. With twitching tail and bristling hair, and eyes

fixed ravenously on its prey, it crouched low to the dust in the rocky hollow, then leapt upon him. And Samson, un-armed as he was, its breath smiting hot upon his cheek, its rankness in his nostrils, met unmoved its furious onset.

And the spirit of the Lord that was his strength came mightily upon him. With one hand he seized the lion by the shag of beard upon its chin, with the other its upper jaw, and with a single wrench of arm and shoulder he rent it asunder limb from limb as easily as if it had been a kid. He

[ 257 ]

stayed to recover his breath, then flung its carcase out beyond the narrow track, pushed back through the thicket into the gorge and continued his journey to Timnath. There he made his way to the house of the father of the young Philistine woman, and talked with her; and as he talked with her his love increased, so that it seemed an anguish almost beyond bearing to part from her and to return to Zorah.

When some days afterwards he was climbing up through the gorge beyond the vineyards of the Philistines on his way home, he turned aside out of the track to look for the carcase of the lion he had killed. He found it there; but the flies of the air and the insects of the dust had picked its bones clean and white, and its hairy hide was dried up in the violent heat of the sun. Stooping, he discovered that a swarm of bees had made their hive within the arching ribs of its dry body, and already there was a rich store of honey. He was hot and hungry, and with the palms of his hands he scraped out a fragment of the oozing comb and refreshed himself with its honey as he went on his way. When he reached home he gave some of the honey to his father and mother, but he uttered no word concerning his encounter with the lion, or that he had found the honey in its dried-up carcase.

Convinced at last that they would never consent to his marriage with the young Philistine woman, he himself went down alone and persuaded her crafty father that she should be given to him for wife. This done, he prepared for his wedding feast, which was to be held, not, as was the custom in Israel, in his own house, but in the house of the Philistine. Many guests from among her kinsfolk and friends were invited, but none of his own people; and of the Philistines some had long been known to him, and one of them was his bosom friend. Apart from the women, thirty young men in all, perfumed and anointed, sat down with him at the feast, which continued, as was the way with the Philistines, for seven days.

The mornings were spent in singing and dancing, and in contests of strength and skill. At night they feasted. Contests of wit, also, for they asked riddles one of another, eating and drinking and rejoicing together. Samson listened to them, as he sat in his bright-coloured wedding clothes, his fair hair braided in seven plaits behind his head. And while he watched them he grew ever more ill at ease, for though they flattered him to his face, there were many among them who mocked at him behind his back and were hostile to the marriage of one of their kinswomen to a man of an alien and hated race. The thought irked him and he pined to outwit and humble these braggarts. He sat brooding, until, of a sudden, smiling within himself, he stood up and challenged them.

"Hearken, now, all of you, and I myself will ask you a riddle. And if any man among you can give me the right answer to it within seven days of the feast, then will I pay for forfeit not only to him but to each and every one of you a change of finest linen and a robe as splendid as any now upon your backs. But beware of it, for it must be a wager between us. And if you fail to find the answer, then shall you yourselves pay me thirty changes of fine linen and thirty robes as good as mine—one of both from each of you!"

He turned and glanced at his bride who sat beside him in her place. She smiled at him with glittering eyes, and he laughed.

Merry with wine, the young Philistines took up his challenge. "Tell us your riddle," they shouted, "and thou shalt have the answer to it far sooner than we the forfeit!"

Then Samson said: "This is my riddle—

*Out of the eater came wherewith to eat,*
*And out of the strong the sweet?*

Answer me that!"

For the next day or two the Philistines racked their wits to find answer to it, but found none. They were enraged at the thought of this Hebrew triumphing over them, and some of them sought out Samson's young wife and threatened her.

"Did you entice down this boasting young Danite and choose him for a husband merely in order to beggar us all? Who is he that we should load him with robes and fine linen? Take heed, then! If thou canst not coax out of thy husband the meaning of this riddle of his so that we can give him his answer before the seven days of the feast are over, it is thou thyself shall pay the forfeit, for of a surety we will burn down thy father's house and thee inside of it."

At this threat Samson's wife was so sore afraid that with all the cunning she could, she set about persuading Samson to tell her the answer. But at first without avail. When they were alone again together she began to weep.

"Again and again", she said, "have I besought thee to confide in me. But all in vain. To think thou shouldst have made up this riddle out of thine own head and asked it of my friends, my own people, without so much as sharing a syllable of it with me! How canst thou say thou lovest me and yet wilt not share with me this one small secret?"

But still Samson refused to tell her. "Why," he said, "I have not even so much as mentioned the riddle to my own father or mother! How then should I tell thee the answer however much I love thee?"

On and on she continued to pester him, taunting, beguiling, weeping, if so be by any means she could seduce him to confide in her. At last Samson could endure her wiles no longer, and on the seventh morning he told her the answer. And as he lay sleeping in the heat of the day, she sallied out softly and revealed it to the young Philistines.

That night, the last night of the feast, the young men sat in triumph, smiling craftily one at another, until at a late hour Samson reminded them that the seven days' grace he had given them was over, and that his riddle remained unanswered. "Where is the forfeit you promised to bring me," he said, "every man of you a vestment of fine linen and a wedding robe? Have it again, and I defy you to answer me:

> *Out of the eater came wherewith to eat,*
> *And out of the strong the sweet?*"

One and all they sat sullenly knitting their brows and gazing at him as if at a loss, then at a signal they rose and derisively sang out the answer:

> "*Sweeter than honey on earth there is nought.*
> *Nor in stronger than lion can its sweetness be sought.*

What sayest thou to that, Samson? Swoop back on the carcass thou hast hidden in the gorge. Maybe thou shalt find thy forfeit hidden under its skin."

Samson's eyes roved slowly from one face to the other as they stood in mockery around him, and at last he turned his head and gazed full into the face of the woman, who with painted cheek and brow, and head garlanded with flowers, sat beside him at the feast. She stared stonily back at him, but her hands trembled.

"Ay," he said to them all, his rage and his hidden contempt of them working within him, "I see the way of it. Having not the wits of a man among you, you crept off and bribed the woman."

Blazing with fury at her treachery and at the crooked and paltry fashion in which his guests had cheated him, he set off that night with a few young men of his own tribe valiant enough to go with him. And they came down before day-break to Askelon, the chief city of the Philistines, which reared its towered walls on high above a pallid sea. There they hid themselves, and out of their ambush waylaid and slew thirty of the men of Askelon and plundered them, and brought back the clothes they wore in payment of Samson's wager with the young Philistines.

But his anger against the woman whom he loved and who had deceived him was not abated. He refused to see her and returned to the house of his father. At this, without word to Samson, his father-in-law, the Philistine, dealt with him even more treacherously than had his guests; for he robbed him of the daughter he had given him to wife and be-stowed her in marriage on one of the Philistines who had been at the wedding feast—even on the young man who was Samson's bosom friend.

As time went by, and knowing nought of what had been done in his absence, Samson's anger against his young wife began to wane. "Surely", he thought within himself, "she cheated and beguiled me not of her own will but for fear of how my enemies might revenge themselves against me." He pined and fretted for her company, being by nature generous and forgiving. In spite of her deceits, he still loved her. So, a little before the wheat harvest, he forgot his pride and went down again to visit her, taking with him for a present and a token of his forgiveness a young kid. But when he reached her house and asked to see her, her father came out to speak with him, and refused to admit him.

"What! is it thou?" he said, averting his eyes and cringing before him. "We thought never to see thee again. How couldst thou have forsaken my daughter within a few days of her marriage! She grieved for thee, and to console her, and for her own honour's sake, I have given her in marriage to thy friend."

But even as he said the word, he quailed at the wrath burning in the young man's eyes. "Of a truth I lament for thee", he continued hastily, "if it be that thou still lovest her. But how shall it profit us to go back upon the past? What is done, is done; and thou thyself art to blame for it. But come, now, take heart: she has a younger sister who is even more beautiful and desirable than she is. I pray thee let me bring her to thee now, and thou canst take her in marriage instead."

Without a word Samson turned himself about and left him. His heart raged in him like a furnace, yet he shuddered as if stricken with cold. "What now!" he thought. "How shall I avenge myself: how punish so vile a treachery? Truly there is no evil I can wreak on these treacherous and insolent Philistines that can wipe out so foul a wrong as this! By the vows that I have vowed to the Lord I will be even yet with these enemies of Israel! Mine be the day and the hour!" And as he went his mind seethed with grief and anger.

# The Foxes in the Wheat

Midway on his journey back to Zorah he sat down to rest awhile in the shade of a tree that arched its boughs over the gorge through which his path lay homewards. Absent in mind, for it was fixed on one thought only, he fondled the kid that still lay within his arm; and he turned his eyes and looked out from his eyrie across the shallow downlands of Philistia. The sun was setting, and as far as sight could reach, stretched to the white sands of the sea the fenceless ripening wheat-fields of his enemies, interwoven here and there with dark-green vineyards and silvery groves of olive.

And as he sat, brooding and motionless, his gaze fixed on the scene stretched out beneath him as if in the peace and unreality of a dream, the wild creatures he had disturbed began to return to their haunts again as if no human creature were by. Jackal yelled to jackal; and almost at his feet from its lair in the ravine a fox presently stole out, and couching itself down on the warm rock began to preen its coat, taking its pleasure, and basking in the heat of the sun.

Samson turned his eyes and watched it without stirring. And suddenly, as though a secret voice had spoken, a wild fancy leaped into his mind. He threw back his head and laughed. The kid awoke, bleating; the fox leapt into the air and was gone. The sound of Samson's mocking laughter pealed on through the ravine, and the sunbeams caught the glint of his bright hair.

The days that followed were spent in frenzied labour to carry out the stratagem he had devised. First he fenced in a natural hollow at the foot of the mountains from which a rocky channel or dried-up watercourse, steep on either side, dropped down towards the plain. This done, he set to work digging pits and setting gins and snares wheresoever he knew was the resort of the wild foxes and jackals. He lay in wait by day in the clefts of the mountain gorges, and at night in the moonlit vineyards, and chased down and caught with his own hands these wild, fleet-footed and timid creatures.

As he caught them, he carried them off and caged them up in the pen he had prepared for them. From this they could neither leap out nor in any wise escape. There he left them to their own devices until the hour when he should need them. He toiled on without rest, urged on by one sole furious desire—to teach these accursed Philistines a lesson they would never forget. His strong-boned face and limbs scorched by the sun, his blue eyes gleaming, he was taut and tense in every sinew, yet supple as a serpent; and when he had captured as many of these creatures as he wanted for his purpose, he spent tedious hours in preparing bundles of little torches or fire-brands of kindling-wood which he smeared over with pitch and left to dry. And at last his work was done.

When then all was in readiness, he rose up one night in the small hours and went down to his pen or hollow in the rocks. It was the season of harvest full moon, and her bleaching rays streamed down on every motionless tree and rock. He straddled over into his pen and into the midst of the host of snarling beasts and by her light he caught them as he wanted them, one in one hand and one in another. They struggled, yelped and snapped at him, but were powerless to resist. He dragged them tail to tail, then bound up one of his little torches or fire-brands in the middle between each two tails.

When all this was to his liking, he rested. The moon sank low, her bright face paling as the hues of dawn began to well into the dark crystal of the east. Moment by moment the light grew stronger, until the whole firmament was dyed with the colours of sunrise. At length the burning orb of the sun itself gilded the mountain-tops and from the rock where he sat in watch, above the scurrying and infuriated animals in the pen, Samson could survey the countless acres of the Philistines' corn-lands, now showing like a vast sea of milk, for they were swathed in a pearl-pale low-lying mist.

Little by little in the heat of the morning the mist began to lift and waver and vanish away, until the wide unrippled miles of wheat-fields, dry as tinder and white as lint, lay fully exposed, shimmering in the faint airs that stirred under the vault of the blue sky. For by far the greater part of their corn was as yet unreaped, though here and there on rough patches of stubble it stood in stooks or sheaves—and all sweltering in the ardour of the sun.

Then Samson strode down to the neck of the pen where the wall of rock so narrowed that there was only passage-room for two or three foxes abreast. He took fire and the torches he had made, and with one blow of his foot broke down the hurdle which lay across this outlet, and seizing the couple of foxes that were nearest, he kindled the torch between their tails and set them free on the very outskirts of the fields. And so he continued.

Instantly after, now here, now there, and in the twinkling of an eye, and to and fro, as the frenzied creatures ranged—

quarrelling, fighting, scurrying this way and that—rose up
and ran jets and spurts of flame, scarcely visible at first in
the blaze of day. But they spread like wildfire, billowing on
in ever-widening eddies across the plain, like ripples of
water on a pool, but soon surging together and circling on
and on, until wide stretches of the mounded plain roared
together like fire in a furnace, and in the wind raised by
their own heat.

When, his last captives set free, Samson climbed up on
high upon a rock and once more surveyed the country of
his foes, it was no longer a sea of mist or of ripe grain his
eyes beheld, but of fire; and a prodigious column of smoke,
black as a storm cloud, towered up into the heavens, visible
for leagues, and to ships far out to sea. He looked and
laughed.

The fire raged on, past human hope of its being quenched
or beaten out. So fervent was the heat and so dense the
smoke that the Philistines could only watch it from a distance, helpless to draw near; until at last not only the standing corn and what was reaped and in sheaves, but many of
their vineyards and olive-yards were no more than a
smoking and smouldering waste of ashes. They were beside
themselves with fury and dismay. It seemed beyond the wit
of man to have wreaked such widespread destruction in but
a few hours.

"Who is it that hath done this? What enemy hath done
this?" they cried one to another. "Away, away with him!"
Indeed it was the law of the land that if by mere mischance
even one of their own people set fire to so much as an acre
of their fields at harvest-tide, he paid for it with his life.

When they were told that this was the work of Samson—
the Hebrew son-in-law of the Timnite—and that he had
done it to avenge himself against them because his wife had

been taken away from him and given to a friend, their rage turned to consternation. Mortally afraid to meet such an enemy until they were prepared, a band of these Philistines that night went up by stealth at dead of dark and encircling the house of the father of the beautiful young Philistine woman, they set it on fire and burnt it to the ground. And he himself and his daughter whom Samson loved and his whole household perished. Thus they thought to wound one whom for the time being they feared to strike.

When Samson heard of it, tears gushed out of his eyes. He forgot the woman's faithlessness and deceit and remembered only that he loved her. A furious and bitter hatred filled his heart. "So be it," he said; "if this is their way of it, I will avenge myself against them seven times over."

He armed himself and went down in his fury, and not one of them escaped with his life. Then aware that he had now raised all Philistia against him like a nest of hornets, he turned east and fled away until he came to a desolate precipitous steep of rock called Etam. This he scaled and there concealed himself in a cave or fissure in the face of the rock, where wild goats and ravens were his only company.

Spies carried news of where he lay, and the Philistines dispatched a troop of soldiers in pursuit of him, with orders that they were to take him alive and bring him down. They marched north, crossed the border, and raiding the country of Judah, encamped that night in a rocky valley named Lehi, not far distant from Samson's lair. On hearing this the men of Judah took hasty counsel and sent an envoy to the captain of the troop of the Philistines to demand what cause they had for invading their country when they were in treaty with them, and had done them no mischief.

The envoy returned with the message that while the Philistines agreed that they had no quarrel with the tribesmen of Judah, they were come up to capture Samson of Zorah, the chieftain of the Danites, who had ravaged their harvest-fields, and now lay in hiding in the rocks of Etam. "Bring him down alive," they said, "surrender him into our hands, and we will go in peace."

The men of Judah had no mind to resist them. They feared the evils that would follow if they opposed the lords of the Philistines. Setting a guard at the base of the height they climbed up by the way Samson had gone, and when they came in sight of the cave where he lay in hiding, they blew a blast upon a horn, summoning him to show himself and to come out and parley with them.

He had chosen his eyrie so well that it could be approached only by men in single file, but armed though they were, and many against one, they had heard too much of his prowess to attempt it.

When Samson appeared in the mouth of the cave they reproached him for having been the cause of the Philistines' raid into their country. "Who art thou," they said, "a stranger and a Danite, to bring this danger upon us? Knowest thou not that we are under the lordship of the Philistines? We have heard of thy burnings and pillagings, but can see no reason for such folly."

"Even as they did unto me," Samson answered, "so only have I done unto them."

Then said the men of Judah: "Thy feud is not our feud. We will have none of it. Come down then and surrender thyself into our hands, else we ourselves will starve and smoke thee out."

But none dared draw near to him.

Then said Samson: "Listen to me, traitors of Israel and cowards that you are. I will consent to give myself up on one condition—that you vow to me by the gods of the

Philistines—for of the God of Israel you know nought—
that you will do me no harm yourselves, nor set upon me
unawares and murder me, but will deliver me over in safety
to the captain of the Philistines."

To this they agreed, swearing by Jehovah that no harm
should befall him whilst he was in their hands, but that they
would merely bind him and give him up to the Philistines.
Then Samson came down from his stronghold in the rock
and submitted himself to them. They bound him fast with
leather thongs, and led him away from Etam to the camp
of the Philistines.

When the Philistines saw the enemy they feared and
hated approaching them, dragged along like an ox to the
slaughter, bound fast and at their mercy, they raised a yell
of triumph. At sound of it a frenzy seized upon Samson. He
shook his head, and lifting his face looked steadfastly on
them, and the spirit of the Lord God of Israel which was the
secret of his strength and which never in any danger forsook
him while he kept true to his vows as a Nazarite, leapt up in
him like a flame. He heaved his mighty shoulders and the
thongs that pinioned his arms snapped and fell off from him
like flax burnt with fire. With a wrench he snapped the
bonds that gnawed into his wrists, and running, and stooping over the carcass of a wild ass which a myriad flies had
but just stripped of its flesh, he snatched out its sharp-sided
jaw-bone, and with this for his only weapon advanced
against his foes.

At sight of him radiant in his wrath and suddenly, and as
if by sorcery, freed from his bonds, the Philistines were
seized with terror. They turned and fled. But Samson was as
fleet and sure-footed as the wild black goats that ranged the
crags of Etam.

"This for Israel!" he cried as one after another he smote

them down. "This for the Lord God Jehovah! And this for my own right hand!" Exulting in his strength, he pursued and smote them until he was weary. Then sated and exhausted, he flung himself down to recover his breath and to rest himself upon a rock in the valley. And as he sat, with none but the dead to share his solitude, he sang a song of triumph.

*"With the jaw-bone of an ass,"* he sang, *"heaps upon heaps!*
*With the jaw-bone of an ass hath Samson slain his thousands."*

Then he flung the bone out of his hand, and from that day this valley was called Ramath-lehi, which means, Place of the Jaw-bone.

It was now high noon; the air of the rock-strewn waste in which he sat alone shimmered with heat like molten glass, and buzzed with the low drone of flies. The sun beat down upon his head, its only shield the close-braided locks of his thick hair. His pulses throbbed. He was parched and stricken with thirst and near fainting, and he wandered to and fro among the barren rocks, scarcely able to see by reason of the blinding dazzle of the sun and his own weariness. It seemed that in the midst of his triumph he would perish miserably for want of but a sip of water. And in his agony he prayed to the Lord to deliver him.

"Thou hast given thy servant this great victory," he groaned, "shall he now die of thirst, and his body fall into the hands of thine enemies!"

The Lord answered his prayer, and lo, from out of a cloven hollow in the rock there gushed water in a clear cold stream. Samson knelt down in the hollow, and cupped his hands and drank, and drank again. He was refreshed and revived and his spirit returned to him. To this place was given a name which means, Hidden Well-spring of Prayer; and though three thousand winters have come and gone, its waters flow in Lehi to this day.

The years went by, and Samson was chosen to be judge or chieftain over the region of Israel where he dwelt. Now there was peace between his own people and the Philistines, and now war. But so long as he lived, there was never a time when his foes were not secretly conniving to seize or ensnare him and to avenge themselves for the shame and evil he had done against them. But he defied them and they dared not attack him openly.

There came a day when Samson went down even to the great walled city of Gaza, and alone. Now this Gaza was

one of the oldest cities in the world. It lay furthest south of
the five chief cities of Philistia—a long day's journey from
Samson's hills. Amid its wide-spread gardens of palm and
olive it stood upon a hill two miles east of the Great Sea, and
was on the coastal highway of the caravans from Tyre and
Sidon and Damascus journeying down to Egypt. Muffled
in the cloak he wore, Samson entered in by the great gate
of the city a little before nightfall, and he went into the
house of a woman that lived there. At the usual hour appointed by the governor of the city the gates were shut and
strongly barred and bolted. But unknown to Samson, one
who stood idling at the gates, and who had cause to remember him, had seen him knock, and enter the house of the
woman, and had recognized him.

He followed on after him, and setting another man of
Gaza to keep watch on the house, he himself hastened with
his news to the governor of the city, who debated how he
might take Samson alive or kill him. Seeing that it was now
night, and there was no risk of his escaping out of the city
while the gates were shut, they determined to wait until
daybreak and to kill him then, for any attempt to seize him
at close quarters in the darkness would be at a heavy
cost.

But Samson remained in the house of the woman for but
a few hours. At midnight, when all was still and the streets
deserted, he rose, and bidding her farewell stole out
cautiously into the darkness. He peered this way and that;
there was no light showing and naught stirring, yet, like a
lion that snuffs at a snare, his mind was filled with a vague
mistrust; and he turned swiftly and passed on until he came
to the city gates. And when he reached them, behold, they
were stoutly barred and bolted against him. He stayed a
moment, glancing about him and listening, for it seemed

the sound of a footfall some paces behind him had of a sudden
ceased.

At this he smiled within himself, and even while the
watchman in the tower above—so smitten with terror at
sight of him that he dared not challenge him or sound the
alarm—stared down from his niche in the wall, Samson
seized the great doors of the gate and lurching now this way,
now that, wrenched both them and their timber-posts out
of the thick masonry of the tower, and heaving them up on
to his shoulders—posts, bar, locks and all—he set out into
the open country and carried them off to the top of a hill.
There in mockery and derision he set them up one against
another for a perch to the wild birds; and there they were
found by the Philistines, who as soon as morning was come
had sallied out in pursuit of him, and found him not.

# Delilah

Time went by, and as, while he was young and ardent and impetuous, after but one glance into her face, he had come to love the beautiful young daughter of the Philistine of Timnath, so again, when he was a man of full age, he came to love another Philistine woman. Her name was Delilah; she lived in the valley of Sorek and not far distant from the village of Zorah, green then with trees among the hills, where Samson himself was born.

His mother and father were now dead, and he lived alone, going down day by day to visit Delilah in the valley of vineyards beneath. When word of this was brought to the ears of the five princes or lords of the Philistines, they came to the house of Delilah and communed with her in secret.

"This man Samson," they said, "as thou knowest well, is the enemy of us all. From the days of his youth even until now he has been the pest and bane of thy people and the sworn adversary of their gods. Yet year by year he grows in power and authority, puffing up these Hebrews with such pride and trust in him that they have come to think of him as half-god and half-man and invincible. But think not it is thee thyself we blame for that. Far from it, since it has been put into thy power to win from him the secret of his strength and valour. So strange and unnatural a thing cannot lie in his own bodily force alone, but must depend upon some magic or mystery connected with the God he worships. Do thy utmost then to entice and to persuade him to confide in thee this secret. It may be that he wears some charm or amulet which thou canst steal away."

While they talked with her, and reasoned with her, though at first she resisted them, Delilah's mind was wavering between her love for Samson and her fear of the vengeance these tyrants would wreak against her if she refused to do as they bade her.

Seeing this, they tempted her at last with a bribe. "It is not in our minds", they said, "that thou shouldst stain thy hands with his blood, but only that thou shouldst entice his secret out of him and so deliver him helpless into our hands. We swear unto thee that though he shall be repaid in full for all his insolence and bloodshed and evil, his life shall be spared. But thou shalt indeed have worked a marvel, and thy name will be famous for all time among the women of Philistia. Moreover, we will each one of us pay over to thee in reward eleven hundred pieces of silver." They watched her closely. And in greed of this great reward Delilah hesitated no more and consented to betray Samson into their hands.

When next he came to visit her, and they were sitting together in the cool of the evening, she began to question him of the days when he was young and when his father and mother were yet alive. She asked him of his bringing up and of the sports and pastimes of his youth, and when he had first come to know how much fleeter of foot and more supple of body he was than any boy of his own age.

"I have heard tell", she said, "that even in thy childhood fear was utterly unknown to thee, and that there was none to compare with thee in craft and daring. Tell me," she said at last, and as if the thought had at that moment come

harmlessly into her mind, "tell me, what is the secret of thy marvellous strength? What charm or talisman hast thou that fills thee with such frenzy, and makes thee invincible against thy foes? I burn with pride in thee, Samson; for I know that only by making thee utterly helpless could they ever hope to subdue thee into their power."

Samson told her freely of his early days in Zorah, but no further. When she persisted in her questions, he rose, stretched out his arms, and stood gazing out of the window towards the vineyards on the hillside already darkened in the shades of night, and from which the last wrack of twilight would soon be faded away.

He smiled within himself and turned back to her. "Why,"

said he, "if I were bound fast with seven raw bow-strings—
bow-strings, I mean, that have never been dried, so that the
knots would not slip—then my strength would ebb clean
out of me, and I should be empty, defenceless, weak as any
other man."

Joy filled Delilah's heart to hear it. On the morrow she
set out forthwith and carried this news to the lords of the
Philistines, and, before evening, returned again to her
house, bringing with her seven undried bow-strings.

A little before nightfall, and when Samson had promised
to visit her again, there stole in to the back parts of her
house a company of picked men, chosen by the lords of the
Philistines for their strength and valour. These she concealed within, in an inner chamber, bidding them stay there
and watch and wait. "Abide here", she said, "without so
much as stirring foot or finger until I cry out, and call you
in. Then come quickly, seize him, and be gone!"

She had prepared dishes of fruit, and bread and wine
against Samson's coming. Flowers sweetened the house. All
was still and in readiness. And presently after she heard his
footfall and his knock upon the door. She rose and admitted
him into the house and they sat and ate and drank together.

When he was content and at ease, she laughed and showed
him the seven bow-strings. "See," she said, narrowing her
eyes and half-whispering, "I have done as thou didst bid
me. Now let me bind thee, merely in sport, and thou shalt
be wholly at Delilah's mercy; for we are utterly alone together, thou and I."

Samson himself put out his hands, and she bound him
with the seven bow-strings, knotting them one upon another, and making them fast. And Samson sat smiling at
her, feigning that his strength was gone and that he was
wholly in her power. So for a while they jested together,

until suddenly, as if some hint of danger had reached her ears, she turned, sprang aside, and cried in warning: "Alas! Samson, beware! The Philistines be upon thee, Samson!"

Gazing swiftly about him like a lion brought to bay, Samson leapt to his feet, and with a twist of his wrist snapped the bow-strings that bound his arms as if they had been no more than a strand of tow touched off by fire. And at sound of the snapping of the bow-strings the Philistines in the inner room were seized with terror, slipped away into the darkness and were gone.

Delilah herself trembled at sight of him and was filled with rage and chagrin, but she pretended only to be vexed at his having deceived her. "Why didst thou deceive me?" she asked him. "What have I done that thou shouldst have no trust in me? I bound thee in sport with the bow-strings just as thou toldst me to, and when but to test thee I called out that there was danger, they fell away from thee as if thine was the strength not of one man but of twenty. I have never seen the like before. But speak truly now and without mockery; are there no bonds strong enough to bind thee— none? So that even if thou wert in deadly peril thou couldst not escape?"

Samson laughed aloud and said: "What are bow-strings? Thou couldst have netted me in like a fish with them, yet still I should have broken free."

She continued to press him for an answer, coaxing and flattering him, until at last and merely to get peace, he said: "I told thee but half the truth; but if I were bound fast with seven brand-new ropes, such as are used for harnessing oxen but have never been chafed or strained, I should become as weak as water; ay, with less strength in my bones, Delilah, than thou hast thyself."

So Delilah made ready the ropes, the supplest and strongest that the lords of the Philistines could provide. And when she and Samson sat together once more, she rose up and stole to door and window as if to make certain that they were alone. Then she came and stooped and kissed him.

"See now, Samson," she said, "here are the ropes. And now I am going to bind thee; and truly thou shalt be made to go down upon thy knees and plead for forgiveness before I set thee free." And she bound Samson with the ropes. When she had made them fast, and sported with him awhile, he heeded so little what she had done that he became drowsy, and all but fell asleep. Having assured herself that the liers-in-wait were at hand in their hiding-place, Delilah drew back of a sudden, leapt up and cried shrilly, as if in fear: "Samson, O Samson, the Philistines be upon thee!"

From out of a dream Samson rose up where he sat, and stretched his arms. And he burst asunder the ropes knotted about him as if they were pack-thread. And when Delilah realized that he had deceived and outwitted her a second time, tears of rage filled her eyes. But she turned and restrained herself, pouring out her reproaches, as if she were weeping only because he had made mock of her.

"Why, and what danger could there be?" she taunted him. "Are we not alone? The mighty one of Israel is as timid as a hare. Have I ever proved false to thee in anything? Surely no man who has any courage in him would lie and lie again! I am of no more importance in thy sight than a child that must be put off with any idle tale that comes into its father's head."

And as Samson soothed and solaced her, gazing fondly into her dark narrow face, her cheeks inflamed with weeping, he was so much blinded by her beauty to the treachery that was in her heart that he was almost persuaded to tell her his secret. But he remembered his vow, and heeded the warnings of the voice within him, though he was loth to obey it. And as he sat brooding his eyes wandered from Delilah's face and fixed themselves upon her loom.

And when once more she dried her eyes and besought him by everything he held dear to vex and cheat her no more, but to confess his secret, "Now hearken," he said; "but first, I entreat thee not to enrage me again with warnings that danger is near. I might believe it to be the truth and be moved once more to teach the Philistines, who as God knows are the enemies of Israel, that it is for no love of them that day after day I venture over the border. It may be I have told thee foolish stories, but why shouldst thou desire to share a secret that I have sworn never to reveal? It is thou who art deceiving me. But now, hearken! Bow-strings and ropes, thongs and bonds are less than nought to me. My strength is in me myself. And if thou shouldst weave the seven braided locks of my hair into the web of thy loom yonder, the virtue would be gone out of me, and I should be weak as a sheep in the hands of the shearers."

Delilah laughed and was satisfied. And when next evening, wearied out by the heat of the day, Samson had laid himself down to rest awhile, and had fallen asleep close beside her loom, she softly and warily wove his long hair into its web, and twisted and beat it close in together with her weaving pin. When she had finished this handiwork and stayed to watch him a while, it seemed to her impossible that any man of his own strength, whether human or divine, could win free again.

Still as a child he lay in his sleep—this Samson, matchless among men for might and beauty and for courage. For a moment her heart wavered and she sickened of her treachery. But memory of the bribe soon to be hers, and of his deceits in the past rose up in her, and with a gesture of contempt the woman turned stealthily towards the inner room; and having assured herself that the captain of the Philistines with his men were in their hiding-place, she cried suddenly and wildly as if in terror: "Oh, Oh! Alas! Alas! The Philistines be upon thee, Samson!" And she roused him from his sleep.

Samson awoke, gazing drowsily about him, and he raised himself upon his knees. Then, as if he were merely drawing tent-pegs out of sand, with one heave of his shoulder he wrenched out not only the web of the loom but the posts also that held it securely to the ground, and he stood up upon his feet. And Delilah flung herself flat upon the ground and wept.

When for the third time the lords of the Philistines knew that Samson had deceived Delilah, they were bitterly incensed against her, and sent word that she should have but one more opportunity of winning the bribe they had offered her. Moreover, they warned her that if she failed yet again to deliver Samson into their hands, they would burn down her house over her head.

At this message Delilah's face wanned with fear. As the days went by she could neither eat nor sleep for dread of the vengeance overhanging her; and she gave Samson no peace.

He brought her gifts, but she refused to be comforted. "How canst thou say, 'I love thee'?" she repeated again and again, sighing and weeping.

"What mockery and folly and what lies! I am weary of it all, and will see thee no more. What love can be where there is no trust? Three times hast thou mocked at me, made me a laughing-stock, and put me to scorn. I am done. Keep thy secret, I will have none of it!"

Whereupon she would lay her head upon his shoulder and fall to weeping again. And Samson's soul was vexed to death.

He could get no rest from her upbraidings, and in mere weariness at last he heeded no more the voice of divine counsel within him. He reasoned with her, entreated her, but all in vain. She sat sullen, shaken with sobs, and refused to answer him. It was on the verge of night. Samson arose and stood gazing out over the starry valley towards the darkness of the sea; and his heart was distraught with sorrow and bitterness.

"Listen," he said, turning himself about, and looking earnestly into her face. "It is true that until now I have told thee nothing but idle tales. What deceit was there in that? What profit could it be to thee, seeing that we love one another, to hear what should never be told? But now I am sickened to the soul, and utterly weary. Remember only this, that I would not reveal what I am about to tell thee to anyone but thyself for all the wealth of all the lords of Philistia. And if thou have any true love or kindness for me in thy heart, breathe not one word of it, I beseech thee, lest my enemies should triumph over me. Here now is the truth and all the truth.

"Even before I was born my mother vowed that my life should be devoted to the service of the God of Israel. He alone is my strength. For I have been a Nazarite ever since I was a child. And though in much I have done amiss, I have kept faithful to my vows. And as a token of their obedience, it is one of the vows of the Nazarites that their hair shall never be shorn, nor any razor come near it. It is a sign and showing of their service to the Lord. So, then, is it with me. Bind the seven locks of my hair in seven looms, and I would pluck them out of the ground like a weed. But if I were to be robbed of them altogether, then the well-spring of my life would be dried up within me. The spirit of the Lord would die out in me. Shamed and abandoned, I should have no more strength than a beast abandoned in the wilderness.

"But how is it possible for thee to find any reason in what I tell thee. It is between me only and the Lord God. And now, Delilah, let there be peace between us, else we meet no more. And I entreat thee let no word of this be ever so much as whispered of between us again."

# He is Betrayed

Delilah listened in silence, but her heart exulted within her, eager as a vulture for blood, for she knew of a certainty that Samson had told her the whole truth and had kept nothing back. She dried her tears, and smiled at him fondly, clasping his hands. The night beyond the windows was utterly still. Not an owl called, or jackal wailed.

Next day she herself hastened in secret to the prince of the Philistines who was governor of the city of Gaza. "I am come, and alone," she said, drawing aside the veil over her face; "and of thy life let no man hear of it. Have patience yet once more. Let the men be in their hiding-place to-morrow as soon as night has fallen, and let them bring with them the money that has been promised me. Many times has this Hebrew Samson cheated me in the past, but if I have not this time decoyed his secret out of him for good and all, then let them bring fire too, and burn my roof-tree over my head. Ay, and make ashes of a woman deceived! But do thou assure thyself that not a word be spoken of this; have patience; all is well."

When the morrow night was come, Samson and Delilah supped again together. She had made ready of her best—dainties and delicacies from the palace of the Philistine lord, fruit and wines and flowers. And it seemed to Samson that never had Delilah loved him as now she loved him. His misgivings and remorse died down in him, and he was comforted; and being weary he laid his head down upon her lap. And singing under her breath an old childish lullaby, Delilah soothed Samson to sleep.

When by his deep and placid breathing she knew that slumber lay heavy upon him, she stayed her singing, and called softly to the man that was in wait in the inner chamber to come into the room. And as she herself directed him, he sheared off one by one the seven heavy braided wheat-brown locks of hair on Samson's head as it lay within her lap. But though an evil bitterer even than death itself was creeping upon him, he was lost to the world and did not so much as even stir in his dreams.

When the barber had taken himself off, Delilah gently drew in a pillow beneath Samson's head, and so, little by little, withdrew herself. Then she rose, and with lamp shaded in her hand, stood looking down upon him, shorn of his hair, and now muttering uneasily in his sleep. She shivered with horror and hatred to see his shaven head, and drew in a deep sighing breath. Then narrowing her eyes and stooping a little, she almost laughed aloud. "Peace, fool," she muttered as though to herself, and taking a pace or two backwards, she snatched up one of the thongs that still lay there, and lashing the sleeper she cried in a shrill and frenzied voice: "Wake, O, wake! Arouse thee, sluggard! Samson! Rouse thee! Thy God is in need of thee! The Philistines be upon thee, Samson!" And yet again she smote him with the thong.

The words echoed into his mind as though from out of a vast and hollow sepulchre. Dreadful shapes swarmed out upon him in his dreams. He groaned and turned heavily in his sleep. But presently as she watched, intent, he stirred again and he raised his head, his eyes opened, and dazed and trembling, he peered stealthily about him. In the light of her lamp Delilah smiled on him, but there was no meaning in her smile, and Samson stared on at her as though he could not assure himself who this woman was.

But gradually the full meaning of her cry broke in upon him. He sat up, his eyes still fixed on her, in wonder of what cold horror had stolen into his blood.

"I will arise now", he whispered to himself, "and shake myself as at other times." He laboured heavily to his feet, but endeavoured in vain to rid himself of the deadly weakness and languor that had come upon him. He put out his hand towards Delilah as naturally as a child to its mother, for his mind was still numb with sleep.

Then he lifted his head, and at the same moment perceived the woman cat-like and smiling, and the liers-in-wait that spied in upon him from the inner chamber. With a lamentable cry like that of a beast wounded to death, he leapt towards them, but stumbled and fell, rose up and fell again, and knew that all was lost.

And the Philistines seized and bound him, many against one, and he could not resist them. They led him away to Gaza. And the news of his downfall ran like wildfire throughout Philistia. The streets of the cities buzzed with it.

The lords of the Philistines, when he was haled before them in their place of assembly, mocked at his entreaties to be put out of his misery. They summoned their torturers, who bored out his eyes and blinded him; and they set him to labour at a mill for grinding corn—for there were no streams and so no water-mills in Gaza.

There, in the company of slaves and felons, he sat, day in, day out, turning the upper stone of the mill upon the nether stone. And while he toiled on, he could hear the coming and going of the people in the streets, for the mill was near the city gates which in a night long gone he had rooted up, posts and all, from their masonry, and set up on a high hill in derision of his enemies.

Now, shackled with massive fetters of bronze he groped on through life in an endless narrow dark; helpless, his eyes gone. At night he lay in a dungeon, haunted with bitter waking dreams of radiant light and freedom—spring-time in Zorah, and the mountains lit with the sun. His only comfort was that at night he was alone, for the lords of the Philistines had given command that all day he should be closely watched, and whipped and goaded on.

But seeing at last there was no strength or spirit left in him, the governor of the prison-house gave him in charge of one of his sons who was little more than a child, and who delighted in tormenting him. Strangers came from near and far to stare in wonder upon him who of old had been the hatred and dread of all Philistia, and now was no better than a beast of burden and humbled to the dust.

But while Samson languished in this misery of mind and body, the hair upon his head—whose unshorn braids had been the symbol of his service to the Lord—began to grow again, and strength to well back into his limbs and sinews. In spite of his torments he asked no mercy of his foes, nor revealed by the least sign that strength and hope were reviving in him again.

Now there stood in Gaza a temple of one of the gods of the Philistines, the god Dagon. In shape, it is said that from his loins upwards, the image of this god of wood and gold and ivory was in the likeness of a man, but from the waist downwards, he was scaled and finned and tailed like a fish. It is said also that Dagon was the god of the harvest. Stark upon his pedestal, there he stood; the glory and terror of the

Philistines. And his vast temple with its wide flat roof and central pillars was built outward from beyond the city above the steep of the hillside on which were reared the city walls.

And the day of the yearly feast of Dagon drew near, when his priests in their garbs and deckings of gold and gems would make sacrifice to their idol. This, the lords of the Philistines had decreed, should be a festival of triumph and jubilation beyond any that had ever gone before, for had not their Dagon delivered into their hands their mighty enemy, the judge and chieftain of Israel, who all his life long had been the unconquerable foe of Philistia, and now was nothing but a mockery and a jibe?

The day drew near, and by every road and track and by-way—and the high-road from Jerusalem ran not far distant —a great press of people from all parts of Philistia flocked into Gaza. Its streets were thronged, and its walls and houses resounded with music and song, dancing and merriment. At the hour appointed they flocked into the great temple until it was overflowing with a host of men and women, the bright and garish colours of their raiment blazing in the light of the sun. In numbers there had never in Gaza been seen the like before. And in the midst of the feast, when this vast multitude was hot and elated with wine, there went up a cry to the lords of the Philistines, where they sat in state in their high places.

"Bring in Samson! bring in Samson! that he may make sport for us!" From wall to wall, from gallery to roof, the clamour spread. Every face was turned in one direction, and their turbulence increased to a frenzy as they shouted for Samson and sang the praises of their god.

So the lords of the Philistines sent word to the keeper of the prison-house that Samson should be brought into the temple, and the tumult sank down into a profound hush.

But when, shuffling and groping, Samson was led in by the lad who had charge of him and appeared in the midst of the temple, a wild prolonged yell of hate and triumph went up from the throats of all assembled there. The walls trembled at sound of it. And Samson, mighty even in ruin, goaded on like a beast by whip and cry, was compelled like some poor mountebank to make sport for them all until they were weary.

At length even the most pitiless of his persecutors were sated of it, and Samson stooped himself low, sick and exhausted. Then he turned to the lad who was at his side and asked him to lead him a little nearer to the two central columns or pillars which held up the roof. "I pray thee," he muttered, "let me abide there unseen and rest awhile, for I am spent and can make sport no more."

And the lad did as Samson asked of him.

The people ceased to watch him, for the priests of Dagon were at their frenzied dancings again, to the sound of drum and cymbal and instruments of music. And Samson, laying his great hands upon the pillars, stood there alone in the midst of the temple. He heard about him the shouts and clamour of this great concourse of Philistines, and the wild barbaric pealings of their brazen instruments. The noise of the multitude was like the noise of a sea in storm breaking on a rocky shore. And as he listened, his heart in sullen fury beating heavily in his body, the spirit of the Lord as of old began to move in him. And he lifted up his sightless face and prayed.

"O Lord God," he said, "I pray thee remember me, and have compassion upon me. Give me back my strength again this once, O Lord God, and for but a little while, that I may take vengeance on these Philistines—thy enemies and mine —if only for but one of my two eyes!"

With his prayer, his life revived within him and a still splendour of light filled his mind like the radiance of the sun. And he laid hold upon the two main pillars of the temple, one with his right hand and the other with his left hand, and he cried suddenly in a great voice, "Lord God of Israel, let me perish with thine enemies!"

Then he bowed himself, and with all his might thrust against the pillars on which the roof of the temple was borne up.

A dreadful silence fell upon the host at his shout, and even while, appalled, they watched, the pillars began to bend and crack and topple beneath the thrust of his mighty shoulders. There came a rending and a crash that resounded up into the cloudless dome of heaven like the tumult of an earthquake. And the walls and the roof of the great temple of the Fish God lurched inwards and downwards and descended upon his image and his priests and upon all who were assembled there, in a horror of lamentation and confusion. Thus Samson perished, in triumph, in the midst of his enemies.

The dead that Samson slew at his death were for might and number more than all those he had slain during his life. And when dark was come, his kinsmen and the friends of the house of his father, Manoah, came down secretly, and bore his broken body away, and buried it in a sepulchre hewn out of the rock between Zorah and Eshtaol. There lies the dust of Samson to this day.

# SAMUEL

# The Childhood of Samuel

I n the days when the temple or tabernacle was at Shiloh —a little town on a rounded rocky hill encircled by hills yet steeper, and by deep valleys on all sides but the south—Eli and his two sons were priests of the Lord. And there lived then in Ramah a man whose name was Elkanah. He had two wives, one of them named Hannah and the other named Peninnah. Now Peninnah had children; they were her pride, her love and delight. But Hannah had no children.

The village of Ramah, with its low white-walled houses, lay in a wild region, also among hills, the hills of Samaria, green with woods that fringed the swift waters of streams never dry. And year by year Elkanah with his whole household used to journey from Ramah to Shiloh, which lay about twelve miles distant, to worship at the temple, bringing with him his offering for the sacrifice, as did all the faithful in Israel.

At the feast that followed the sacrifice, he divided the good things among his household, his children and his servants. He gave to each one of them according to his share; but to Hannah he gave more than to the others, for he loved her very dearly. When Peninnah saw this she was filled with jealousy. She hated Hannah for her gentleness and beauty, and because Elkanah loved her. And she never ceased to fret and pester her, and to taunt her because she had no children. She made her life a burden and Hannah knew not where to go to hide her grief and to be out of hearing of Peninnah's bitter tongue; for, of all things in the world, the one secret desire of her heart was that she might have a son.

Now one day, at the usual season of the year, when Elkanah and his household were gone down to the temple at Shiloh and were together at the feast, Hannah sat weeping apart from them. Her heart was forlorn within her, and she could neither eat nor drink for sorrow. Peninnah's smiling face was dark with scorn; but her husband who could not bear to see Hannah unhappy, drew her apart to comfort her.

"Tell me, Hannah," he said, "why art thou weeping? And why dost thou not eat and rejoice with us? Come now, dry thy tears and grieve no more. Am I not better to thee even than ten sons!"

Hannah tried in vain to smile at her husband, but his love and gentleness seemed only to make her burden the more difficult to bear. She rose up and left him in haste and fled away to the temple to pray.

There she found herself alone, except only that Eli the High Priest was seated not far distant in his chair, and near the pillar that stood before the entering-in of the temple. And as Hannah prayed, she wept bitterly and she poured out all her troubles; and in her longing she vowed a vow to the Lord.

"O Lord of Hosts," she said, "I beseech thee to look in pity upon me. To remember me and not forget me. Thou knowest all things, and in what trouble I am. If only, O Lord God, thou wouldst of thy compassion give me a son, then I myself would give him back to thee, and would devote him to thy service his whole life long. I entreat thee to take pity on me, for my sorrow is almost greater than I can bear."

She continued to pray, and Eli, the High Priest, being seated at but a little distance from her, could see the changing expressions on her face. Her lips moved, but he could hear no words, only the sound of her weeping, for she prayed silently in her heart. And she looked so wretched and so woebegone that he thought she was drunken with wine. At last in his anger he rebuked her, accusing her, and bidding her go away and hide her shame.

Hannah stayed her tears and drew near. "Indeed and indeed, my lord, it is not so," she said. "I entreat thee not to think such shame of me. I have not tasted wine to-day, but being in great trouble I came here alone to pray. It is because my spirit is cast down with sorrow that I have been weeping; but I have poured out my soul before the Lord and he has comforted me."

When Eli heard this and looked into her face, he knew that what she had said was the truth, and he reproached himself for having spoken harshly to her. He smiled at her tenderly and lifted up his hands in blessing. "Go in peace," he said, "and may the Lord God of Israel have compassion upon thee and grant thee thy petition."

Hannah bowed herself before him. "May thy servant", she said, "find grace in thy sight."

Then she went her way, and returned to the house in Shiloh where her husband was lodging. The sadness of her mind seemed to have vanished away like the mist of morning that falls in dew. She sat down to eat, and Elkanah saw that her face was changed, and was no longer wan and overshadowed with care; and he rejoiced, but said nothing. Next morning they rose early and, having worshipped at the Tabernacle, the whole company of them made ready to return home.

Hannah's prayer was answered. The Lord remembered

her, and a son was born to her, whom she called Samuel, which means, Asked of the Lord. And as she sat gazing into his fair, small, solemn face, or talking softly to him as mothers are wont to do, or lulling him to sleep, it seemed that her life was like a tree that has come to its blossoming, and she was at peace with all the world.

The day came again when Elkanah prepared for his yearly journey to Shiloh to bring his offering to the Tabernacle, and to keep the Feast. But Hannah remained at Ramah. "Be not displeased with me or take it amiss," she said to her husband, "if this year I do not come down with thee to Shiloh but stay here quietly at home. When the child is weaned and has grown a little older, I will myself bring him to the sanctuary and into the presence of the Lord, and he shall remain there for ever. As thou knowest, Elkanah, even before he was born I vowed to give him into his service. How could we ever be grateful enough for this blessing, and how can I ever thank thee for all thy love and kindness!"

Elkanah smiled at her and kissed her. "Do whatever seems best to thee," he said. "Stay with the child then until he is weaned and is of an age when thou thyself canst take him to Shiloh. And may the Lord bring everything about according to thy prayers."

So with Peninnah and her children he set out on his journey; and Hannah in happiness and peace such as she had never known since she was a child at her own mother's knee, was left alone with Samuel.

When he had been weaned and was old enough to need her close care no longer, she herself made preparations to take him to Shiloh. For her offering she took with her three young calves, three bushels of flour and a bottle of wine. With a servant to protect and attend on her, mother and son

set out together on this, their first and their last long journey
together. When she was come to Shiloh she presented her
sacrifice to the two priests, Hophni and Phinehas. And she
herself with her small son was afterwards brought into the
presence of Eli. He searched her face in vain; he did not
remember her.

"It is no wonder, my lord," she said, "that my face is
strange to thee. But it may be thou wilt remember how in
time gone by a woman came alone to the temple to pray
and stood in thy presence. She was in great trouble and

affliction of mind. And my lord, when he knew this, was gracious to her and gave her his blessing, and bade her go in peace in the hope that her prayers would be answered. Well, my lord, I am myself that woman, and am now happy beyond words to tell."

Then Hannah took Samuel by the hand, and gently urging him on, presented him to Eli.

"See, my lord," she said, "here is the child himself, my first-born, whom I vowed, if he found grace in thy sight, to give into thy charge and to lend him to the Lord. As long as he liveth he shall be lent to the Lord. And may he bless him even as he hath blessed me!"

Tears were in her eyes and her heart welled over with joy and gratitude. And the old man stooped and took the child by the hand, and kissed him and blessed him. And from that day forward Samuel was left in the care of Eli, and was a comfort to him. There he lived and there in a little room alone he slept. And he helped in the services of the Tabernacle, obeying the High Priest in all that he did. Child though he was, he was girded like the priests themselves with a tunic of fine linen and with a girdle of embroidered needlework; and, with Eli, he ministered before the Lord.

Every year, too, when his mother came with Elkanah to Shiloh to keep the Feast, she brought with her a little coat that she had made for Samuel to wear when he was not in the temple. She listened while he poured out to her all that had come about since last they had met. She rejoiced in his happiness and to see how every year he grew in stature and understanding, though her heart ached when the time came again to say good-bye. And Eli blessed Hannah and her husband for the most precious gift which it had been in their power to make. "May the Lord reward you! And for this child that you have lent to him may he give you many to be a comfort to you throughout your lives." And Hannah had other children, three sons and two daughters; but Samuel was her first-born, and she loved him very dearly.

Eli was now old and growing feeble, and in the last few years of his life when he should have been at peace with God and man, he was in misery and distress because of the evil reports that came to his ears concerning his two sons, Hophni and Phinehas. They lived in open and shameless sin, and were feared and hated by all who came to the temple. They cheated the poor and simple of their offerings and abused the helpless. But because they were priests of the Lord none dared to resist or to accuse them openly.

Eli alone had authority over them. But though he reasoned with his sons and rebuked them, his heart was divided between his love for them and his hatred of their wickedness. He pleaded with them, beseeching them to pay heed to him before it was too late.

"If one man sin against another," he said, "God of his mercy may be appeased and bring peace between them. But if a man who is consecrated to his service sin against God himself, to whom then shall he fly for refuge? Who then shall intercede for him?"

But his sons only mocked at him behind his back, and went their own way from one wickedness to another. And Eli withdrew himself more and more into solitude with only Samuel to wait upon him.

There came at last to Eli a man of God who arraigned him face to face. "I am come by the will of the God of Israel," he said, "to declare his judgment against thee and against thy two sons, the abhorred of all Israel. In the days when the people languished in misery and slavery in Egypt did not the Lord choose from among them one to be his priest and his anointed, and to stand before him at his holy altar? As with him, the Lord's chosen, so with his son that came after him, and so with thee thyself and with thy sons. They were consecrated and set apart in his service, and in that only. But where now is the honour and glory of the highest? Thy sons have brought shame and disgrace on the worship of the Lord. Their very name is a byword and a cause of loathing and hatred. Thou knowest it, and hast rebuked them; but hast done nothing.

"Hearken, then: the dreadful day of reckoning draws near. They that honour the Lord, the Lord will honour; but they that despise him shall be forsaken. A time comes, and that soon, when of thine own blood and lineage there shall be left none honoured in Israel, and of those that come after thee not one shall survive the flower of his age. The Lord will abandon thee, and will choose a man faithful and true to be his priest in thy stead, and even thy memory shall be a shame. As for thy two sons, disaster and disgrace lie in wait for them; they shall die together on the same day, and thou shalt know it for a sign that what I have foretold will surely come about. Ay, and thy children's children shall be outcasts, and shall come and crouch before the gates of the temple begging for but a morsel of bread and a pittance of silver to save them from starvation. Thus saith the Lord."

And the man of God went out from the presence of Eli, leaving him alone. The old man sat on in the growing darkness, shaken and forlorn, striving to pray, but beset with horror and confusion.

He had been warned, he was sore afraid, and yet in his weakness of will he failed to give heed to it.

His eyes had now begun to grow dim, and his sight to fail him. And to Samuel was given the charge of trimming and filling with oil the seven lamps of the six-branched golden candlestick that stood before the veil in the Sanctuary, where also was the table of Shewbread and the Altar of Incense. This he did so that they should burn on without danger of their light failing through the hours of darkness.

Beyond the veil of the Sanctuary, embroidered with its cherubim in purple and scarlet, was the Ark of the Covenant of the Lord, the holiest and most precious thing in the keeping of the priests. Above it knelt its cherubim of gold, one at either end of it, their wings outstretched and over-arching it; their faces ever gazing one upon the other in the peace and silence of the holy place.

But few came now to worship in the temple. It was forsaken even of its priests. Yet Eli still forbore to banish his sons from its service altogether, and to disgrace them publicly before the people. He loved them and was weak. He trusted by prayer and sacrifice to save them from the horror and death that had been foretold, yet kept himself apart from them, and deceived his own mind with the hope they might yet repent and turn again.

There came a night when Samuel, having tended the golden lamps of the candlesticks and filled them with oil, laid himself down to sleep in the little room set apart for him in the Sanctuary. He was young; and sleep came swiftly and without dream. But in the darkest hour of the night he awoke; and, still and clear, he heard a voice calling him, "Samuel, Samuel!"

He answered: "Here am I," rose from his bed and ran to Eli and asked him what he needed. "Here I am," he said, "for I heard thee calling me."

Eli turned his face towards him in the gloom.

"I called thee not," he said gently. "Be not troubled; lie down again and sleep."

[ 303 ]

So Samuel went and lay down again, and composed himself to sleep. And yet again he heard a voice calling him: "Samuel, Samuel!"

He rose instantly and returned to Eli, saying: "See, here I am, for indeed I heard thee calling me, and no one else is by."

But Eli, though disquieted a little, answered him yet again: "Indeed I called thee not, my son. Some dream is in thy mind. Lie down again and rest."

But no sooner had Samuel returned into the quiet and darkness of his room than for the third time he heard a voice, infinitely near and yet as if from very far, calling him: "Samuel, Samuel!"

For the third time he went back to Eli, and besought him to tell him what was amiss. He feared that being old and nearly blind Eli had need of him, and it might be had called him in his sleep, or in pain. And Eli perceived that it could have been no earthly voice that Samuel had heard, but the voice of the Lord, summoning him in the secrecy of his mind and heart. And in his weakness and infirmity Eli trembled at the thought that the voice of God had been heard by the child.

But he said nothing of what was in his mind, and bade Samuel not to be afraid or distressed if he should hear the voice calling him again. "For surely," he said, "it is the voice of God thou hast heard. Go back again, then, and lie down; and if yet again thou hear the voice, then thou shalt say, 'Speak, Lord, for thy servant heareth.'"

So Samuel, as he was bidden, went back again and lay down. But sleep was now far from him. His mind was like a pool of water under the stars. And the Lord came, and out of a silence deep as the sea Samuel heard again the voice calling him by his name.

And he answered, "Speak, Lord, for thy servant heareth."

The voice said to Samuel: "Take heed, for I am about to do a thing in Israel at which the ears of all who hear of it shall tingle, and their hearts be shaken with dismay. In that day, even as I have spoken, shall come the destruction of Eli and those of his own blood. Even as I make a beginning so also will I make an end. He knew well that his sons were vile and that they have blasphemed against the Lord, yet he did not restrain them nor shame them in their wickedness. On his sin and on theirs, then, shall fall my judgment, and on those therefore that shall come after them; nor shall it be set aside by any sacrifice or offering."

Grieved and terrified, Samuel lay awake until the twilight of morning began to steal in upon him. Then he rose and opened the doors of the temple. And the beams of the risen sun swept in upon his face and flooded the bright woven draperies around him with their light. But his heart was torn with sorrow, and he was afraid. And he went not as usual into the presence of Eli, for he dreaded the questions he might be asked, and to bring sorrow upon him.

But presently after Eli himself called Samuel in a voice solemn and gentle, "Samuel, my son."

And Samuel went in to him, and said: "Here I am, my lord."

Then Eli turned his head, though even in the full light of the morning he could not see Samuel where he stood beside him, because his sight was dim. He stretched out his hand towards the child, and said: "Tell me truly, my son, what is it that the Lord said unto thee this night that is gone? Hide nothing from me however grievous it may be. If thou keep anything back from me, may the Lord do unto thee even as he has ordained to do unto me!"

And Samuel told him every word, as the voice had spoken, and hid nothing from him.

Eli listened in silence, then stricken and trembling, turned his face away: "Enough; go in peace," he said. "It is the Lord; let him do what is good in his sight."

# The Capture of the Ark

Time went by, and as Samuel grew up towards manhood his mind grew also in knowledge and wisdom, and the Lord was with him, revealing to him in the silence of his own heart what he should do and what he should say. And he obeyed it without fear or doubting. His was the vision to foresee what is hidden from those whose minds are obscured by the things of this world, and to foretell what shall come to be. And it became known throughout Israel from Dan in the north to Beersheba in the far south, that the Lord had revealed himself through Samuel in Shiloh. The faithful flocked again to worship there, putting their trust in him as in the prophet of God.

But no peace was yet to be in Israel. There came a day when its enemies the Philistines mustered an army and declared war, and marching north-east into Benjamin, pitched their camp on the slopes of Aphek above the passes into the country of Benjamin. And the Israelites gathered in their thousands, and encamped over against them on the lofty ridge of Eben-ezer. In the battle that followed the army of Israel was divided, and the full strength of neither one side nor the other was engaged. And though the tribesmen fought stubbornly, the day went against them. They were driven back across the lower ground and withdrew to their camp on Eben-ezer, leaving behind them, dead or wounded, four thousand men.

The chieftains of the tribes met next day in council to consider the causes of this defeat. "Surely", they said one to another, "if the men of Israel had felt in their souls that the Lord Jehovah was with them, to them would have been given the victory." But they doubted even while they said it, and to renew confidence in their troops and to fire them with zeal and courage, they determined to send to the temple at Shiloh and to bring thence the Ark of the Covenant into the camp.

"Then shall the men of Israel see with their own eyes that the Ark of the Lord is with them, and they shall trust

[ 308 ]

in it as in a sure aid and defence against the enemy, deeming themselves unvanquishable."

Messengers were at once despatched to Shiloh. But when Eli was told of their errand, he was greatly troubled. How could the chieftains of the army know that this was the will of God? How could they so guard the Ark in the dangers of the long journey through the wild uplands of Ephraim and in the peril and tumult of war, that its safety should be assured? If the least harm or desecration befell it, surely the reproach to Israel could never be absolved and he himself would never cease to mourn. He entreated his sons Hophni and Phinehas to consider well before they obeyed the orders that had been sent.

But they paid no heed to him. They were filled with exultation. Would not the great victory that might follow bring them honour, and cleanse away the evil repute into which they had fallen? They overruled their father and themselves lifted the Ark from its resting-place in the Holy of Holies and came with it, and brought it into the camp at Eben-ezer into the midst of the army; and a multitude accompanied them on the way thither.

When the blaring of the rams' horns of the priests was heard in the camp, the tribesmen flocked to see it, borne in on high, the sun blazing upon the wings of its golden cherubim. And all Israel shouted with a great shout, so that the earth rang again. So wild was the noise of their acclamations, echoing like thunder in the height of the morning, that the Philistines mustered on the slopes of Aphek heard it. They were dismayed, and questioned what evil omen this might be. Spies were sent out, and at nightfall reported that the Ark sacred to Jehovah the God of the Hebrews had been carried by its priests into their camp in solemn splendour, and that the whole army exulted because of it, and was elated with sure hope of victory. News of this spread from mouth to mouth among the troops of the Philistines.

"Woe, woe unto us," went up the cry. "Never has there been the like of this before. The mighty god of Israel is come down to fight against us, even Jehovah who smote the Egyptians with plagues, and mocked at the hosts of Pharaoh. Woe unto us!"

Fearing that his troops might break into open revolt, the commander of the army of the Philistines gave orders that at daybreak next morning his troops should be mustered in battle array, and he sent heralds to make proclamation throughout the camp: "Be bold, be strong, O ye warriors of Philistia! Quit yourselves like men, and fight even to the death. For truly death is a better fate than to languish in slavery under these vile Hebrews, as they themselves have languished under us. The day of victory has dawned. Quit yourselves like men, and they shall be scattered like chaff before the wind."

The trumpets sounded. The army of the Philistines with their chariots and spearmen, like grasshoppers for multitude, advanced through the valley to the attack; and long and furious was the fray. The sun rose high, and the battle raged and increased in frenzy. But Israel was smitten. They broke and fled in disorder, every man to his tent; and there was a very great slaughter, for there fell of Israel that day, either slain in battle or smitten in flight, thirty thousand footmen. And the Ark of God that had been in the rearward of the battle was taken, and the sons of Eli, Hophni and Phinehas, its priests, were slain before it, and it was bespattered with their blood.

Since dawn that day and while the bitter conflict was still raging, the advantage being now with the one side and now with the other, Eli had sat in his high seat at the wayside near the temple. It stood on a terrace of rock above the vineyards in the valley to the north of Shiloh. He was now of a great age, being ninety-and-eight, his hair and beard were white as snow and he was blind and feeble. As he sat there, apart and solitary, his trembling head sunken on his breast, his mind was in confusion, and his heart trembled with fear for the safety of the Ark of the Lord. Samuel alone, who waited upon him and tended him in his blindness, was of his company.

The hot and cloudless day drew on. The sun began to decline into the west, its level beams smiting with gold the white walls and low flat roofs of the little town. Except for the cries of the children at their play, there was little sound or stir in its streets, for none but the women and the old men, and those unfit to fight, were left within it. These went in silence to and fro about their business, for they knew that their safety, and their very lives, hung on the fortunes of the day.

Samuel touched gently Eli's hand that lay upon his knee. He gazed tenderly into the forlorn and aged face. "The day draws on," he said. "I will go now and see if there has come any rumour into the town of how the battle has gone. Rest in quiet here, my lord, and I will speedily return again."

He hastened away to where he could command a view of the track that led in from the south towards Shiloh. There he stood and watched. And a little after sunset, when the first shadows of night had already enfolded the temple, there came running, wounded and spent, and staff in hand, a man of the tribe of Benjamin who had escaped from the forefront of the battle. His clothes were rent. From head to foot he was white with dust, and he had scattered dust upon his head in token of the woe and calamity that had fallen on Israel. In his haste he mistook his way to the temple and

followed the street within the walls that led to the market-
place; and as he ran on into the town he proclaimed his
dreadful tidings. And Samuel came again to Eli; but said
naught.

"What sound is that I hear as of a man crying out and in
grief?" said Eli to Samuel. But Samuel could not answer
him on the instant, his heart was cold as stone within him,
for he had seen the fugitive from afar and had divined his
errand.

"It is a man running," he said; "he seems to be all but spent."

"What manner of man is he?" said Eli. "And whence has he come?"

But before Samuel could answer him, there broke out within the city a wild and sudden outcry, shrill wailings and lamentations. When Eli heard it, he turned, trembling, to Samuel.

"I beseech thee, my son," he said, "hasten and bring me news of the meaning of this tumult."

And Samuel himself, stricken with a dreadful foreboding, went into the city and brought back the Benjamite himself into the presence of Eli.

He bowed himself before the High Priest, and Eli lifted up his face as if to look at him, and said: "Tell me, my son, who art thou, and what news is this thou bringest; keep nothing back from me."

And the Benjamite said: "I am he that hath escaped this day but only with his life from out of the battle. I am wounded to death. Woe, woe, my lord! The armies of Israel have been routed by the Philistines, and have been smitten with a terrible slaughter. When I left the battle they were fleeing in terror, every man for himself, and there was no hope left."

Eli listened on, stark and motionless, and said nothing.

"To thee, too, my lord, do I bring most grievous tidings," said the Benjamite, but his voice was faint. "Thy two sons, Hophni and Phinehas, who were with the Ark in the ranks of the battle, are slain. And the Ark of God has been taken by the Philistines."

When Eli heard that his two sons were slain, his body shook as if with palsy, but when he heard also that the Ark of the Lord had been taken, his senses left him. Darkness swept over his mind; and he fell from off his seat backward by the side of the gate, and his neck brake, and he died; for he was an old man, and heavy.

With their captives and their plunder the army of the Philistines returned in triumph into their own country. But of the spoil that they had captured from Israel the Ark of God was their supreme boast, and this the five lords gave for a trophy into the charge of the city of Ashdod, which with its gardens, its battlemented walls and towers lay, amid its dunes, but a little inland from the coast of the Great Sea, though the very site of it is now no more than a heap of shifting sand.

A tumultuous concourse of people filled the streets, shouting with joy and hooting insults against the Ark, as it was borne in through the gates of the temple of Dagon, and they surged in after it with such vehemence that some among them were flung to the ground and crushed and trampled to death. Since the day that Samson, the mighty champion of Israel, had been led blinded and helpless into Gaza, there had been no jubilation to compare with this. And the priests made sacrifice, chanting their hymns of praise and dancing in frenzy before the worshippers in the temple. They set up the Ark beneath the gloating image of the Fish God himself, as though his nostrils might snuff up the incense of their victory; and there it lay.

# The Ark is Restored

The hours of dark drew on, the multitudes dispersed, the brazen gates of the empty temple were shut, and the priests withdrew to their own sleeping quarters in the city. The crescent moon that had hung in the heavens in the brief twilight of evening sank down beyond the waters of the sea, and the faint rumour of the tide upon the shore could be heard in the silence of night.

Early next morning the priests returned to the temple. They opened its gates and entered in. But when they were come within, they stood motionless, for behold, their god was fallen upon his face upon the floor, and lay prone as if in obeisance before the Ark of the Lord. They were perturbed and questioned one another. But no sound had been heard in the night, and though they searched the temple, its gallery and precincts, they found nothing else amiss, and all avowed they had left their Dagon safe the evening before.

So the priests, having bound themselves by a solemn oath to secrecy, lifted up the image and restored it to its place upon its pedestal. All the next day the people of Ashdod came in throngs to visit the temple, countrymen and strangers also from distant parts, and darkness fell, and again the gates were close-shut and barred and bolted. That night, though none dared remain within its walls, a strong watch was set. The hours went by and the east lightened, and no danger had showed, nor had any man or shape of man come out from the temple or gone in.

Yet when the priests arose on the morrow morning and opened the gates, not only was their god fallen flat upon his face again upon the floor, but the palms of his ivory hands had been snapped off and lay on either side of him, and his carven head had rolled off his neck to the very threshold of the temple. Only the scaled and gilded tail of him and his defaced trunk or stump remained unbroken.

At this evil omen the priests forbore to meddle with him again. His pedestal was left empty, and none but they had access to the temple. They strove in vain to keep this matter concealed from the people, and rumour of it spread abroad. And while the Ark of God was still in the temple and in the keeping of the priests, a grievous and contagious plague or pestilence broke out in the city. In a few days it had swept across the country-side to the villages round about Ashdod on the coast and in the plain. So great were its ravages that the chief men of Ashdod and the priests of Dagon met together and resolved that the Ark should remain in their city no longer.

"For of a truth," they said, "this pestilence that has come upon us is the vengeance of Jehovah, the God of the Hebrews, who in the darkness even of the first night that his Ark came hither struck down Dagon, our god, as if with a thunderbolt. Worse still is in store for us while the Ark remains in Ashdod."

So they sent messengers; and the lords or tyrants of the five cities met together in council. They debated and argued, but he who was prince of Ashdod remained stubborn in his refusal to be responsible for the safety of the Ark a day longer.

"From the hour it entered our gates, it has brought nothing but trouble on the city," he said. "The temple of Dagon is deserted; the priests shake with dread; the people die like flies; and I will have none of it."

The lords of the other four cities scoffed at his faint-heartedness and refused to believe him. "When", they said, "this Ark of the Hebrew Jehovah was captured you clamoured to set it up as a trophy in the temple at Ashdod, and the people welcomed it as if their valour alone had given it into their keeping. What folly then is this? Surely if this God of Israel had power to avenge himself against us, he would have fought with them and given them the victory. Was that so? Take thy priests to the carcass-strown steeps of Eben-ezer and let them see for themselves!"

But the prince of Ashdod paid no heed to their mockery: only repeating yet again that he himself would not be answerable for the safe keeping of the Ark a day longer.

Since nought they said could persuade him otherwise, it was agreed by them at last that the Ark should be taken to Gath. But as it was with Ashdod, so it was with Gath. For immediately pestilence broke out there also and spread through the city from street to street, house to house, like a canker in the skin, bringing with it terror and destruction. The whole city was filled day and night with the sound of wailing. Nevertheless, the princes of the Philistines stubbornly refused to be warned by it, and commanded that the Ark should be taken from Gath to Ekron.

This was done under cover of night, but report of it ran swiftly and the people broke out into open revolt. An unruly mob assembled before the windows of the house of the lord of Ekron, shouting demands that the Ark should be removed at once from out of the city and accusing him of having betrayed them into the same disaster as had already overtaken Ashdod and Gath.

He quelled the riot with a high hand; but as they had foreseen, so it came about. The Ark had lain but a few days in Ekron when the same fatal pestilence began to fret its way from one end of it to the other. And so great was the destruction that the streets were all but empty of way-farers, the market-place was deserted except of the dead, and the doors of the houses of the living were shut and sealed close in dread of its contagion. The cry of the people went up to heaven, and the visitation of God was heavier in Ekron than it had been in any other city where the Ark had rested.

Seven months had now gone by since the defeat of the Israelites and the capture of the Ark. And the lords of the Philistines were in consternation at the calamities that had fallen upon their country. They were at their wits' end to decide what they should do to pacify and assuage the people, for the helpless terror that had come upon them only increased the ravages of the pestilence. And tales were whispered that spectral visitants of the Avenger himself had been seen in the dead of dark, walking the streets and gaz-ing in at the windows, and that voices had been heard, gab-bling in a strange tongue.

The princes summoned their priests and diviners and asked their counsel. "See now," they said, "what shall be done to free ourselves of this Ark of Israel? The mere thought of it fills the people with terror. Consider the mat-ter, and if it be you decide that the Ark should be restored to the Israelites, declare in what manner shall it be returned, and what shall go with it?"

The priests and diviners when they had debated the mat-ter returned to the lords of the Philistines. They reminded

them of the centuries gone by when their enemies the
Hebrews had languished in slavery in Egypt, and what
afflictions and disasters had fallen upon Pharaoh, the lord of
Egypt, when he refused to allow them a few days' grace
from their bondage in which to worship their God and to
make sacrifice to him.

"As it was in those days," said they, "so may it be in
these. The vengeance of Jehovah the God of Israel that
smote Pharaoh has smitten Philistia. Our counsel then is to
send back this Ark to the Hebrews, together with a peace-
offering to their God. If you had been content with your
victory over the Israelites, it may be he would have paid no
heed and would have been pacified. But by seizing on his
Ark, the symbol of his power, you have defiled what is his
and his only. He is Jehovah, and mighty against his
enemies."

The princes of the Philistines listened in silence. They
were divided among themselves, and were sullenly loth to
swallow their pride and to acknowledge openly not only to
their enemies but to their people their own humiliation.

"Tell us now," said they to the diviners, "how can you
assure us that the disasters which have befallen us, this
plague and wasting sickness, this folly of horror and stagna-
tion, are the vengeance of Jehovah of the Hebrews? Has
plague never before smitten a country? Is it anywhere always peace and sunshine, and never storm and tempest?
Who can say whence and why these evils come upon the
world? Is man always in some hidden and inscrutable
fashion responsible for the ills that befall him? Haply this
sickness and all its evils will soon be over, and our cities free
of it."

But they disputed with more confidence than they felt,
and feared what might follow if, like Pharaoh before them,

they held out till all was lost. Having privily debated the matter yet again, they determined at length to follow the counsel that had been given them by the priests and diviners.

They sent for their most skilful craftsmen in goldsmiths' work, and they caused five images of fine gold to be fashioned, one for each of the five chief cities of Philistia—Askelon, Ashdod, Gath, Gaza and Ekron. These images were to be for a peace-offering to placate Jehovah the mighty God of Israel who had afflicted them with pestilence and death.

They were enclosed in a wooden chest or coffer of the rarest workmanship also. A new cart was made ready, a cart that had never been in use before; and two milch cows, the finest of their herds, were set apart, beasts that had not been broken to the plough or borne yoke, and whose young calves had been taken away from them and shut up in a byre. Then the Ark with its rings and its staves was lifted up by the priests of Ekron and laid within the cart, and a canopy of fine embroidered linen was placed over it and over the golden cherubim. And the coffer containing the five golden images was laid beside the Ark.

All this was done as the priests of Beelzebub had counselled. "By this", they said to the princes, "shall be divined the truth of the matter. If when the milch cows that draw the cart are allowed to go free they remain where they are, or following their natural instinct, wheel about and return to their calves, then it shall be proof that this Jehovah of the Hebrews hath no care or thought for his Ark or heed of his worshippers. Then shall it be made clear that the pestilence that has ravaged the country is nothing but an evil chance that could not be avoided, and for which some other remedy must be found.

"But if without pause or bidding these dumb beasts when

they are set free take their way from the gates of Ekron towards Bethshemesh, then shall you know that this pestilence in very truth and deed came of the vengeance of their Lord God Jehovah, and that only by a miracle have we ourselves been saved alive from his wrath."

So all was prepared; and overnight strict watch was set that none should draw near the Ark, lest it should be touched and defiled. Next morning at sunrise—and the dawn broke marvellously fair, for it was the season of harvest—the priests assembled, and the princes in their pomp of state, and a multitude of the people. But not a cry broke the silence. The day of victory was forgotten; only care and awe showed on their faces as they followed after the cart containing the Ark of God under its embroidered canopy, and the coffer with its golden emblems laid beside it, as it was drawn by its milk-white cows to the gates of Ekron.

There the priests performed their strange and barbarous rites, and at the hour appointed the milch cows were allowed to go free whithersoever they chose to wander. And it was forbidden on pain of death for any man to hinder or lead or drive or entice them on.

As soon as those who held their bridled heads had withdrawn, without pause or hesitation they moved slowly on, out of the morning shadow of the city walls and into the glare of the sun. And forsaking the high-road that stretched away from the gates of Ekron they turned aside south-eastward into the wild and trackless plain towards the valley of Sorek.

Following on behind them, but at a distance, came the priests and the princes and the multitude of onlookers from Ekron and the country round about, and they watched what should befall.

And behold, under the bright bare blue of the day, and

lowing mournfully in longing for their calves as they went, the cows continued on their way. They turned neither to the right hand nor to the left, except to avoid the rocks and hollows in their path. It was as though some unseen herdsman, some voice inaudible, were haling them on, for the course they took would lead them direct to the mouth of the valley of Bethshemesh, a city of Israel which lay over against Zorah, the birthplace of Samson, and was the nearest village of the Israelites beyond the Philistine border.

When they were come to the border and the roofs of Bethshemesh were in sight, the princes of the five cities with the priests and diviners and the concourse that had followed close after them, turned back, and went no farther. They had had their answer.

Now it chanced that this day the men in the valleys of Bethshemesh were in the fields reaping their wheat. It was near noon, and hot and still. And as, sickle in hand, they toiled on at their labour, they heard the lowing of cattle, and looked up; and they saw approaching them from the direction of Ekron a cart, brand-new and of strange work-manship, and drawn by two milch cows.

They marvelled at the sight, and hastened out to meet it, for though the beasts harnessed to it came on without pause, turning neither to one side nor to the other, nor stayed to graze, they were without reins, and no man sat above to drive them or walked at their heads to lead them on their way.

The cart came on until it reached the field of a man named Joshua, and there the beasts, as if at the biddance of a voice they had heard, came to a standstill, opposite a great flat-headed stone that was in the midst of the field.

Then the harvesters drew near to the cart. They lifted up the embroidered canopy and the sun in heaven smote down upon the outstretched wings of the cherubim within. It was as if a dazzling lamp had been kindled in the splendour of noonday. And they saw the Ark of the Lord and the coffer of wood containing the golden images which the princes of the Philistines had commanded should be set beside it. They were like men demented with joy and astonishment at sight of it, and sent off messengers far and wide to carry the glad tidings. And they themselves unharnessed the Philistines' sacred cows, hewed in pieces the timber of the cart, and offered them up as a sacrifice to the Lord. The smoke of the sacrifice rose up in the windless air of the morning and was visible even to the Philistines who still watched from afar, on the towered walls of Ekron.

But the Philistines, though they had surrendered the Ark of the Lord continued to oppress the Israelites and to hold them in subjection. And Samuel, who was now acknowledged throughout Israel as a prophet, and was made judge over Israel, mourned for Eli, and ministered no more before the Ark. A shrine was made for it in a house upon a hill that was appointed for its resting-place; and a Levite named Eleazar was sanctified to its charge. But Samuel returned to dwell in Ramah, in the house where he was born.

# SAUL

# Saul and Samuel

Samuel was judge over Israel as long as he lived. Every year he went in circuit through the country of Benjamin. First to Bethel, where Jacob on his solitary journey from Beersheba at the oncoming of night had lain down in a desolate place, stones for his pillow, and had seen in his sleep a ladder standing upon the earth, the height of it touching heaven, and there, descending and ascending, the multitude of the angels of God between earth and heaven. From Bethel Samuel went on to Gilgal, where was the circle of memorial stones taken up out of the bed of the river and set up by Joshua. And from Gilgal Samuel went to Mizpeh, where the tabernacle now was and the Ark of the Covenant of the Lord.

In each of these cities he held his court or assize, and heard the grievances which the people brought before him, and administered justice. He was a judge wise in counsel, grave, austere and upright. Thus he spent his life, having little rest in it. And when he had finished this circuit, he returned to Ramah, the hill-side village where he had shared his childhood with his mother, and where he now lived alone. There he had built an altar and a sanctuary.

He was now old and beginning to be infirm, and the burden of long travel and of his office had grown too heavy to bear unaided. And he made his two sons, Joel and Abiah, judges in Israel. But as soon as they had been set up in

power and authority over the people, they showed themselves as base as had the sons of Eli; except only that
Hophni and Phinehas, being priests consecrated to the
Lord, had brought shame on his worship. But they gave
false judgment, took bribes, and favoured the rich against
the poor.

This evil could not continue long. The government of
Israel had become like a fruit rotten at the core. The
southern tribes were still under the domination of the
Philistines, and paid tribute to their princes. And powerful
nations ruled over by hostile kings menaced Israel on every
side. The people were divided among themselves, and the
land was seething with unrest and discontent.

In these straits the elders met together and came to
Samuel in Ramah to lay their complaint before him and to
make a petition.

They saluted him gravely. He took his seat among them
and asked the reason of their coming.

They said: "We, the elders of Israel, have met together
and have consulted one with another and are of one mind in
what we have come to ask of thee. We know thy wisdom,
thy integrity and uprightness. Thou art the prophet of the
Lord and thy name is revered throughout Israel. But behold, thou art now an old man, and no longer able to control and direct the people as in days gone by, and thy sons
whom thou hast set in judgment over us walk not in thy
ways. They are covetous and corrupt. They are feared and
hated of the people.

"How then can we ourselves do justice in lesser matters if
it can be bought for money in great? Moreover, though
Israel be at peace, it is a peace that cannot long endure.
Enemies beset us on every side, and there is none to guide
and govern us. Our desire is that a leader shall be set over

us, strong and upright, a man of power. Why should not Israel be like the nations around them, knit together in one, and ever ready for war? That is our plea. Make us a king to reign over us!"

Samuel heard them in silence. Many of them had been children when he himself had come to manhood. What knew they of Israel's need? But some among them were almost of as great an age as himself, and his heart sank within him as he looked into their faces and listened to the shameful charges they had brought against his sons. He remembered Eli and his anguish of mind when he himself as a child had pronounced the doom of God against his sons, and the day of disaster when the Ark of the Covenant had been taken.

And though the thing displeased him—this demand for a king—he promised to consider it, to ask counsel of God, and to meet the elders again. He was wounded at their ingratitude after he had served them faithfully his whole life long. The thought that he himself was in part responsible for their discontent pierced him to the heart. He sat bowed down with sadness, alone.

His mind returned to the past, and dwelt on the mercies that had been shown Israel, and the wonders that had been revealed since they had been set free from their woes and slavery in Egypt. Had not the Lord God been their king, their guide, and their counsellor? How often had the people —and even their elders—forsaken him, to humble themselves in shameless worship of the false gods of the heathen —Baal and Astarte. Yet when in affliction they had repented them and turned to him again, he had been merciful, and had raised up deliverers to set them free.

Now, envious of the powerful and hostile nations around them, his enemies and theirs, they had abandoned their faith in him and were pleading for an earthly king to reign over them, heedless of the evils that might come of it. At this thought shame came over him. He had in truth been thinking only of himself. It was the Lord God they had rejected. What was any grievance of his own compared with that?

In remorse he laid his cares and sorrows before the Lord, and remained in silent communion until it was revealed to him what answer he should make to the elders and how he should act.

When they came before him again, he told them all that had been put into his mind to say to them.

"You have demanded that a king shall be set over you, to reign in Israel. Hearken then, while I make clear to you what will be his way and manner of ruling.

"He will command, and you must obey. You will put all authority into his hands; and his least word shall be your law. Even when the tribes are at peace, he will choose of the choicest young men of Israel, and will surround himself with an army, with chariots and with horsemen, and fleet-footed runners to run before his chariot whithersoever he goes. He will take your own sons from you and compel them to serve him. He will himself appoint officers from among them, and set captains over thousands and captains over hundreds, to lead his troops into battle and die at his behest. The people will be forced to plough and to reap for him; to forge him weapons of war, to make him chariots with their metal-work and their leather-work, their harness and equipment. And he will reign in pomp and splendour.

"And how shall he reward those that serve him unless you yourselves pay him revenue and fill his treasuries with gold? He will seize the richest and goodliest of your fields, of your vineyards and your groves of olives, and bestow them on his officers and servants. Heavy taxes will he lay on you, even to the tenth part of your seed and of your harvest, of your flocks and your herds, of your men-servants and your maid-servants. Of every hundred of your sheep and oxen, ten shall be his. Ay, and he will choose out all that please him from among your daughters, the loveliest and the comeliest and the most skilful, to be his embroiderers and perfumers, his cooks and his bakers. And who shall say him nay? This is the way and manner of a king.

"Pay heed to me, therefore, I entreat you, while there is yet time. A king once made cannot easily be unmade; and the day will come when you shall bewail and lament because of this king whom—covetous of the pride and glory of Egypt, Ammon, Moab, Edom—you yourselves have set in mastery over you. Then shall you cry to the Lord to be freed from his tyrannies. And you will cry in vain. For how shall the Lord listen to you then, if you pay no heed to him now?"

But the eloquence with which Samuel had told of the power and splendour of a kingdom only inflamed the imagination of those who heard him; and his warnings fell on deaf ears. They refused to be guided by this wise old counsellor who had given his whole life to their service.

They cried again: "Nay! Nay! a king: a king! We will have a king to reign over us. Then shall we be like the great nations around us. And he will do justice without fear; and will favour no man. And he shall lead us forth to war, command us in battle, and bring glory to Israel."

When Samuel knew that nothing he could say would move them from their purpose, he dismissed the elders; and they returned every man to his own house to await the day when he should summon them and all the chief men of the tribes of Israel to assemble at Mizpeh, there to make known to them what man among them was to be king.

Now in the village of Gibeah in Benjamin there lived at this time a man named Kish. He was the head of his family, well-to-do, and of standing in his clan; and he had an only son whose name was Saul, now in the flower of his life. In looks and stature there was none to compare with him. His eyes were of a strange clearness and brightness, and he towered head and shoulders above any man in Israel.

From his childhood he had spent a quiet and retired life with his father, and now had charge of his flocks and herds. He was known to few beyond his own family, and was not only of a natural modesty but inclined to conceal himself from the notice of his fellows. He was at times, and without cause, as it seemed, moody and downcast and dark in mind. But soon his gloom would depart from him, and his whole being would awake and shine. He could be as swift and resolute in action as a sword flashing in the sun. And when aroused, he was capable of stubbornly insisting at all costs on following his own will. He was born to be a great captain and leader, and was to win glory in Israel, though at last pride, jealousy and faithlessness gained the mastery over his better nature, brought him to ruin and darkened his fame.

Now it chanced one day that some of his father's asses, which had not yet been broken in to saddle and bridle, strayed away from their pasturage and were lost.

When Kish heard of it, he bade Saul take one of his servants and set off speedily in search of them.

For two whole days they looked for them, wandering in every direction through the waste and wooded solitudes of the mountains. Thus they covered upwards of forty miles. On the third day they turned south and sought them in a country of hills and cultivated valleys called Zuph. They pressed on, following the windings of a stream, until they came in sight of a walled village or city that lay on the slopes of its hillside among rich vineyards and olive-groves.

They were footsore and weary, and they sat together on the rocks in the shade of a tree, and in the coolness of running water, to rest and to eat. They shared between them their last half-loaf of bread, a cluster of raisins and some figs, and Saul told his servant that he had decided to look for the asses no further.

"It is all in vain, and I am weary of it," he said. "Let us turn home again; for peradventure my father has by now given up all thought of the asses and is troubled only for our safety."

But the lad was loth to return to his master without the asses, and he told Saul that in the city yonder he would find a seer who if they asked his counsel would give them his help.

"He is a holy man," he said, "and of great renown among the people, for all that he foretells concerning the future surely comes to pass. So it may be with us. Let us go into the city and seek him out; and it may be he will tell us where the asses are to be found."

"But how", said Saul, "can I ask this great man to help us unless I can offer him some fitting present in return? There is not a crust left in our wallets, and I have nothing whatever that I could ask him to accept. What hast thou?"

His servant looked, and answered that he had one small piece of money left—a quarter of a shekel of silver. "It is little enough", he said, "to give this man of God. But if thou offer it and explain that it is all we have, it may be of his grace he will accept it and will tell us our way."

"Well said," Saul answered, rising instantly to his feet. "We will go at once into the city and ask where we shall find him."

So they set off towards the city together, its walled-in

clustering white houses shining clear against the blue, only narrow silver fleeces of cloud dappling the sky above its roofs. And as they were slowly mounting the hill-side towards its gates, they met a company of damsels who, laughing and talking together, and with their pitchers on their heads, had come down to the well-spring to draw water. Saul asked them if the seer of whom he had heard were still in the city and, if so, where he might be found.

One and all they came to a standstill, and their dark eyes gazed wonderingly at him, for never before had they seen a man to compare with him in looks or stature.

[ 334 ]

"The seer is here indeed," they made answer. "Hasten on and you will surely find him, for he came hither this very morning. There is to be a sacrifice this day in the sanctuary. The feast will soon be ready and he himself will be there. Delay not a moment then, and you will overtake him before he goes up to the high place where the guests who have been bidden are even now awaiting him to bless the sacrifice. You could not have come at a better time."

Saul thanked them and, turning away, hastened on with his servant. And when these two were come a little beyond the gates of the city and into the main street of it, they saw an old man, dressed in a long white tunic and a mantle of fine wool, who had but just shut-to the door behind him, and come out of his house. And though Saul was unaware of it, this old man was the great prophet Samuel himself.

Anxious thoughts concerning the mission which had been deputed to him by the elders had been continually in Samuel's mind since they had presented their petition. And, on the morning of the day next before that on which Saul had come into the city, it had been revealed to him that on the morrow at this same hour a stranger of the tribe of Benjamin would be sent to him, and that this was the man chosen of the Lord to be prince over Israel.

When then he raised his eyes and perceived Saul and his servant hastening towards him, he stood still and looked. And a voice in the silence of his mind cried, "Behold, this is the king!"

He was filled with joy, and waited there in the street until Saul should come up with him.

Saul bowed low in greeting before Samuel. He asked if he could direct him to the house of the seer who he had heard that day was in the city. Samuel looked up into his face, marvelling within himself at sight of him. His own sons whom he loved were severed from him beyond recall. They had brought him into reproach. Not only admiration but a tender longing and affection welled up in him as he answered this stranger.

"I am myself", he said, "the seer whom thou seekest. I knew of thy coming hither and have much to say to thee. This day thou and thy servant shall be my guests and shall come with me to the feast at the sanctuary that is even now made ready. To-morrow I will speak with thee alone, and will tell thee all that is in thy heart to enquire of me. As for the drove of asses which thou hast been seeking these three days gone, think no more of them, for they have been found."

He paused, then laid his trembling hand on Saul's arm. "There is but one word I would say to thee now," he added. "Look into thine heart and tell me! To whom shall come that which is desired above all things in Israel? Is it not to thee, and through thee to all thy father's house?"

Saul was filled with wonder and abashed. He gazed on into the countenance of Samuel—a face aged but serene, though marked with the cares and griefs of a long life. It was now lit up with a strange peace and happiness. Seer indeed he must be, Saul thought within himself, for he had not only read a stranger's thoughts and foreseen his errand, but could speak of the future as if it were an open book. But what was the meaning of this dark adjuration? He bowed himself again before Samuel. "Am not I a Benjamite," he said, "the least and smallest of the tribes of Israel; and are not my kindred the least among the clans of Benjamin? Why askest thou this of me, then? Thy words are past my understanding. I entreat thee to make them clear to me."

But at this time Samuel made no answer to Saul's question. He smiled at him and signed to him to go on before him. So they went on their way together, mounting the steep narrow rough-paved street that led to the sanctuary which crowned the hill-top and overlooked the walls of the city and the green terraces in the valley. It lay amid the mountains, and southward stood Jerusalem.

And Samuel brought Saul and his servant into the great room or parlour which had been prepared, and where his guests, about thirty in all of the chief men of the city who had been invited to the feast, were awaiting him. He bade these two young strangers seat themselves, the one on his right hand, the other on his left.

Now as was the custom at such a feast, a special portion of the meat that had been offered up in sacrifice had been set apart for the prophet himself. And Samuel sent word to the cook that this should now be served and should be set before Saul. The cook did as he was bid. He brought in the dish—and welcome was its savour to them both, as they had eaten little since dawn—and he laid it down before Saul. Then said Samuel: "Come now, it was for thee the feast has been kept waiting, and now thou art here. Reach forth thy hand then; eat and drink and may God give thee his blessing."

So Saul ate with Samuel that day, sitting in the chief place beside him, the guest of honour.

When the feast was over and they were come down again together to Samuel's house, he led Saul up on to its flat roof, which like the rest of the houses within the gates of the city was surrounded by a low stone wall or battlement. Here there was cool and quiet after the heat of the day. They watched the lovely countryside around them veiling itself in the shade and peace of evening, and where none could disturb them they talked together long and late. And under a canopy of leafy branches that had been set up for him on the roof and where a bed had been spread for him, Saul lay down that night to rest.

But though he was wearied out, he could not sleep. He watched the stars, as, wildly refulgent in the blue of night, they wheeled from east to west. His mind was restless with his thoughts, now hot with ardour as he pondered over what Samuel had foretold, and now dark with doubt. But weariness at last overcame his senses, and he slept.

# He is made King

At daybreak next morning Samuel arose and called Saul where he still lay slumbering on the roof of the house, and awoke him.

"Up now," he said, "and I will send thee on thy way; and I myself will go with thee for I have a thing of great moment to say to thee."

So, presently after, they left Samuel's house, and went out into the empty street, the three of them together, the prophet and Saul and Saul's servant. And when they were come down from out of the city gates into the valley and were concealed from the eyes of any who like themselves had risen early and might now be looking down from the housetops above, Samuel bade Saul tell the lad who was with him to pass on in front of them.

"But do thou", he said, "stay here with me, that I may reveal to thee the will of God."

The air was fresh in the cool of the morning and sweet with the growth of summer.

They waited until Saul's servant had vanished out of sight. Then Samuel took a horn or vial of holy oil and poured it upon Saul's head, and anointed him with the oil.

"I do this", he said, "as a sign and token that the Lord of hosts hath chosen and anointed thee to be king over his people Israel. Thou shalt reign over them and shalt com-

mand and lead them in war; and if in all things thou follow
his will as it is declared to thee, then shalt thou save them in
times of peril out of the hands of their enemies. Know then
by this that the Eternal hath himself anointed thee prince
of his inheritance."

Samuel looked earnestly at Saul as he stood with bowed
head before him. He had never seen a face so fair with
promise. He laid his hands upon Saul's shoulders, drew his
head down and kissed him; for stranger though Saul had

been until yesterday, the old man's heart had gone out to him in loving affection.

The beams of the newly risen sun gleamed on the locks of Saul's hair burnished by the holy oil. He was moved to the soul by what Samuel had said to him, and he turned falteringly not knowing how to answer him, marvelling and afraid. And Samuel seeing this, and having in their talk and converse together the evening before watched the expressions of his face as they revealed the moods of his impulsive nature, strove to reassure him. For token and proof that he had spoken truly, he foretold what would happen to Saul on his way home to his father at Gibeah.

"When", he said, "we are departed one from another this day, and thou hast begun thy journey home, thou shalt meet two men near the rock-hewn sepulchre of Rachel. They will greet thee and will tell thee that the asses thou hast been seeking these three days past have been found, and that thy father has no longer any thought of them but only of thee, and is troubled for thee, fearing that some evil chance has overtaken thee, and knowing not what to do.

"When these men have gone their way and thou shalt have left them and come to the sacred oak that is at Tabor, thou shalt meet with three other men on their way to the sanctuary at Bethel, there to sacrifice to the Lord. One of them will be carrying his offering of three young kids, another three loaves of white bread, and the third a skin of wine. They will salute thee, and will give thee two of their loaves of bread, one for thyself and one for thy servant, which thou shalt accept at their hands.

"And at length, when thou shalt come to the hill of God at Geba where the officer in command of the garrison of the Philistines is stationed, and thou art nearing home, thou shalt meet a band of prophets coming down from the sanctuary above, chanting their prophecies to the music of psaltery and tabret and pipe and harp. And the spirit of the Lord shall enter into thee and fill thee with exaltation, and thou thyself shalt utter prophecies. Thou shalt be a changed man.

"When then these signs and tokens which I foretell have come to pass, doubt no more, but follow all that thine own soul divineth, for the Lord God will be thy strength and help. Be bold in the service of the Lord."

Then Samuel blessed Saul and bade him farewell until they should meet again; and Saul and his servant went on their way. As Samuel had foretold, so it was. Near the rock-hewn tomb of Rachel—where in the bare and stony way of Ephrath, after the birth of her son, the beautiful mother of Joseph and Benjamin had laid herself down to die—there they met two men who told Saul that his father's asses had long since been found and restored to him.

"Hasten on," they said, "for thy father is in distress for thee and fears only for thy safety."

When they came to the solitary sacred oak on the plain of Tabor, they met also three wayfarers who with their offer-ings of wine and bread and kids were on their way to the sacrifice at the sanctuary at Bethel. They greeted one an-other, and when they parted, the man who carried the loaves of bread, seeing that Saul and his servant had no food left, gave them two of his loaves, which they broke and ate as they journeyed on together.

Few words were exchanged between them, for Saul's mind was overcharged with thought. In a single day his in-ward life and being seemed to have changed their course, like the dark waters of a river issuing from the gloom and solitude of a forest into the light of noonday.

And last, when they came to the foot of the hill of God

which is at Geba and were nearing home, their ears caught strains of music from the height.

And lo, a company of prophets were descending from the sanctuary, accompanied by musicians playing upon a psaltery or lyre, a tambourine, a pipe or flute, and harp. Their music rang wild and sweet upon the air, and as the prophets came on, they leapt and danced, chanting in shrill high voices, and proclaiming their prophecies.

They drew near, and Saul stood where he was, motionless and intent, his eyes fixed hawklike, his face transfigured as he listened to their wild chantings. It was as though his soul within him had escaped like a bird from out of its cage.

And the spirit of the Lord fountained up in his mind. He became rapt, and filled with a strange ardour and exaltation, and scarcely aware of what he did, he mingled with the company of the priests, and himself joined in their chantings, and uttered prophecies.

Now, amid the throng of the curious who stood near and watched and listened as the procession of the prophets passed by, there were a few—friends of his own father—who recognized him. They knew how quiet and simple a life he was wont to lead, and were astonished to see him in such a company. They eagerly questioned one another.

"Surely", they said, "this is the young man who lives on the outskirts of Gibeah! What change is this? What can have happened to him? Is Saul also among the prophets?"

Another standing near overheard the question, and curious to learn more, asked: "Who, then, is this young man's father?"

They answered: "His name is Kish. We know him well. He would be as much amazed as we are ourselves to see this sight."

In times soon to come, when Saul's name had become re-

nowned throughout Israel, the people remembered this day
and the question became a proverb or byword among them:
"Is Saul also among the prophets?"

When to the great comfort of his father Saul had been
restored to him safe and well, and he had refreshed himself
after his journey, his uncle drew him aside and questioned
him. Strange rumours had reached his ears.

"Tell me," he said, "which way did you go, and what
kept you so long?"

Saul told him that after he and his servant had spent two
whole days among the mountains in search of the strayed
asses, they had turned south, but had still been unable to
find them.

"I myself", he said, " had given up hope of ever seeing
them again, and had decided to turn back. But the lad with
me said that in a city near at hand—the walls of which we
could clearly see from where we sat—we should find a man
of God, a seer, who might consent to help us, and would of
his wisdom reveal whither they had strayed. We had little
enough with us for an offering; but so we did."

He turned his strange bright eyes away, his face haunted
by some inward light or influence that his uncle had never
seen there before, and the meaning of which he could not
divine.

"And what was the name of this seer?" he said.

Saul sighed. "It was the prophet, Samuel," he answered.

"Prophet, in truth!" said his uncle, and watched him
closely as he enquired: "Tell me, what did the prophet say
to thee?"

"He received me graciously," said Saul, "telling me to
have no further care for the asses since they had been
found. He knew all."

And though his uncle still continued to question him,

Saul told him nothing more—said not one word of the secret thing that had come to pass between himself and Samuel but one day gone, when, in the first beams of sunrise, the great prophet had anointed his head with oil and hailed him prince of Israel.

Soon after this—and it was drawing near the season of the first harvest, when almost continual fair weather brings to ripeness the barley-fields of Canaan—Samuel summoned the men of Israel to an assembly at Mizpeh in Benjamin. Day by day, hour by hour, they came flocking in from near and far—the chief men of every clan and family, with their servants—long slow caravans and throngs of those who had joined together in company, having met at the by-ways and continuing on together, with their beasts of burden and their baggage.

On the wide slopes of Mizpeh the camp was pitched. There they hobbled their beasts; and their baggage was heaped together in a mound upon its outskirts.

At the hour appointed by Samuel they assembled in their host, sitting cross-legged upon the ground in the wide open space before the doors of the temple, within which, in the Holy of Holies, lay the Ark of the Covenant. They had set themselves in order according to their tribes and clans, a great multitude, men old and young, rich and poor, and all of the lineage of the sons of Jacob and Joseph.

Samuel himself sat in his high seat at the entering-in of the temple; and round about him stood the priests of the Lord. He had summoned the tribesmen of Israel to come together that all might bear witness to the election of the Lord's anointed, the king who should henceforth reign over them. As was the custom in Israel in affairs of great moment, the divine will was to be openly revealed by the casting of lots.

Among the priests stood the High Priest. He wore a robe

of fine linen, embroidered about its hem with pomegranates in needlework—blue and purple and scarlet. Bells
of pure gold were sewn between the silken pomegranates
round about the hem, and tinkled as he moved. Upon his
head was set a crown or mitre, and above his brows on the
forefront of the mitre was a plate of pure gold, engraved, as
with the characters of a signet, with the words "Holiness to
the Lord".

From his shoulders hung an ephod or apron of fine
twined linen, also embroidered in gold and blue and purple
and scarlet. And upon his breast, with its braided chains of
gold, was the breastplate of judgment.

Set in fine gold in four rows upon the front of this breastplate were stones of great price, and each one of these was
engraved with the name of one of the twelve tribes of Israel.
In the first row there gleamed a sardius, a topaz and a car-
buncle; in the second row an emerald, a sapphire and a dia-
mond; in the third a flame-coloured ligure, an agate and an
amethyst; and in the fourth row a beryl, an onyx and a
jasper. They burned in the splendour of the sun that from
the ample skies poured down its radiance upon the garish
host assembled there.

Within the fold of the breastplate lay a flat sacred crystal,
the one side of which was called Urim, the other Thummim.
On the side which was called Urim was graved the Ineffable Name, the name of the Lord God, the Eternal. But
the side called Thummim was smooth and plain.

When the divine oracle was to be consulted and lots were
to be drawn, and it had been made known what question
needed divine answer, the High Priest thrust his hand
within the breastplate and withdrew the stone. And according to which of the two sides of the stone came uppermost, either Urim or Thummim, such was the answer that

had been revealed: either Yes or No, as it had been ordained.

When all was in readiness, and silence had fallen upon the host stretched out before him, Samuel bade the chief man of every tribe draw near. From their places in the throng the twelve came forward, and stood before Samuel and the High Priest. And the whole multitude watched under the blue tent of the day. Then the High Priest, having prayed, thrust his hand into the breastplate of judgment and drew the lot for each tribe, from Reuben onwards. And as for one after another the stone when he drew it out showed the side that was called Thummim, the chief of that tribe returned to his own place in the throng. For the lot was against him.

Last came Benjamin, the least of the tribes of Israel. And when the High Priest drew out the stone yet once again, it was Urim that was revealed. And it was proclaimed to the assembly that out of all Israel the Lord God had chosen the tribe of Benjamin. Wild voices broke out at the hearing of it, cries of amazement, incredulity, dismay and exultation.

Then Samuel bade the chiefs of the clans of the tribe of Benjamin draw near, and the lot fell on the clan of the Matri. Then followed the heads of the households of this clan, with Kish himself among them, and the lot fell at last upon Saul.

"Saul! Saul!"

The shout pealed out from a thousand throats; the tribesmen leapt to their feet to acclaim their king.

But behold, when they sought for Saul that he might show himself before the people, he could nowhere be found. A furious clamour shook the air, some calling his name, others questioning who and what he was, and why he was absent; others enraged at the affront which they deemed to have been laid by a mere Benjamite upon the chieftains of

Israel. And as still he refused to show himself, and none could bring word of him, the assembly was in a tumult.

Samuel sat unmoved. His faith in Saul was as yet unshaken. He had divined his wayward nature, at one moment ardent and assured; and then, cast down, self-distrustful and faint-hearted. Had he not already anointed Saul king, knowing that he would be the Lord's chosen? What wonder Saul had been seized with misgiving at the ordeal before him and had fled away in dread of standing alone in the intent and searching gaze of all Israel. He loved him the more in that he had not vaunted himself, or shown himself overbold before them. He waited in patience.

When it became certain that Saul was not present among the host before him, the High Priest consulted the oracle again, praying that it might be revealed whether or not Saul were near at hand and if peradventure he had hidden himself. It was declared that he was in hiding. They sent then in haste to search for him everywhere throughout the vast encampment, and he was found at last in hiding among the baggage.

But when he stood in the presence of the High Priest, had gazed once into Samuel's face, then turned about to confront the mighty throng, in countenance and bearing he looked a king indeed. For in stature he towered head and shoulders above any man present there, of all the tribes of Israel.

Then Samuel rose, and bade all be silent. He cried in a loud voice to the multitude: "Behold, and see now! He whom the Lord God of Israel hath chosen to be your king stands before you. Of a truth there is not one among you to be compared with him."

And there went up an acclamation of joy and triumph: "God save the King! Long live the King!"

Then Samuel took a scroll of parchment, and for proof and witness that the elders of Israel themselves had demanded this change in the government of Israel, he wrote in it a record of all that had been done that day, and this record was laid up in the holy place in the Tabernacle.

Until long after nightfall the tent of Kish where Saul was with his father was thronged continually with a concourse of strangers. Many of them had journeyed from remote parts of the country and they wished to see and speak with their king face to face. They brought him presents to do him honour and for proof of their allegiance.

And when Saul returned to Gibeah, there went with him a band of men, whose hearts God had touched, to bear him company, and to be his body-guard as was befitting a king. They were men valiant and fearless, and from that day on were devoted to him and to his service. But there were many others at Gibeah who in envy and discontent revolted openly against him.

They murmured one to another: "How shall such a man as this save Israel in the hour of need! Until this day we have never even so much as heard this Benjamite's name. What hath he done that he should be foisted up over us? A mighty man of valour in truth!—who when he was proclaimed King of Israel was found hiding among the stuff!"

They envied and despised him, refused to do him honour, and brought him no gifts. But Saul at that time made as though he had not heard them.

He returned home to his wife and his son Jonathan. And when the feasting and rejoicings of his kinsmen and of those who dwelt in and around Gibeah were at an end, he continued to lead the simple life he had led of old. He went about his daily work in his father's fields and vineyards, as other kings of small nations had done before him. He awaited the day when Israel should be in need of him, and he could prove himself a king not only in word but in deed.

# King Nahash

That day was soon to come, for no long time after the assembly at Mizpeh, Nahash, king of the Ammonites, summoned his tribesmen to war, and led his host against the great walled and fortified city of Jabesh. He coveted the rich and fruitful region of Gilead and lusted to drive the Israelites once and for all across the Jordan. But this stronghold of Jabesh which— seven miles east of the river—stood on a lofty tableland and on the ancient road from the Red Sea to Damascus, lay in his way. He could do nothing until it was reduced and captured. The defenceless people that dwelt in the villages round about it fled before him and sought refuge within its gates. And Nahash went up and laid close siege against the city. His tents clustered thick about its walls, and though the men of Jabesh repelled the furious assaults his tribesmen made against it, he beset it so closely that not so much as a sack of corn could be smuggled through its gates.

Weeks went by, and there came no relief. Day by day the store of food in the city dwindled. The horrors of famine came upon the people and a dreadful sickness broke out among them, so that even among the watchmen on the walls some were found at morning stark and dead at their posts. The city was reduced at length to such desperate straits that all hope was abandoned of holding out many days longer.

Undefeated, but broken with grief and despair at the

miseries around them, the chief men of Jabesh sent out envoys to King Nahash announcing that they would surrender the city and would agree to any terms he might im-
pose, provided only that he made a covenant with them to
spare the lives of all within it, to withdraw his tribesmen
from their territory, and molest them no more.

King Nahash himself received the envoys who had been
sent out to him. They abased themselves before him, and as
he listened to their hollow voices and watched their faces,
wan and haggard with famine, he laughed aloud. The name

of this king meant *serpent*, and the guile of the serpent was in his countenance as with flat and crafty eyes he glanced at the officers that stood about him, and bade the envoys get them back into the city.

"Tell them that sent you hither," he said, "this shall be my covenant. Fling open your gates and surrender yourselves forthwith! And for token of my clemency, I will gouge out the right eye of every man among you who has resisted me. One of every man's eyes, I say, from out of his head! Yea; and from this day forward you shall look crookedly and askance one at another, and shall be a shame and reproach to all who see you and the scorn of your enemies. For verily," he said, "there is in all Israel none now to heed or to help you!"

Enraged at this foul boast the chiefs of Jabesh determined to fight on, but, to gain time, pleaded for a seven days' truce. "And if", they said, "when the seven days have gone by, no ransom shall have come, then will we surrender ourselves into the hands of the king, and he shall do with us as seems best to him."

Assured that he had the city and all within it at his mercy and could beat off any attack that might be made upon him, Nahash agreed to a seven days' truce. He invited the envoys that had been sent out to him to eat and drink and make merry, and laughed the louder when they refused, and, turning back, stalked off like spectres and were admitted into the city.

Under cover of night there crept out of Jabesh a few picked men. They were to make their way through the camp of the Ammonites, cross the Jordan, scatter themselves among the tribes of Israel, and do their utmost to raise a force strong enough to come to their aid, and to raise the siege.

On the morrow the miserable pittance of food allowed to every man, woman and child yet alive in the city was halved. And death within its walls took far heavier toll of them than had the spearmen of Ammon.

The messengers came to Gibeah, and when they told the people of the straits to which the inhabitants of Jabesh had been reduced by famine and sickness, and the insults that Nahash the king had heaped upon them, grief and horror came on all who heard. The streets resounded with the women's lamentations.

It was the hour of sunset, and Saul was returning home from the fields with a yoke of his father's oxen. He had been ploughing after the ingathering of the barley harvest. When he saw the commotion in the streets and heard the wailings and lamentings of the women, he questioned one who stood by.

"What aileth the people that they weep?" he said.

Those near at hand gathered about him, and the two messengers from Jabesh were brought into his presence. They told again of the disaster that had overtaken their city and the vile revenge that Nahash would wreak upon its defenders unless immediate help were sent. And as Saul looked into their ravaged faces and heard the dreadful story of their wrongs and of the insolence of King Nahash, his mind went up in a flame of fury, and the spirit of the Lord came upon him.

Snatching the iron two-edged sword from out of the leathern sheath of one of the messengers, he turned himself about and with his own hand struck down the oxen that he was leading in from the fields to his father's house, and hewed their carcases in pieces before their eyes.

Then he lifted up his bloody hands above his head, and he cried with a loud voice to those who stood by: "Which of you is on the Lord's side? Which on the Lord's side? Jehovah calls to war!"

They answered him with one voice, "Ay!" And he chose from among them the hardiest and fleetest of foot, and sent them out through all the coasts of Israel. And to each was given a fragment of the slaughtered oxen. Whithersoever they went, he commanded them to summon the people to arms, and bid them flock with all haste to the standard that he would set up at Bezek.

"Vow unto them", he said, "by the life of their king that whosoever cometh not out after Saul, so shall it be done unto his oxen as I myself have done unto these."

The messengers sped on by plain and valley and mountain, from village to village, city to city, and whithersoever they went, they called the people to war. And when the men of Israel heard the threat that Saul had uttered against those who should refuse to follow him, the fear of God came upon them. With one consent they flocked together to Bezek—a mighty host.

Now Bezek lay to the west of the Jordan and some five and twenty miles from Jabesh towards the east. But the tribesmen of Israel were scattered far and wide, and travel was slow; and five full days went by while they were mustering at Bezek. The morrow would be the last of the seven days of respite which the men of Jabesh had covenanted for with King Nahash. Saul sent for the messengers and told them to win their way back into the city as covertly as they had come out, and to assure those who had sent them that on the morrow deliverance would come.

"Say this unto them from King Saul," he said. "Be strong and fear not! Verily before to-morrow's sun mounts hot above your heads your woes shall be avenged."

Soon after nightfall the messengers made their way by

stealth through the Ammonite camp. They knocked secretly on the gate, gave the countersign agreed upon before they set out, and the watchmen let them in. Never came messengers more welcome. The silence of death was over the city. Its defenders after waiting so many days in vain had concluded that the messengers who had been sent out had been captured or had perished. They had resigned themselves to their fate. Tears rained down their faces; exceeding great was their joy.

And even though dark had now fallen, an envoy was at once sent out by torchlight to King Nahash bringing him word that on the morrow at noonday all within the city would surrender themselves to his mercy, if he were then prepared to receive them. It pleased him well; the hour of his vengeance drew near.

Lulled into a false security, the camp of the Ammonites soon lay hushed in sleep. The night was starry but dark; their watchfires burned low; and even the sentries drowsed at their stations.

But the army of Israel encamped at Bezek was awake and stirring and already in battle array. Saul had divided his troops into three companies. At midnight they forded the Jordan. And when they had reached the further bank one of them turned to make a circuit towards the north, and one towards the south, while Saul himself, in command of the third division, marched east.

Thus the camp of the Ammonites would be surrounded that night on every side, and secret orders had been given that all three companies were to advance to the assault together at daybreak.

The night drew on. There came the first gleam of dawn flushing the east. And about the hour that ends the morning watch the trumpets of Israel sounded. Shouting their battle-cry, the three companies converged together, and swept down upon the camp of the Ammonites while they were still heavy with sleep.

They had gone to rest thirsting for the bloodshed and booty of the morrow. They awoke to disaster and defeat. They fought fiercely, but were thrown into confusion, and, all order abandoned, broke and fled. And the tribesmen of Israel pursued them eastward until the sun had risen high into the heavens in the heat of the day.

So complete was the rout of King Nahash and his host that there remained not two of them left together, and he himself barely escaped with his life. Thus did Saul keep to the letter the vow that he had made to the men of Jabesh.

When the pursuit was over, he withdrew his troops across the Jordan and mustered them at Gilgal. There on the naked and terraced mountain-top of rock had been reared up the circle of memorial stones by Joshua above three centuries before. His troops were drunken with victory. Like their great captains, Barak and Gideon and Jephthah, before him, Saul had proved himself a resolute and valiant leader. And those of them who had sworn fealty to him when he had been chosen king at Mizpeh and who from that day had never swerved in their allegiance to him, remembered the malcontents who had scorned and rejected him, crying: "Who is this Saul the Benjamite that he should reign over us! Away with him!"

They came before the king and demanded that these rebels and traitors should be instantly put to death.

"Why should they share this day in thy triumph? They are unworthy to live. Let them die!"

But Saul refused to listen to them.

"Nay," he said, "this is not the hour for vengeance, and there shall not a man be put to death this day. Not mine the victory; it is the Lord God Jehovah who has wrought salvation in Israel."

And Samuel himself came to Gilgal, and there, without any dissenting voice, Saul was once more solemnly proclaimed king, and sacrifices were offered up and libations poured out to the Lord, and Saul and all the men of Israel gave thanks to Jehovah, and great were their rejoicings.

Then Samuel spoke for the last time before the people. He reminded them how their elders had laid before him their petition that a king should be chosen to reign over Israel.

"And now behold," he said, "your king himself is here to lead you. Glorious indeed is he! He has proved himself worthy of his crown. As for me, I am an old man and grey-headed. Yet, as you know well, I too have been a shepherd of Israel, even from the days of my childhood until now. Have I at any time wantonly done anything amiss? See, now, I stand before you and challenge you to declare if you have anything against me. Speak out without fear before the Lord God and before the king, his anointed one! Have I accepted bribes? Whose ox have I taken? Whose ass have I taken? Whom have I defrauded? Whom have I treated harshly? Is there a man among you who can solemnly avow that any gift of his has ever blinded my eyes to justice? If there be such a one, let him now rise up and testify against me, and if he accuse me of having accepted a bribe or of having sold justice for money, then will I restore it."

At sight of Samuel pleading his cause before them—an old man, bowed down with age and infirmity, who had devoted himself to their service his whole life long and now had been set aside, the people were seized with remorse. They answered him with one voice that they had no charge whatever to bring against him.

Then said Samuel: "The Lord God, then, is this day

witness, and your king, his anointed, is witness between us. You have found nothing against me?"

And they answered: "Be God our witness."

Then said Samuel: "If in the years that are gone I have kept faith with you as you yourselves have testified, hearken to me now, for it may be that I shall not come before you again."

And he recalled to them the mercies which had been shown to Israel since they had first become a nation. Nevertheless, again and again they had proved faithless and had forsaken the Lord and humbled and defiled themselves in worship of the false gods of the nations around them. They had sunk into sloth and apathy. Enemies had risen against them, triumphed over them in battle, and oppressed them.

Yet when they had repented and returned again to the Lord, had he not taken pity on their sorrows, heard their prayers, and raised up for them leaders valiant of heart, subtle of mind, and skilled in war?

Had they forgotten Moses who had been sent to save Israel in days of old? Far-sighted, wise and fearless, had he not defied the might and tyranny of Egypt, shattered the pride of Pharaoh, and redeemed Israel from thraldom? How many valiant captains had God raised up for them in the time of need? Joshua, who after their long wanderings in the wilderness had led Israel into Canaan and divided it among them. Ehud, who had destroyed King Eglon of the Moabites. Barak, who had so utterly defeated the hosts of King Jabin, with his nine hundred chariots of iron, that Sisera the commander of his armies had been compelled to flee on foot and, wearied-out, meet in sleep his shameful end at the hand of a woman, armed only with a tent mallet and a nail. Gideon, too, who with but three hundred men had discomfited the hosts of Midian and Amalek.

"Yea," he said, "and even Samuel himself who stands before you now—hath he not fought for Israel? Nevertheless when but a little while gone you were seized with terror of Nahash, King of Ammon, did you, remembering these things, put your trust in God? Nay, you murmured among yourselves, and in thanklessness and folly forgot that Jehovah was your Saviour, and demanded that a king should reign over you. And you refused to listen to my warnings. 'A king! A king shall reign over us!' This was your cry.

"Behold, then, here is the king whom you have chosen, the king of your desire, the Lord's anointed! Serve him faithfully. But be not puffed up with pride. If you fear and honour the Lord he will never forsake you, nor will he reject your king. But if you refuse him and rebel against him, then shall his hand be lifted in wrath against you, even as he punished your fathers before you. He will abandon you. How shall he be the shield and defender of those who deny and defy him? How shall the light of his countenance shine upon those who choose the dark? Stand now, and see, for the Lord God in his heavens shall even this day reveal a wonder before your eyes.

"Are not the wheat-fields of Canaan ripe for harvest? Comes ever in Israel storm or rain at this season? Lo, I myself will call upon Jehovah, and the thunder of his voice shall rend the firmament, and there shall be rain and lightnings. And you shall tremble with fear of such a marvel, and your hearts shall melt within you, knowing your wickedness and the wrong you have done in demanding a king."

At these words a great silence fell upon the host. On one side of the bare open plain, where they were encamped, far mountains lifted rugged slopes faintly coloured in the haze of heat. On the other, beyond fantastic hillocks and through thickets of acacia, tamarisk, willow and the white-flowering juniper, flowed the swift and turbid waters of the Jordan in its wide sunken channel, the lair of wolf and leopard, and the resort of the lapwing, the crested hoopoe, and the loud-sounding bittern.

In the presence of the host Samuel prayed to the Lord. And behold, in the skies that had been for weeks past fair and serene and overwelling with sunlight above the wind-less earth stretched out beneath them, leaden and louring clouds began to gather, heaping themselves on high. The gloom of storm drew over the hoary circle of stones; its shadow darkened the plain. It was as though night had come back upon the day. The upturned faces of the host wanned as they watched, and a dreadful foreboding filled every mind. And there suddenly swept down from heaven a tempest of wind that sucked dense whirling veils of dust into the air. The multitude was terrified at its fury. They cowered beneath the deluge of the rain. The thunder broke upon their hearts like the wrath of God pealing through the firmament. The gloom was riven with lightnings, and the wilderness around them, mountains to river, stood spectral white in their glare.

They looked with dread upon Samuel, and were smitten with the fear of God. A long low wailing rose from among them and was heard in the hush of wind and thunder. And the people besought Samuel to intercede for them. "Pray for thy servants to the Lord thy God," they implored him, "lest we die. We have in truth added to all our sins a great evil in desiring a king to reign over us."

Calm returned between earth and heaven as swiftly as the storm itself had broken. The sun in glory shone out daz-zling clear, its beams glittering like quicksilver on the pools and runnels. After the tumult came the singing of birds, and the stones of Gilgal smoked in the blaze of heat.

Then Samuel bade the people put away their fears, since they had confessed and repented of their wickedness.

"Serve the Lord from this day forward, with all your heart," he entreated them. "And for his own name's sake he will never forsake you. Hath he not himself chosen Israel to make of you in times to come a very great nation? Turn not aside then from following after him, in desire for earthly vanities. What are these but things of nought which can only net you in and entangle you ever the more closely in the bonds of your own folly?"

His voice trembled, and he bowed his head. "As for me," he continued, "God forbid that I should ever sin against him in ceasing to pray for you, and to intercede for you, even to my last breath! Nor will I ever refrain from showing you the way of goodness and truth. But if you refuse him and do wickedly, then disaster shall come upon you, defeat and captivity, and you shall perish—yourselves and your king."

# *Jonathan*

For some years after the defeat of King Nahash and the Ammonites, there was peace in Israel. Nevertheless it was a peace that could not be of long continuance. The tribes in the south of Canaan were still under the overlordship of the Philistines, and were compelled to pay tribute and to trade with them. In order to levy this tribute, to control and keep watch on the country and to quell any show of rebellion, the lords of the five cities had stationed officers in different parts of the country.

Saul, then, in much was a king only in name. Until by force of arms he could fling off the domination of the Philistines, Israel could never be a free people. This was his secret aim and desire, and with this end in view he gathered about him a standing army. He chose from among the tribesmen who had fought at Jabesh three thousand of the best men in Israel for strength and hardihood and valour: archers, slingers and spearmen. The rest he dismissed and sent them home with orders that they were to hold themselves ever ready to take up arms for Israel and to fight under him whenever, as in times past, the need came to summon them to war.

He then divided his standing army into three equal companies, each one of them a thousand strong. Of chariots and horsemen he had none. One of these companies he stationed above Michmash, a village on the steep-cliffed heights above a ravine, where ran the great highway between Gilead and the coast. To hold this Michmash was to hold the key of the defence of all central Canaan. Here Saul himself set up his standard.

His second division was stationed on the ridge near Bethel. The third, under the command of his son Jonathan, was on the heights of Geba, which lay on the other side of the valley looking towards Michmash. With these forces he held the pass beneath.

Now at this time Saul's son, Jonathan, was in the flower of his youth. Like his father who loved him and delighted in his company, he was of an impetuous and wayward spirit and impatient of control, but true and faithful. He had not the mighty stature of the king, but was as bold and hardy as a she-lion with her whelps, and was of a rare ease and grace of body. He exulted in all martial exercises, and was renowned as an archer and for his skill with the sling. He pined to prove himself a soldier and a leader of men.

At Geba, where he was stationed with his thousand, there was a small garrison of the Philistines. The officer in command of it was vainglorious and insolent. He had openly flouted the king and opposed by every means in his power the establishment of his army. In all his dealings with Jonathan he used him with contempt. The young prince was by nature courteous and sensitive, and he burned with anger at this Philistine's insults.

There came a day when there were high words between them. At an affront against Israel fouler than any that had passed this man's lips before, Jonathan rose up in a fury and smote him where he sat. Then he fled out of the house. And of the Philistine garrison not one escaped with his life.

But report of his wild action speedily reached the princes

of the five cities. They determined to stamp out the flame of revolt before it could spread further. They gathered together an army—chariots and horsemen, and footmen—as the sand on the seashore for number. By way of the pass of Beth-horon, it marched against Israel.

Terror seized upon all who heard of it; the roads flocked with fugitives. So sharp was the fear and dread of the Philistines, the ancient and implacable enemy of Israel, that many even of Saul's picked troops deserted the king and fled into hiding. When he mustered those that remained with him, he found that they were only six hundred men in all.

Powerless to oppose the advance of the Philistines with a force so weak and unstable, he withdrew across the valley to Geba where Jonathan was stationed. And the Philistines seized Michmash, encamped there, and fortified it. From thence they sent out raiders in three divisions, with orders to ravage the country, to slay and spare not. One of these divisions took the road to Ophrah, which lay five miles north-east of Bethel; the second turned west towards the valley lying between the upper and lower villages of Bethhoron; the third went east, following the border track above the gorge of Zeboim, one of the deep and rugged watercourses of that region, and infested with hyenas.

Thus they despoiled the land of Benjamin on every side, pillaging and burning as they went. So dire were the straits to which the people were reduced that they abandoned their villages, and with their wives and children fled for safety into the mountains. There, venturing out only after nightfall, they hid themselves, wheresoever they could find a refuge—in the caves and thickets, among the rocks of the lofty gorges, and even in the dried up water-pits. Many crossed the Jordan and fled into the country of Gad and Gilead.

When the three companies of raiders had finished their work, they retired with their plunder to Michmash where the main garrison of the Philistines was stationed. They had left a deserted waste behind them. And traitors went with them, tribesmen of Israel who for terror or in the hope of gain had forsaken the cause of the king and joined the ranks of his enemies.

Meanwhile Saul, with the few tried and trusty men left to him, remained in his camp on the outskirts of Geba. His tent, with his standard set up before it, was pitched near a pomegranate tree which grew—with its narrow leaves and bright red and crimson-cupped blossoms—not far distant from a threshing-floor on the bare open hill-top. Here, after harvest, the grain was trodden out by oxen to be winnowed by the wind. From this point of vantage watch could be kept on the neighbouring heights of Michmash across the valley.

And with the king at this time was a priest whose name was Ahiah. He was of the lineage of Eli, but not of direct descent, and he wore the ephod of the Lord.

Jonathan also was with his father. His wild deed of violence against the garrison at Geba had been the cause of the vengeance of the Philistines. He grieved bitterly at what had come of it. He had watched afar off the drifting flamelit smoke-clouds in the darkness above the peaceful villages which the raiders had left burning in their wake, and had listened to the tales of horror told by those who had escaped their vengeance and who had sought refuge in the camp.

The faces of his men, who loved and trusted him, were dark with despair. And though his father refrained from reproaching him, Jonathan knew how sharp the stroke of this disaster had been. For hours the king would sit without

speech, his eyes downcast, his countenance heavy with gloom.

Jonathan yearned to bring him comfort, to find grace again in his sight, and above all to strike a reviving blow that would redeem what was past. But how could this be while the army of Israel remained inactive and sat idle in their tents; while not a trumpet sounded, and the people, homeless and terrified, shared the wilds with the beasts.

There came a day when a spy whom he had sent out from Geba brought him back word that the lords of the five cities had withdrawn part of the army they had sent against

Israel. And though the forces of the Philistines that remained still far outnumbered those under the king, yet were they not so strong but that some valiant exploit, such as had given the victory to Gideon against the Midianites, might bring them low.

As he lay that night, brooding and sleepless, he devised a plan which, whether it succeeded or not, would almost assuredly cost him his life. The thought of it burned like a fire-brand within him. The next morning early he drew aside his young squire or armour-bearer, and they went out together from the camp where no man could see them, and where they could talk in secret.

And Jonathan told his armour-bearer all that was in his mind. Now between Geba and Michmash lay deep and wide ravines, with valleys debouching into them on either side. And on the one side was a lofty crag or peak of rock named Bozez or "the Shining" —because when the sun smote down upon it, it gleamed like burnished metal; and on the other a crag named Seneh, "the Thorny". Bozez was to the north over against the garrison of the Philistines, and Seneh was to the south in face of Geba. The whole region was rugged, wild and precipitous. But Jonathan knew it as he knew the palm of his hand.

This then was his stratagem: that they two, himself and his armour-bearer, should sally out in disguise when night was down, and having descended into the ravine beneath, should make their way to the foot of the cliff beyond whose summit was the camp of the Philistines, scale it, and attack the outpost that guarded the crag, and as if from the eyrie of an eagle kept watch upon the valleys.

"Even", said Jonathan, "if we make this venture alone, thou and I together, against these accursed Philistines, even though it be but a step between us and death, peradventure the Lord will work a wonder, and with his help we shall be the means of rousing all Israel. I am sick to the heart as the days go by in waste and despair. But with God nothing is impossible. And who is to declare how he shall save his people, whether by many or by few, yea, or even by you and me alone?"

And his armour-bearer, who was also young and valiant, vowed that he would follow him to the death. "Do all that is in thine heart," he said, "and I am with thee; my life with thy life. But we must come upon them by stealth. And how shall we scale the crag or even get within bowshot of this outpost and not be seen?"

"Well said," said Jonathan. "But to that too I have seen a way out. For see, now: when we have come to the foot of the crag, we will show ourselves, and the watchmen looking down and shadowing us out in the darkness will take us for belated night-farers, fugitives from the raiders, who under cover of the dark are stealing home. If, when he challenge us, he cry 'Hold! Stand where you are until we come down to you!' then will we wait for them there in our places. But if, boaster that he be, he dare us to come up, then will we go up, and woe be to him!

"This then shall be the sign to us; if he say 'Come!' we will go, and I vow even thou and I alone while still we breathe will show a wonder! The Lord will have delivered them into our hands. These vile Philistines boast there is not a mouse left stirring in Israel, but Jehovah will fight for us, and that shall be our sign."

When all that Jonathan had devised was made clear between them, they returned into the camp. They spoke of it to no man, nor did Jonathan say one word concerning his stratagem to his father the king. He knew its dangers, and what small hope there was that he should escape with his life. And he feared that his father might forbid the venture, and prevent him from pursuing it.

On a night of no moon, and when all the camp was still; armed, cloaked and muffled, Jonathan with his armour-bearer stole silently forth from out of his tent. Soon lost to sight in the pitchy dark, they descended into the valley. And no man challenged them. Prowling nocturnal beasts their only company, the dismal yell of roving jackals their sole music, they pressed on through the ravine, strown with sunburned rocks. Its air, though it was night, was parched and hot as an oven. They made their way betwixt the two precipitous crags of Seneh on the one side, dense with thorn and bramble, and Bozez naked and faintly glimmering on the other, their summits looming black against the star-sewn sky.

Not a breath of wind stirred the leaves, the dense ravine was sultry and stagnant, as though bodeful of some strange disaster. But thus these two came out at length at the foot of the lowermost slope of the crag on which was stationed the outpost of the Philistines.

Huge rounded boulders and scrub bushes lay scattered around them; and when they had rested themselves, whispering together, their pulses drumming them on, they stole out from their concealment and showed themselves in the open.

The clatter of their footfall reached the ears of the watchman above. He peered down at them through the gloom, and discerned their motionless shapes against the pallor of the rocks. Whereupon he called back mockingly to his fellows: "Hey, now, come and see a marvel! Behold, some of these vile Hebrews have come creeping out of the holes wherein they have hidden themselves."

A brief silence followed. And as Jonathan and his armour-bearer, muffled in their cloaks, stood gazing upward, the watchman was joined by other soldiers of the guard who peered down at them likewise. And they bawled in derision: "Hey, there, come up, you two! And we will show you a thing you shall never forget!"

Jonathan made no answer, but turned aside with his armour-bearer and vanished out of sight of those that looked down from above. When they had tarried awhile, and all was still once more, he whispered to the young man: "Lo, now; heardest thou that, 'Come!'? It was the sign! Follow me close, for verily the Lord God of Israel hath delivered them into our hands."

They threw off their cloaks, and girding their weapons out of harm's way, began to scale the rocky precipice that frowned down upon them in the darkness, towering sheer above their heads. Hand and foot from rock to rock and ledge to ledge, pausing only to take breath, Jonathan climbed on, and his armour-bearer climbed after him, until they came out upon the summit of the crag. Then with a shout that rang wild through the night and echoed on from steep to steep they ran in upon the Philistines.

And the Philistines fell before them. Many of the watch were asleep, and none was ready. So sudden and vehement had been the assault that they made no pause to discover the numbers of their assailants, but in terror turned and fled. And Jonathan pursued after them, slaying as he went; and his armour-bearer slew after him; until in that first slaughter—within a space in breadth but half a furrow of an acre of land—about twenty men lay dead.

Then sang Jonathan's bowstring, and they chased those that remained alive along the ridge as they fled towards the village and the camp. Their cries rent the dark, and roused the garrison, who, confused with sleep, supposed that the whole strength of Israel was advancing to the attack. Fear bred fear in the stagnant gloom, and amid this tumult, of a sudden the solid rock itself beneath them began to tremble, and the earth quaked, and there was a very great trembling.

A furious wind followed the earthquake. Shouts of "Jehovah!" rose to heaven, and terror fell upon the host throughout the camp, and over the open country, and on the pitiless plunderers who had returned in triumph from their raidings. All was confusion. And the night drew to an end.

And the watchmen of King Saul on the heights of Geba looked out across the valley in the first faint dusk of dawn, and behold, the whole army of the Philistines was in commotion, surging hither and thither as they fought one against another, beating one another down. And their tumult struck faint upon the ear. They gave the alarm. The trumpet sounded. And when the men of Israel were mustered in their ranks, every man under his own captain, and the roll was called, it was found that Jonathan and his armour-bearer were not there.

Then Saul sent hastily for Ahiah the priest, and bade him: "Bring hither the Ephod!" He was at a loss, yearning to join battle with his enemies, yet in doubt whether or not this was the will of the Lord Jehovah.

But even while he was still speaking with the priest, the rout and clamour in the enemy's camp on the heights of Michmash went on and increased more and more. And when Saul heard it, his spirit awoke fiercely within him; he doubted no more. He bade the priest draw back his hand, refrain from consulting the oracle, and follow him before Israel, bearing the ephod of the Lord.

Then King Saul set his army in battle array—spearmen and bowmen. And he himself, filled with a frenzy, and tarrying not to question whether he did right or wrong, vowed a vow before them all and laid an oath on them every one. "Cursed be the man", he cried, "that tasteth food this day until the evening. Cursed be he! For now is the hour of my vengeance against the enemies of the Lord."

And they answered him with one voice: "Yea!"

They raised the war cry, and descending into the ravine now veiled milk-white with the mists of morning, advanced to the attack. And lo, when they came to the camp of the Philistines, and the light of day grew clear, and the sun shone, the whole host of them was in wild conflict, horsemen and chariot, none knowing friend from foe. Every man's sword was against his fellow, and there was a very great confusion. In the midst of it Israel swept down upon them; and they broke and fled.

Moreover, when the Hebrews that had treacherously joined the ranks of the raiders saw that the victory was with the king, they turned against the Philistines and fought with the Israelites under Saul and Jonathan. Report also that the Philistines were in flight spread far and wide, and the troops who had deserted the king, and the people who were in hiding among the forests and caves and mountains of Ephraim, flocked to Saul's standard, and followed hard after him in the battle.

So the Lord saved Israel, and the battle passed over and westward through the valley, and beyond the pass of Bethhoron. Ten thousand men of Israel fought with Saul that day, and the pursuit was scattered over all the mountainous country of Ephraim.

But as the day drew on and the sun rose high in the heavens and the heat increased, the men of Israel began to be sorely distressed for want of food. When the trumpet had sounded at dawn, few had broken their fast, and none since then had tasted a morsel, as Saul had decreed.

And those who were with Jonathan in the pursuit came soon after noon to a rocky waste where grew a few sparse trees, casting a dappled shade. And in the hollows of the rocks, above which the air shimmered like crystal in the heat, there was an abundance of honeycomb now deserted by the bees that had made it. The honey itself was oozing out from the crevices in the rocks, and revealed this hidden store. All who had heard the king's vow sped on, and tasted not, for they feared the curse that he had spoken.

But Jonathan, who knew nothing of it, and was even worse spent than any with him since he had neither stayed to rest nor eaten since nightfall, thrust into the honeycomb the battle-club that was in his hand and dipped it into the honey. He put his hand to his mouth and ate of the honey. Light came back into his eyes, and he was refreshed.

When one of those who came running after through the wood chanced to see it, he said to Jonathan: "Knowest thou not that thy father the king straitly charged the people with an oath saying: 'Cursed be the man that tasteth food this day'?"

Jonathan was sorely troubled, and ate no more of the honey. But he answered the man, and said: "Of a surety my father when he made such a vow knew not what trouble he would bring upon the troops of Israel. For see, now, though I have tasted but little of the honey, it has renewed my strength and refreshed me. How much better would it have been if everyone had done likewise and eaten freely of the spoil they have taken. Would there not by now have been a much greater slaughter among the Philistines?"

He continued the pursuit and hastened on. And Israel chased and routed the Philistines until, following the river, they came down through the valley of Ajalon and into the plain, above the city of Gath. There they turned back, for they were utterly exhausted. And they rushed upon the booty they had captured, and took of the sheep and oxen and slew them there where they found them, without offering any as a sacrifice of thanksgiving. They were famished and in distress.

When report of this was brought to Saul, he was angered that they had dealt unfaithfully with him, and he feared the wrath of God. He bade those who were about him roll a great stone that stood near into the open. Of this he made an altar. Then he sent out heralds: "Disperse yourselves among the people", he commanded them, "and bid every man you meet bring hither to me whatever living creature he hath taken from the Philistines, and let them be slain here before the altar of the Lord that they may eat, and sin no more by refraining from sacrifice."

The people obeyed, and every man of them, from that hour on and far into the night, brought his spoil to the altar, and all that was needed for food was slain there, and the blood sprinkled upon the stone. This was the first altar King Saul set up to the Lord.

The sun was now set, and dark was come. Seeing then that strength had returned into his troops, and that they were rested and renewed, Saul summoned his captains to meet him in council, and Ahiah, the priest of the Lord, was with him.

"The night comes," he said, "and the Philistines peradventure may think that our pursuit is at an end and that they are safe. Let us then up and follow after them before morning shall give them time and light to rally, smite them until daybreak and leave not a man of them alive."

His captains agreed. They were eager to follow him and filled with exultation. "Do whatever seems good to thee," they said.

But Ahiah the priest intervened between them. "Let not my lord", he said, "be in too great haste to decide in this matter, but first let us draw near to Jehovah, and pray for his guidance. Unless it be his will that Israel go down after the Philistines, thou shalt not prevail against them."

Saul consented, chafing at the delay. The priest withdrew and made entreaty to the Lord, but returned again to the king, troubled in mind, for though he had prayed long and earnestly, no assurance had entered into his soul of any answer to his prayer. And he counselled Saul to discover with whom lay the guilt of having transgressed that day.

Saul turned away from the priest in fury. His one desire was to seize the opportunity night gave him to press on after the Philistines and overwhelm them in such a disaster that for years to come they would never venture to raid the borders of Israel again.

But he remembered his vow and the curse he had uttered. God was against him. His kingdom was at stake. He had not the strength to stand alone. Why was not Samuel at his side, he asked himself again and again. And as he thus debated within himself, his wrath increased against the unknown transgressor who had estranged God from him and kept him back from the full glory of his vengeance.

He bade his captains stay with him, and sent out messengers to summon the chief men of Israel into his presence. They came in haste. Many of them had been wounded in the battle, and had but hastily bound up their wounds, and all were dishevelled and bloodstained, and covered with dust after the long pursuit. Last to come was Jonathan, who in certain hope that his father would continue the pursuit, had seized a moment in the lull that had followed the first onset to snatch a little sleep. Saul greeted him with a troubled smile, and Jonathan sat down beside him.

Then Saul stood up before the assembly and spoke: "God who watcheth over Israel", he said, "hath been very gracious to us this day, yet in the midst of our triumph it seems that by some man or men among us a wanton offence hath been committed against him, though how I cannot tell. What say you all? Shall we not by some sure means detect and discover this transgressor? Shall he not suffer for the outrage that he hath done against Israel? And how else shall this be made known—unless any of you can yourselves bear witness against him—except by consulting the oracle of God? Ay," he said to them, laying his hand on Jonathan's shoulder, "and even though the guilt lie with my own son Jonathan, he shall surely die."

And there was not one among them that answered him.

Then Saul sent a messenger to bring in Ahiah the priest, bidding him prepare to consult the oracle of God. The priest came in to them, clad in his linen ephod with the breastplate of judgment upon it. Its gems faintly glistened in the light of the torches. Then said Saul: "Let the oracle first declare whether the blame be with Israel or with Israel's king. And thou thyself, Jonathan," he added, "shall be of thy father's company."

So he bade the priest cast lots between all Israel on the one side and himself and Jonathan on the other.

"Is it your will", he said, turning again to the people, "that I should ask the Lord God Jehovah with whom lies the blame—on this side or on that?"

There was no voice to question it. "Do what seems good to thee," they said.

Then Saul called upon Jehovah before them all. "Lord God Jehovah," he cried, "I adjure thee to declare if the evil that has been done this day be with Israel or with me myself and my son Jonathan."

And Ahiah the priest thrust in his hand beneath the breastplate—*Urim* for Israel, and *Thummim* for Saul and Jonathan. And behold, when he withdrew his hand, the face of the stone which was uppermost was engraved with the Ineffable Name. The lot was against Saul and Jonathan.

None stirred or spoke. Saul's face darkened. He gazed at the priest, unable in his confusion to take in the full meaning of what he had said. But when it swept in upon him, and his glance roved on from one face to another of those gathered together around him, his mind was in bitter conflict. Zeal for the cause of Israel and the dread of breaking his vow had led him on to make his challenge; and now an awful doubt assailed him. But it was too late to draw back.

"Cast lots again," he bade the priest harshly. "And this time be it between me and my son Jonathan, and may God give the judgment. For as the Lord liveth, whichever one of us is shown to be guilty he shall die the death."

At this, cries of dissent arose on every side. Many started to their feet, entreating him to hold his hand. But the will of the king prevailed over them, and once more Ahiah drew the sacred stone from out of the breastplate, and cast the lot between Saul and his son Jonathan. And the lot was against Jonathan.

Then Saul turned himself about and gazed in fear and sorrow into Jonathan's face. "Tell me, my son," he said, "what hast thou done?"

And Jonathan told him everything that he had done that day, confessing openly before them all—how he himself as he ran in the forefront of the pursuit of the Philistines had come to a rocky hollow where a few sparse trees gave their shade and where wild bees had hidden their secret store of honey-comb, and how he had tasted of the honey, being sore spent.

"And even", he said, "as the sweetness was in my mouth, one running after me told me of the curse which thou thyself hadst uttered against any man that tasted food this day. I vow that until then no word of it had reached my ear. And I ate no more of the honey, yet was so refreshed by it that I stayed not from chasing after the Philistines until night came down. But now, seeing that I have sinned against the Lord, though I did it unwittingly, there is nought to say. Lo, I must die."

Saul heard him out in silence; his face grey as in death. Then he rose. "Be God himself witness this day between me and thee, Jonathan," he said. "And if I transgress against him, may he do unto me—and more also—as I do unto thee. Thou hast thyself confessed thy sin, and thou must die."

At this there broke out a loud and tumultuous outcry among all those assembled there.

"God forbid! God forbid!" they shouted. "Shall Jonathan die who hath wrought this great salvation in Israel! Two against a host! As the Lord liveth, there shall not one hair of his head fall to the ground! The Lord of Hosts was with him."

Those that stood near ranged themselves about Jonathan as a bodyguard, to defend him against his father. And the king was powerless to resist them. Without another word said, he turned away from them and withdrew himself, and went into his tent alone.

The tumult died away and silence fell upon the camp of Israel. That night they advanced no further, and the remnant of the army of the Philistines that had escaped the slaughter returned unmolested into their own country.

# King Agag

There was war with the princes of the Philistines as long as Saul lived, and in his last dark days, when his kingdom was divided, he himself, wounded and in flight with his sons, and pursued by their archers and charioteers, died a miserable death. And his body was hung on the wall of Beth-shan.

But for many years he remained undisputed king over Israel, and proved his valour and leadership. He led the armies of Israel against their enemies on every side, against Moab, whose king Barak in years long gone by endeavoured in vain to bribe Balaam with his divinations to curse Israel. These were the people, worshippers of Chemosh, whose king Eglon had been slain by Ehud, judge of Israel, with his own hand, two hundred and fifty years before.

Saul warred also against the wandering tribes of the Ammonites, whom he had defeated at Jabesh; and against Edom, whose territory was far south towards the desert of Sinai, and in the north he defeated the King of Zoba.

And his sons, Jonathan and Ishbaal, fought with him. The names of his daughters were Merab and Michal. And Michal, the younger of them, was very fair and beautiful and of a quick, resolute spirit. The name of the captain who was commander-in-chief of the army under Saul himself, was Abner. He was a cousin of the king's, the son of his father's brother.

During the first few years of his reign Samuel remained

the king's chief counsellor. In matters of moment Saul sought and followed his advice, and did him honour. So far also as his great age admitted, Samuel continued to administer justice, and he was feared and reverenced throughout Israel as the prophet chosen of God to reveal his will to the people. But as Saul waxed in power and his conquests won him renown, even the thought of any authority to which he himself must bow began to vex and burden him. His confidence in his own wisdom increased; he became wayward and despotic, and the desire to amass riches had entered into his soul.

Now of the ancient enemies of Israel there was none they hated more bitterly than the Amalekites. Even when, four hundred years gone, the Israelites were but a host of wandering and fugitive tribesmen in the Arabian desert, Amalek had been their unrelenting and treacherous foe. They had harassed Israel without mercy, cutting off and massacring any feeble stragglers whom they found lost and helpless in the wilderness.

At Rephidim in those far days, after a long and stubborn conflict, Joshua had defeated them in battle, and Moses had watched and prayed on a hilltop the whole day long, the vantage now going to the one side, now to the other—the staff of God in his hand. But the Amalekites, one of the oldest races of man on earth, were of a fierce and untamable spirit, and they had recovered their strength. In the days of the Judges they had allied themselves with King Eglon of Moab; and, afterwards, with the Midianites they had raided the southern borders of Canaan, destroying the people's crops, their flocks and their herds, and had spared no living thing.

Moses himself had made written record for a memorial that there would be no enduring peace in Israel until the power of Amalek had been finally broken, and they had been blotted out.

When Saul had established himself in his kingdom, and Israel was at peace, there came a day when Samuel set out to visit him at his house in Gibeah. Long time had passed since they had met. The king had neglected and ignored him. But to all outward appearance he greeted the prophet graciously and with the reverence due to his age and office. He dismissed his attendants and led him into a quiet inner chamber where they could talk alone.

And Samuel announced to Saul that he had come before him with a message from the Lord. "I would first recall to thy mind", he said, "the day when I was sent to anoint thee to be king over his people. Thou wast then, even in thine own sight, of little account in Israel. Is it truth that I have spoken? Dost thou still acknowledge his authority as it is made manifest through me, his prophet; for apart from him, I ask nothing of thee, nor claim any right to intervene between thyself and thy people?"

Saul bowed his head in assent.

"Hearken, then," said Samuel, "unto the words of the Lord who has sent me hither to thee this day. Thou hast grown strong and mighty; thy word is law in Israel. And now it is the Lord's will that the grievous wrongs which Amalek did against his people after they had been redeemed from Egypt and were as yet a nation of wanderers without a country, weak and ill-armed, shall be avenged, and that justice shall be meted out to them. Arise, then. Gather together thine armies; proclaim a holy war. Summon all Israel to thy standard; and march against Amalek. As for their king, Agag, spare him not, nor any of his people, man, woman or child, nor anything that is his or theirs. They are accursed. Take no spoil or plunder, nothing; neither ox nor sheep nor camel nor ass. Utterly destroy them. Even as the Amalekites vowed to do unto Israel, so do thou unto them."

Saul heard him in silence; his eyes bent upon the ground. The thing said pleased him greatly, though he misliked the manner of it. He had long looked with envy on King Agag and lusted to go out against him, and defeat and despoil him. And now Jehovah himself had declared his will. Proclamation of a holy war against such an enemy as this would rouse all Israel, and victory was assured. He lifted his head. His keen dark strange eyes rested a moment on Samuel's face, then faltered and turned away. He vowed solemnly that in all things as Samuel had bidden him, he would obey.

As he had foreseen, when heralds were sent from city to city summoning the people to fight against Amalek, they were enflamed with zeal and ardour. They flocked to his standard and joined the army that was already fully prepared for war, and was mustered at Telaim. And Saul numbered the host that was with him: two hundred thousand men of Israel, spearmen, slingers and bowmen, and ten thousand men of Judah.

Word came to the king that the Kenites, another wandering tribe of the desert who in times long past had been in alliance with Israel, had now joined themselves with the forces under King Agag. Saul therefore sent an envoy to the leaders of the Kenites, assuring them that neither he himself nor his people had any quarrel with them, but remembered well how of old time they had shown kindness to Israel when they had fled out of Egypt and had crossed the Red Sea into the wilderness. He bade the envoy make known to the Kenites how mighty a host he had gathered together, and to adjure them to sever themselves from the Amalekites while there was yet time; lest in the heat and fury of battle they should suffer the fate that awaited King Agag.

The chieftains of the Kenites, having debated the matter in secret, sent back a friendly answer to the king, raised their camp, and withdrew into the desert.

Then Saul marched south against the city of Amalek where King Agag was encamped. He divided his army to hem him in, and he himself with a strong force advanced under cover of night and lay in wait in the valley. When battle was joined, fierce and bloody was the conflict. And, though the Amalekites fought on bravely and recklessly until the sun was declining in the west and even hope was gone, the armies of Saul prevailed against them, and of the bodyguard of King Agag not a man was left alive, though he himself was taken.

The troops of Israel pursued the remnant of his tribesmen from Havilah even to the fortified city of Shur on the eastern borders of Egypt. And the city of Amalek was taken and the whole camp with all its spoil, and every living creature found therein of the race of Amalek was put to the sword. Except only Agag. He was brought by Abner to the king, who in the flush and pride of victory spared his life to grace his triumph.

And though Saul gave strict orders that of the booty captured from the enemy all that was of little use and value was to be destroyed, he spared the best of the cattle and the fattest of the sheep and lambs. Moreover, the costliest of the Amalekites' tents and raiment, their vessels of silver and gold, the jewels, furniture and weapons of the king, and the ornaments and apparel of his women—these were taken and brought into the camp to Saul.

All else was burned with fire; and throughout that night the skies above the desert were red with the flames of its destruction.

When the troops of Israel had returned from the pursuit,
Saul, with his rich booty in cattle and kind and with King
Agag in his train, returned into Canaan and marched to
Carmel. There he set up a pillar of stone as a trophy and
memorial of his great victory, and thence he went to Gilgal.

That night the word of the Lord came to Samuel in a
vision as he lay sleeping upon his bed. In the silence or
dream the divine call troubled him: "It repenteth me that
I have set up Saul to be king over my people Israel. He
hath rejected me, and hath not obeyed my command-
ment."

[ 385 ]

Samuel awoke, and that night slept no more. He was grieved to the soul for Saul, and angered against the Lord, and throughout the long dark hours until daybreak he prayed without ceasing, interceding for one whom he loved so dearly. Early next morning he set out on his journey to the king. He had been told by men of Ramah, disbanded from the army after the defeat of the Amalekites, who were returning home, that Saul had tarried awhile at Carmel, had there set up a trophy and was now with his troops at Gilgal.

Samuel continued on his way, heavy at heart, but with all speed. He came to Gilgal and, mounted on his ass, made his way through the thronging camp to the king's tent. He dismissed the one servant that was with him, passed by the guard, and alone and unannounced entered into the tent and stood before Saul.

The floor of the tent was heaped up with the most precious of the booty that had been captured from Amalek. Saul himself with the officers who were in attendance upon him sat in splendour. A great feast had been prepared that day, and he himself was about to appear before the army drawn up in readiness to receive him at the sacred circle of stones where he had been proclaimed king.

At Samuel's entry he rose hastily. His mind misgave him at sight of the old man's face, cold and austere, from which every token of tenderness and affection was gone. But having dismissed those who were with him, he greeted him as if all were well between them.

"Blessed be thou of the Lord," he said. "Thou hast come at a fair and prosperous moment, for I have done all that thou wouldst have me do, according to the will of Jehovah."

He seated himself again and invited Samuel to sit beside him. But even as he spoke, he turned away his head, unable to meet the grief and anger in Samuel's eyes.

The prophet stood unmoved before him. "If thou hast done all that I bade thee do," he said, "what means this bleating of sheep in my ears, and this lowing of oxen in the camp of Israel?"

"These sheep, these oxen?" said Saul. "They are the spoil taken by the armies of Israel from the Amalekites. They spared only the choicest of their flocks and herds wherewith to make sacrifice to the Lord thy God. All that remained of the booty I have utterly destroyed."

But his voice rang false even in his own ears. He raised his hand as if to continue speaking, but Samuel broke in upon him.

"Stay," he said, "and I will tell thee what the Lord himself said to me this night that is gone."

With set face Saul sat confronting him. "Say on," he said.

Then said Samuel: "When thou wast a man of nought, who chose thee to be chieftain of all Israel, head and sovereign of the tribes? Was it not the Lord himself who anointed thee? And did he not of late send thee on thy way in the glory of his service to lead Israel against the accursed and idolatrous Amalekites, that again and again have afflicted his people? 'Go,' he said, 'spare not, but destroy them utterly and everything that is theirs.' But what in truth hast thou done? Why hast thou refused to obey the voice of the Lord? Why, like a ravenous bird from out of the mountains, didst thou swoop down upon the spoil and do that which is evil in his sight? By all the love I bear thee, I entreat thee to confess that thou hast sinned and to plead to him for mercy."

A dark frown had gathered on Saul's brow. His voice shook as with eyes averted he answered Samuel.

"Thou dost me wrong," he said. "As the Lord com-

manded, I have obeyed. Did I not send couriers throughout
the length and breadth of Israel, proclaiming a holy war?
Was I of so little account and so cold in my zeal for Jehovah
that none answered or lifted hand from the plough? Thou
thyself knowest this to be false; for when the people heard
my call, they left all to follow me. Two hundred thousand
men of Israel and ten thousand men of Judah—for the
glory of Israel they flocked to my standard. Did I pause or
falter or parley with these accursed Amalekites? Not so; I
marched with my armies against them and having won
away with fair words the tribes of the Kenites from their
alliance, I swept down upon them and utterly defeated
them. The smouldering ruins of Amalek bear witness
against thee. Only Agag, their king, did I save alive, and
this but for proof that he who was the dread and terror of
all Israel is now a mere cringing captive slave and at my
mercy. How then canst thou rebuke me if the men of Israel
in their lust for plunder spared a few of the enemy's sheep
and oxen, and these only the best and choicest, and destroyed—as I bade them—all else. They are but men.
Wouldst thou deny them even that? How otherwise could
they make fitting sacrifice to the Lord thy God, even here
in his sacred place at Gilgal?"

Then said Samuel: "Thinkest thou the Lord God delights in sacrifices and offerings as much as he delights in
them that humbly obey him? Obedience is better than
sacrifice, and to heed faithfully what he bids thee do is
better than any gift on earth thou canst bring him of mere
gold or jewels or any worldly treasure. Knowest thou not
that rebellion against him is wicked as witchcraft, and a
stubborn heart as blasphemous as the worship of idols?
Hearken, now, for it is the Lord himself who speaks to thee.
Because thou hast rejected him, he also hath rejected thee.

As from nothing he raised thee up, so shall he abase thee. The day of thy downfall draws near, and thou shalt be king in his sight no longer."

Saul rose vehemently, his armour clashing as he moved. He strode to the door of his tent. Except for the sentries on watch there, no one was near. He turned, his face transfixed with dread at the old man's solemn maledictions, flung himself on his knees before him, and besought his forgiveness.

"Take back thy words. Have pity on me," he cried. "I see now that I have sinned. I have in truth transgressed and done other than thou didst strictly bid me do. But it was not of my own will. I feared the people, and they prevailed against me. When, drunken with victory, the armies of Israel had driven in the plunder they had taken from the Amalekites, their flocks, their herds, how could I give orders that all should be destroyed? They would have risen in revolt against me; and in weakness I consented to do what they asked of me. I entreat thee now, by all the love and forbearance thou once didst show me, forgive this evil that I have done, and restore me to thy kindness as of old. Come with me even now, that we may pray together and give thanks to the Lord God for his victory in the presence of all Israel."

But Samuel drew back from Saul as he knelt before him. "No," he said, "I will not go with thee. Nor will I show thee honour before the people. In thy pride and avarice thou hast wantonly rejected the Lord, and from this day forth he hath rejected thee."

He turned about to leave the king. In a frenzy of despair Saul seized the skirt of his outer mantle, and it was rent in his grasp. And Samuel's wrath flamed against him.

"Lo, now," he cried, "in fear of what men shall think of thee, thine own hand hath witnessed against thee! For this day hath the Lord rent the sceptre of Israel from thy grasp and shall give it to another who is better than thou. Thinkest thou that the Eternal, the glory of Israel, can be false to himself and turn aside from doing that on which he hath set his will? Thinkest thou the Lord is as man whom he created out of dust, whose heart changes with every wind that blows and who is never of the same mind from one day to another. He hath spoken; and this is the end between us."

But in his horror and misery Saul still strove to persuade Samuel to show him at least the outward marks of honour and respect in the presence of his captains and the elders and people of Israel.

"I beseech thee," he said, "abandon me not now lest Israel be divided and rebel against me, and worse evils follow. For this sake only let it but seem there is nothing amiss. Come now, we will go together and give praise to the Lord thy God!"

At sight of Saul weeping and abased before him, one whom in spite of all his folly and falsities he still loved, Samuel consented to do as Saul asked of him, and they went out together from the shade of the tent into the heat and splendour of noonday.

Saul sent for Abner, and the trumpets sounded. The army of Israel had ranged itself under its captains, according to its regiments and companies, and stood awaiting the king in the wide open space before the great circle of hoary stones. And Samuel bade Abner send a guard and bring King Agag before him.

In sight of the whole host, the captive king was led trembling into his presence. In his silken robes, the emblems of kingship stripped from brow and neck and shoulder, he walked delicately, scarcely able to draw one foot after the other, so sharp was the agony of his soul.

One swift glance into the prophet's face revealed that all hope was gone. He saw the doom that was close upon him. Terror seized him. He turned to Saul, pleading for mercy.

"Of a truth," he said, "thou canst not have held me captive these many days to vaunt thyself over me, the mock and scorn of my enemies, only to destroy me now? Surely the bitterness of death is past?"

Saul looked coldly on him, turned away and made no answer.

Then Samuel himself drew the sword of the king from out of its sheath, and faced Agag. He gazed at him steadfastly and Agag quailed before him.

"Thy sword", said Samuel, "hath slain and spared not. Thou hast made many women of Israel childless. So now shall thy mother be childless among women."

And in the sight of the whole host of Israel he smote off King Agag's head and hewed his body in pieces.

# DAVID

# He is Anointed King
## over Israel

Samuel returned from Gilgal to his house at Ramah, and came no more to Saul. Nor from that day onward, except once, did he ever again in this life speak with the king face to face. Saul hardened his heart against his one true counsellor. In his pride he heeded him not and refrained from asking his guidance. He was a law to himself, inflexible against his enemies, and he fought valiantly for Israel. Yet in spite of his ascendancy and the glory he had won, he found no peace of mind and heart.

He doubted the loyalty even of those most faithful to him, and hours of violence and fury were followed by days of voiceless dejection. The divine grace, that had once been his, no longer guided and comforted him. Thankless and ungenerous, every remembrance of Samuel, and of his loving-kindness when his own need was greatest, only goaded him on to an obstinate enmity. But though he refused to do him honour, he secretly feared him, and his fear engendered hatred.

Nevertheless Samuel remained faithful to the king. His own authority was gone, except as the prophet of God. But neither absence from the king nor the indignities of neglect made any change in his love for Saul. He ceased not to grieve for him, remembering the wondrous promise he had seen in his face when as a humble stranger seeking for the strayed asses of his father, Saul had drawn near to speak with him that morning now long gone by, and the voice within his own heart had cried: "Lo, the king of Israel!"

He strove to put out of mind the king's stubborn ingratitude. He knew well that fear alone of what might follow prevented Saul from showing his enmity and seeking to destroy him. In his desolation he continued to intercede for him. But the word of the Lord came at length to Samuel in his solitude at Ramah: "How long wilt thou mourn for Saul, seeing that I have rejected him from reigning over Israel? Put away thy grief. Fill thine horn with oil, and go; for I will send thee to Bethlehem. There among the sons of Jesse I have found me a king."

And Samuel knew that it was the voice of God that bade him do this thing to his own great sorrow. He prayed earnestly, seeking in vain for reasons against at once obeying it.

"How can I go?" he asked himself again and again. "If the king should hear that such a thought has even come into my mind, he will surely kill me."

But the voice within answered him again: "Doubt not; the Lord will be with thee. Thou shalt take a heifer with thee and when thou comest to Bethlehem thou shalt say that thou hast come to sacrifice to the Lord. And thou shalt call Jesse to the sacrifice with his sons. Tarry then until the voice of God within thee shall assure thee what thou must do. Then shalt thou arise and anoint him whom the Lord hath chosen."

With a heavy heart the old grief-stricken man made his few preparations and at early morning set out with his servant.

The day was fresh and sweet, and as he approached it, the

village of Bethlehem, built on high amid its valleys on the spur of a hill, and surrounded by vineyards, and groves of olive and almond trees, lay still and tranquil as though in a dream. Samuel continued on his way through the fields of wheat and barley, and mounted the steep path that would bring him into the village.

The approach of these two solitary wayfarers had been seen from afar by some of the elders of Bethlehem. They stood in watch, and when they saw that one of them, the old man with hooded head and long silver beard—the ass on which he was riding led gently on by the servant who was with him—was the dreaded prophet Samuel himself, they hastened out to greet him. They bowed themselves before him, filled with misgiving. Why had this messenger of God come now to visit them?

"Cometh my lord peaceably?" they asked him. "Bringest thou good tidings or tidings of evil?"

And Samuel made answer: "Peaceably. Be not afraid. I am come to make sacrifice unto the Lord."

He bade them purify themselves and prepare for the sacrifice and for the feast that would follow after it, and enquired where he would find one named Jesse who lived in the city.

He was taken to his house, and as soon as he was within, he drew Jesse apart and talked with him alone. He asked him concerning his sons, and bade him bring them in that he might sanctify them, and himself prepare them for the sacrifice. To this he bade them come one and all, and to the feast. Jesse hastened to obey him, striving in vain to find a reason why he himself of all the chief men of the city had been singled out for this honour. He made the prophet welcome. He waited upon him and showed him the courtesy and reverence befitting his high office. Meanwhile he had sent out servants to call in his sons from their work or wherever they might be.

When they were ready, each one of them in turn was brought into the presence of Samuel, whose whole mind was intent on the supreme purpose that had brought him to Bethlehem that day.

Eliab, who was the eldest of Jesse's sons, was the first to pass before him. He was a man of great stature and of a bold and resolute face. And when Samuel looked on him he said within himself: "Surely the Lord's anointed stands here with me in his presence!" For in all things that are clear and impressive at first view Eliab was such a man as Samuel himself delighted in. The thought pierced him, for it recalled to memory the day when he had first seen Saul.

But the divine voice within him cried its warning: "Be not misled, look not with favour on this man for the sake of his countenance, his confidence and his stature. He is not the Lord's chosen. The Lord seeth not as man seeth. The eyes of man look only on the outward appearance, but the Lord looketh on the heart."

Then Jesse summoned Abinadab, the next of his sons in order of age, into the presence of the prophet. But neither was Abinadab the chosen of the Lord. Nor Shammah, Jesse's third son. So each one of Jesse's seven sons who were with him in the house was brought before Samuel, and his eyes dwelt on each face in turn with the same grave scrutiny. But still he knew in his heart that none of them was the man whom he was seeking.

So all at last had come and gone their way. Perplexed yet serene, Samuel pondered within himself awhile, then turned to Jesse: "Are these young men whom I have seen", he asked him, "all thy sons? For of a truth none of them is he whom I am seeking and whom the Lord has chosen to honour."

And Jesse answered: "There remains only the youngest of them. He is little more than a child, and very dear to me, and he is now in the fields keeping the sheep."

Then Samuel bade Jesse send at once to fetch him. "We will not sit down to the feast", he said, "until he come hither."

A servant was dispatched in haste. He ran down from out of the city into the pastures that lay in the green valleys to look for the boy and to bring him in. He found him sitting with his sheep, his shepherd's pipe in his hand, and he returned with him to his father.

So David came in from the fields, and stood before Samuel. He was in the first brightness of his youth, being not yet even of the age of Joseph when he set out from the Vale of Hebron in his coat of many colours in search of his brothers. He was blue-eyed and ruddy, with wind and sun, of a beautiful countenance withal and goodly to look to. He bowed himself before the prophet, solemnly, like a boy, and marvelling for what reason he had been called in from his sheep.

The old man gazed steadily into his clear wide eyes; and the voice within him which he had learned to heed and to obey since his own childhood, cried within him. "Arise, anoint him, for this is he!"

Then in the presence of Jesse his father and of his seven sons Samuel arose and took the horn of holy oil that he had brought with him from Ramah, and poured it upon David's head and anointed him.

And Samuel blessed him and talked with him alone. And the spirit of the Lord entered into the heart of David and was with him from that day forward. And Jesse and all his sons accompanied Samuel to the sacrifice that morning and to the feast.

On the morrow David went back to the fields to his sheep, and Samuel himself, his mind burdened with sadness and yet at peace in that his mission had been fulfilled, returned to Ramah.

No word of this reached the ears of the king. But there came a day when Saul fell again grievously sick of the malady that had afflicted his mind in the last few years of his life. Pestered with evil thoughts that he had no power to master or divert, he spent his days in anguish and lost to all sense of those around him. And in memory he dwelt continually on the hour when alone in his tent, rich with plunder of the Amalekites, he had fallen on his knees in supplication before Samuel, and the prophet had foretold that his kingdom would not continue and that he had been rejected of the Lord. No true peace had been his since then. In his pride he had striven in vain against the thought that the well-spring of the divine which had once refreshed his spirit was now parched up for ever. The dreadful conviction assailed him that he had been abandoned of God.

All things that of old had once pleased and satisfied him had become bitter as ashes in his mouth. He was haunted by terrors of the unknown and by vacant forebodings. He lay in his tent, parched with fever, hating the light, rejecting all human company, and pining for death to ease him of his misery. He found neither rest by day nor quiet sleep by night.

As soon as his heavy eyelids closed in slumber, evil and hideous dreams thronged into his mind, and he would awake in a frenzy of fear seeking in vain for help and refuge. Even in the full brightness of morning he would be seized by sudden dread, and with fixed and starting eyes, like a watchman on his tower in the dark of winter, would cry out in a wild hollow voice as though he were pursued by an enemy or a dreadful apparition were come to share his solitude.

His attendants and physicians sought by every means in their power to relieve his malady and to restore him to health; but in vain. Their skill was of no avail to aid him. And when all other remedies had proved vain, they bethought themselves of music, since music has a strange power to soothe a troubled mind and to charm away afflicting thoughts.

When next there came a respite in his sickness, and with mind a little quietened, he was able to grasp the import of what was said to him, his physicians spoke of this. It was, they told him, no bodily ailment from which he pined, spent though he was and sick to death; it must be that some spirit not of this earth but of the divine was troubling him. And they assured him that if only its evil influence could be banished out of his mind, he would be well.

"Let now my lord", said one of them, "command his servants that they seek out a musician who has skill in the playing of the harp. And it shall be when this dread horror of soul come upon thee again, and thou hear the strains of his music, it will soothe and comfort thee, and will banish this evil spirit and thou shalt sleep and be refreshed."

Saul heard them in patience, his head sunken between his shoulders, his eyes hollow and lightless, and he bade them provide him with such a man without delay and bring him to his bedside. His physicians left him. They made inquiry of the king's servants, and one of them told that there was a lad, the son of Jesse the Bethlehemite, who was skilled in music and in the playing of the harp.

"I myself know him well," he said, "for I am of Bethlehem. I have sate beside him in the wild, listening enravished

while he played and sang; and the birds mute to hear him!
Even though he has no more knowledge of the world than
what comes of keeping his father's sheep, he is of a rare
courage and prudence, and of a fair and beautiful countenance. He is one that can be trusted to keep silence, and the
Lord is with him."

When Saul heard this he took comfort. A longing and desire for music, like water to one athirst, had sprung up within him, as it were a gourd in the night. He bade his physicians delay not a moment but send at once to Bethlehem
and bring this young shepherd in.

When these messengers came to the house of Jesse and
told him their errand, he was troubled. It pleased him that
David should have been well spoken of to the king, but
three of his sons had already been taken to serve in Saul's
army, and he feared that he might now be deprived of his
youngest son also.

None the less he made ready a present for the king, the
best he could afford. He saddled an ass, and laded it with
ten loaves of wheaten bread, a skin of wine from his own
vineyard and the choicest of his kids. With a change of
raiment besides, and all that he would need during his
absence, David set out next day. He kissed his father, and
bade him farewell, and hastened away.

He was young, the day was sweet and early, the way new
to him; and he soon thought no more of the fears and misgivings that had troubled his dreams the night before. He
watched the morning colours in the sky as though they
were a forecast of the future, and his ass, though dumb, was
far better than no company at all.

It was dark when he reached his journey's end, and when
the king's physicians had spoken with him privily and
warned him of the condition of the king, he was brought

into Saul's presence. And he took with him his nine-stringed harp.

The royal tent was lit only by the single flame of a lamp which with a cruse of water stood at the bed's head. In the wafting of the air it cast distorted shadows into the gloom beyond. The king lay stretched out upon a low and heavy bedstead, a purple coverlet over him, a pillow of goat's hair for his bolster, and his arms relaxed at his sides. His wasted brows were drawn with anguish, and his face wan. At sound of David's entrance he turned his head, and his dark, brilliant, fever-haunted eyes rested upon the clear young face and found peace there. His heart went out to him; he smiled, and sighed.

David knelt before him, and with a gesture Saul bade him rise and play. So night after night David shared Saul's solitude, broken only by the occasional entry of one of his servants or physicians, until in the cold small hours of morning he himself grew faint for want of sleep, his plucking fingers loosened upon his harp-strings, and his head nodded where he sat.

Then of a sudden Saul, muttering restlessly in his slumber, would awake, start up from his bed, and stare in empty terror into the gloom, as if in challenge of some appalling phantom before his very eyes. He would thrust out his hand, seize upon the spear which stood with his armour at his bedside, and sit trembling and aghast, or be filled with a blind and speechless fury.

And David would come near and reassure him, "Alas, my lord, be not dismayed; see, it is I, David."

He would touch the king's hand to prove that he was near and real, and then would return to his playing. And Saul would be pacified. He would fix his eyes on him and watch him like a child, and drink in with his music the

vision of his face. Even in his darkest moments David had no fear of the king. At that time there was only love between them.

The music he conjured from his harp-strings gave speech to thoughts and feelings no words of his could tell. For alone with his sheep he had been wont, though unwittingly, to let the peaceful scenes stretched out before him well into his mind, to be in memory transmuted into music. And for song he had taught himself melodies and laments so ancient that even the children of the Hebrews had been lulled to sleep with them when their fathers were in thrall to Pharaoh and Goshen was their land of bondage. So Saul's nightmare terrors and evil imaginations would ebb out of his mind and pass away. He would sink back exhausted upon his bed, and fall into a heavy sleep, his haggard face so cold and changeless that it might be that of the dead, or hewn out of stone.

The days went by; his malady gradually left him, and only rest and quiet were now needed to restore his wasted strength and make him whole.

And David returned home again to his father in Bethlehem, and to his customary life in the fields with his sheep. All that had passed during his dark hours of sickness was blotted out of the memory of the king.

# Goliath

When again the Philistines gathered an army together for war, they marched into the territory of Judah, and pitched their camp above the Valley of Elah, and on the steeps of a mountain ridge west of Bethlehem. And the host of Israel lay on the northern height of the valley, so that the two armies were face to face, and in sight one of another; the Philistines occupying the mountain on the one side, and Saul and his army occupying the mountain on the other side, with the wide valley and ravine between them. Through this ravine a pebbly brook coursed down among its rocks from the mountains above.

Now in the ranks of the Philistines at this time was a giant of prodigious strength and girth and stature, whose name was Goliath. He was of the city of Gath, and his four sons who were as yet in their childhood there, grew up to be giants like him; and one of them had six fingers on either hand, and on either foot six toes. From the crown of his head to the sole of his foot Goliath stood six cubits and a span. And he was the champion of the army of the Philistines.

While the day of battle was still in the balance, and neither army moved, morning and evening this Goliath would issue out from among the tents of the camp of the Philistines, stride down into the valley and there, in full view of both armies, would roar out his challenge, defying all Israel. Unlike his fellows in the ranks who were dressed in kilts with a pleated head-cap strapped under the chin, and who, apart from spear and broad-sword, carried only a two-handled shield or wore a cuirass of leather, he was clad from head to foot in armour of brass. A helmet of bronze was upon his head; a bronze coat of mail loose and supple covered his body, the scales of it overlapping one above another like the scales of a fish; and it weighed five thousand shekels of brass. Greaves also of bronze covered his shins, and a javelin of bronze hung between his shoulders. The haft of the spear he carried was like the beam of a weaver's loom, and the pointed head of iron upon it weighed six hundred shekels. And there went out before him a crook-backed Philistine who in stature was a dwarf by comparison, and he carried the giant's shield.

Now when this champion had bawled his challenge, and no man made answer, he would begin to taunt and mock at the Israelites.

"Why, forsooth," he would shout against them, "have you come out in your rabble against the Philistines, and why have you set yourselves in battle array, seeing that the quarrel between us may be decided here and now. Here stand I, a warrior of the princes of Philistia; and there sit you, servants of Saul. If there be any man among you with the courage of a sheep, drive him down to meet me, face to face. For I swear by Dagon that if he prevail against me and kill me, then shall the Philistines become the slaves of Israel, to hew them wood and draw them water. But if, as I surely shall, I prevail against him, and fell him to the dust with this spear in my hand, then shall Israel be the slaves of the Philistines. Hai, now! Yet again this day I defy the armies of Israel. If man among you there is none to meet

DAVID

me, call on Jehovah to smite me with his thunderbolt! Peradventure he will answer!"

He clashed with his spear upon his breastplate, shouting derision. And the troops of Israel who heard him were dismayed. There were many men among them of tried valour and skill in battle, but not one ready to go out against this giant in single combat, with even a hope of triumphing over him. And defeat would bring disaster.

So morning and evening, Goliath would come striding down out of the camp of the Philistines, yell aloud his challenge, and pour out his taunts and insults. And the Philistines laughed to hear him.

Now of the eight sons of Jesse, who was himself too old for the hardships of war, the three eldest, Eliab, Abinadab and Shammah, were serving in the ranks of the army under Saul. But David, the youngest, was with his father in Bethlehem, keeping his sheep.

When one evening he returned home, his father bade him set out on the morrow for the camp of the army of Israel to see how his brothers fared.

"And take with thee", he said, "a bushel of this parched corn, and these ten loaves and these ten cheeses; and run to the camp and bring me news, for it is many days since we had word of them."

The parched or roasted corn and the flat round loaves were for David's brothers, and the curd cheeses were for a present to the captain in command of their thousand. For Saul and they themselves and all the men of Israel were above the valley of Elah, confronting the Philistines.

Next morning, then, as soon as the first flush of dawn appeared in the sky, David rose up and having left his sheep in charge of a herdsman, set out for the camp, a journey of twelve miles. He went rejoicing on his way. After the brief time he had spent in the service of the king, he had fretted at remaining at home with his father, keeping his sheep. He pined to be with his brothers, fighting for Israel.

When he came to the hills on which Saul's army was in-trenched, the whole camp was astir. For army against army, Israel and the Philistines were ready and in array. He heard that battle might be joined that very morning. On fire with eagerness to see what was afoot, David gave all that he had brought with him into the hands of the keeper who had charge of the baggage, and ran off with all speed to seek out his brothers. Their quarters were in the forefront of the camp. There he found them and saluted them. "Peace be with you!" he said. And he gave them his father's message, and talked with them there.

And as he talked with them, his eyes ranged eagerly over the camp of the Philistines on the heights above and beyond the valley. Their bright-dyed tents in the crystal clear air shone in their colours in the sun. He could even count their chariots with their horses and charioteers. And the moun-tain-side was thick with men moving—like an ant-hill in midsummer, when its warriors prepare to sally out to attack a neighbouring tribe.

Curious and intent, he watched every movement, and at the same time questioned his brothers of what he saw, the numbers, the regiments, the commanders, the chances of the battle.

The day was yet early, and even as he watched, there showed a stir on the outskirts of the enemy's camp, and there issued out of it from among the host of the Philistines, smalled in the distance and alone but for his armour-bearer, the giant, Goliath.

With slow and ponderous tread he advanced down the slope into the valley until he was a little beyond midway between the two camps, and a rabble of his comrades followed after him, though afar off.

He came to a standstill, and brandishing his bronze-tipped spear on high, he cried out as he had cried before, and roared out his challenge against Israel. The hoarse echoes of his voice rang among the hills; the sun beat down upon the burnished fish-scales of his armour, and gleamed upon his helm. David could well-nigh see the glittering of his eyes in his great face.

At sight of him he had fallen silent. He stood stock-still like an image carved out of wood, his gaze fixed on Goliath, his heart wildly beating, while his ears drank in the vile and boastful words he uttered. At sound of his mighty voice the Israelitish troops who had been filling their water-pots at the stream-side and those who were on the fringes of the camp, fled back before him, for they were sore afraid. When David saw it, a frown gathered on his brow. He turned to those who stood near.

"Who is this accursed Philistine?" he asked them. "And how comes it that he dare insult and defy the armies of the living God? What man has been chosen to go out to meet him, and what shall be done to him when he hath laid him low, and hath washed away this shame and reproach against Israel?"

The soldiers who stood by told David that no man had yet been chosen or had dared to go out to meet the giant, but that any who accepted his challenge and met him face to face and killed him would not only be enriched with great riches but that the king himself would give him his own daughter in marriage, and from that day onward his father's whole house, whosoever he might be, would be made free men in Israel. And David hearkened, pondering what they said.

But when his eldest brother, Eliab, heard him talking, he turned on him fiercely, hot with anger. He remembered the day when the great prophet Samuel had come to Bethlehem and he himself had been set aside, and this stripling, the youngest of them all, had been blessed by the prophet and anointed with the holy oil. And he had been filled with envy when he heard that David had been summoned to court by the king.

"Who bade thee come idling here," he said, "leaving thy poor little flock of sheep with some herd-boy in the wilds? Oh, but I know thee of old, thy pride and presumption and the naughtiness of thy heart. Thou art puffed up with self-will, and it is not to bring a message from our father that thou hast come into the camp, but to see the fighting."

But David answered him, "What is it I have done amiss? I did but ask a question, and thou canst not deny it is one that needs an answer."

He turned away from his brother, and continued to question those who stood near, and one and all gave him the answer that had been given him already.

"But look now," he adjured them earnestly, "this boaster, monster though he be, is but a man. Weighed down with brass he moves as clumsily as an ox, and his face at least is naked. Why is he allowed to live, defying Jehovah?"

Seeing at length, though he was still little more than a boy, that David's scorn of the champion of the Philistines and his shame for Israel sprang from the courage of his very soul, these men reported the matter to their captain, who himself questioned David, and brought him to the tent of the king.

David stood beside Saul's standard while the captain went within. Then the captain led him into the tent where Saul sat, with Abner and his chief officers in attendance upon him; and David stood before the king. He bowed himself before Saul, and being questioned, said simply what was in his mind. He told the king why he had come into the camp, and how he had chanced to hear the champion of the Philistines shout his challenge against Israel, and that he had spoken only as his own soul had declared.

"Why", he said, "should any heart in Israel be faint with fear because of this man, this enemy of the Lord? Thy servant would himself go out and fight with the Philistine."

The king looked on him and marvelled, questioning within himself where he had seen his face before. But there came back no clear remembrance of the shepherd-boy who had sat beside him as he lay sick, and had solaced the dread and horror in his mind with the music of his harp.

"Of a truth," he said, "there is no doubt of thy valour. But what hope hast thou of prevailing against him? Thou art but a youth and hast had no experience in arms, while this Goliath hath been a man of war from the day when he was first able to carry a spear. He would disdain thee, my son, and snap thee in twain between his fingers."

But David pleaded with the king. He said how in days gone by, when he had sat keeping his father's sheep alone in the wild, at one time a bear and at another a young lion had sprung out from its ambush in the rocks and thickets near by, and had seized and carried off a lamb from his flock.

"So I went out after him," he said, "and chased him, and snatched his prey from out of his mouth. And when, raging with fury, he sprang upon me, his paws upon my shoulders, I caught him, like this, by the beard upon his chin, and with my club smote and slew him at a blow. So indeed, my lord, thy servant killed both the lion and the bear, and so will I do unto this accursed Philistine, for I vow, my lord, I have no fear of him, seeing that he hath defied the armies of the living God, and is himself no better than a ravening beast. The Lord God who delivered me from the paw of the lion and the paw of the bear will deliver me from the spear of this Philistine also!"

Watching David close as he stood before him and marking how his face was lit up and transfigured with the faith and courage of the spirit within him, Saul consented at length to let him go. He glanced at Abner; there was a strange influence in this young man that swept all doubts aside and prevailed over his own ripe judgment.

"Go," he said, "and may the Lord be with thee."

Then he bade his servants bring him his coat of mail and his helmet of bronze. "Thou wilt not venture out unarmed," he said.

There in the king's tent David put on Saul's coat of mail, and his helmet on his head, and girded Saul's sword about the armour as he stood. And the king with his own hand aided him. But Saul was a man of a mighty stature; and thus armed, David essayed in vain to take a pace or two, hoping that he might become accustomed to the burden, for he had never worn the like before. But he could not. He turned with a sigh to the king, and entreated that the armour should be put off him.

He said to the king: "It was in truth a grace and kindness that my lord should array me in his armour, but I cannot wear it, for I am not used to it. Be it the king's will that I go to meet Goliath as I am."

So he went out of Saul's tent with nothing in his hand but his shepherd's staff or club and his sling. When he had gone, Saul turned to Abner, the commander-in-chief of his armies, who had watched all that had passed. He asked him, "Abner, whose son is this youth?"

And Abner said: "As thy soul liveth, O king, I cannot tell."

And Saul bade him make inquiry and discover from whence he came. Then the king and Abner with·their officers followed after David to see what would come of his ordeal.

And David, having left the king, made his way back between the clustering tents until he had come out beyond the fringes of the camp. As he continued on his way down into the valley he came to the brook of water that flowed between the rocks in the ravine, warbling amid its stones, and gleaming in its blue in the sunbeams. It was as though he moved in a dream, but a dream marvellously clear, and with all his senses alert. He stooped and chose from out of the brook's cold waters five of the smoothest pebbles on its bed, and in so doing saw the image of his own face reflected there, and it was as though he had never seen its like before. He put the pebbles into the scrip or shepherd's bag he carried, then rose and went on his way.

At the shout that had gone up from the men of Israel at sight of him, the giant who had turned back towards the Philistine camp wheeled and looked about, and knitting his shaggy eyebrows in the glare of the sun, fixed his stare on David as he rose from the brook-side and, leaping from boulder to boulder, came on down into the valley. Whereat the champion called back a word over his shoulder to his shield-bearer, and advanced to meet him.

And David, his sling in his hand, the sling with which he was wont to drive off the smaller beasts that pestered his flocks, drew near. The men of Israel fell silent, and the armies, clustered black on either height, watched. In the hush of the valley the skirring of the grass-hoppers in the heat of the morning, and the song of the brook-water brawling in its rocky channel, were the only sounds to be heard.

Astounded and rejoiced that after these many fruitless days there had at last come forth a man of Israel valiant enough to take up his challenge, Goliath snatched his shield from the Philistine who carried it, and stood in wait.

But when he could see his foe clearly and what manner of champion this was, little more than a lad, fair and tanned with the sun, in shepherd's clothes and unarmed, his voice pealed out in mocking laughter, and he cursed him by his gods.

"Am I a carrion dog," he cried, "that thou comest out against me with nought but a staff in thy hand? By the gods of my fathers, do but come a little closer, and I will strip the flesh from off thy body and give it to the fowls of the air, and thy bones to the wild beasts to mumble."

Even as he spoke there showed black specks in the height of the sky above the mountain-tops, and vulture and kite came circling overhead against the blue above the valley.

Warily David watched the Philistine, and he stepped alertly pace with his pace and well beyond javelin cast, and circled about him so that at last he should bring the giant face to face with him against the dazzle and blaze of the sun. And as he did so, he made answer to Goliath, calling clearly across in the stillness between them.

"Thou hast come out against me, armed with sword and spear and javelin," he cried. "A brazen shield is on thine arm, and thou art hung head to foot with armour of brass. But if this be all thy strength, beware of it! For I am come out against thee in the name of the Lord of Hosts, the God of the armies of Israel, whom thou hast insulted and defied, and this day the Lord will deliver thee into my hand. And I will smite thee and take thy head from off thy shoulders, and not only thy carcass but the carcasses of the host of the Philistines shall be given this day to the fowls of the air and the beasts of the wild. That all the earth may know there is a God in Israel, and that his salvation is not in sword and spear, nor his battle to the strong, but that he giveth victory according as he decree."

In rage and fury at these words, Goliath raised himself, towering in his might, his blood roaring in his ears, and with lifted spear strode in to smite his enemy down, and his armour clanged as he trod.

And David drew back lightly from before him. He watched every transient look upon the great flushed bony countenance beneath the crested helmet, now full in the glare of noonday. And softly as he sped on, he drew from out of his scrip one after another of the pebbles he had chosen from the brook and poised it in his sling. His first stone rang out sharp upon the champion's breastplate; and the next numbed the hand that held his spear; for David could sling a stone at a hair-breadth, and not miss.

Then of a sudden he turned swiftly, and with the speed of an angel sent from God, ran in towards the giant, whirling his sling above his head as he did so, his gaze fixed gravely on the target of his face. And as he looked, Goliath's heart fainted within him and he was cold as stone. He stood bemused. And David lifted his thumb, set free the stone, and slang it straight at its mark. It whistled through the air, and smote the Philistine in the middle of his forehead, clean between the eyes. The stone sank down into his forehead, and into his brain and, without a groan, the giant fell stunned upon his face upon the ground. The noise of his fall was like the clashing of innumerable cymbals, and the dust above his body rose over him in a cloud.

Before he could stir from the swoon in which he lay,

David ran in, and stood over him. And with his two hands
he drew the giant's bronze two-bladed sword from out of
its sheath, wheeled it with all his might above his shoulders
and at a blow smote off Goliath's head.

Then with his two hands he snatched up the helmless
matted head and held it high aloft before all Israel. And
there went up a cry.

When the Philistines, who had been watching the combat
from the heights above, saw that their champion had been
defeated and lay prone, dead, and headless upon the ground
they fled in terror back towards their camp. A wild clamour
arose as the news of the champion's downfall sped on from
mouth to mouth; cries of astonishment and fear.

Then sounded the trumpets in the camp of Israel. The
Lord had wrought a great salvation, and the men of Israel
and the men of Judah, shouting their war cry, swept down
into the valley and up the slopes beyond, and stormed the
heights of Shochoh. Rank on rank they pressed forward,
beating down all resistance, and the Philistine army broke
and fled. Westward and north-westward the Israelites pursued them through the valleys and ravines until they came
out on to the plain and even to the walls of Ekron and of
Gath. Throughout the whole way to Shaaraim the ground
was strown with their dead and wounded, to the very gates
of the two cities.

Thence the pursuers turned back. And when they had
come from chasing after the Philistines, they plundered their
tents, a rich booty. Laden with their spoil, they returned to
their own camp. And the armour of Goliath was stripped
from off his body, and with his spear, his javelin and his
sword, was afterwards laid up as a trophy in Jerusalem.

When David himself returned from the pursuit of the
Philistines he was brought to Abner, and Abner himself

took him into the presence of Saul. And Jonathan was with his father the king. David came in and stood before them, the head of the Philistine in his hand. Saul looked from the one face, wan and swarthy and dark and shut by death, to the other, young and bright with life and aware, and he marvelled.

He asked David whose son he was, and many another question. David told him that he was the son of Jesse of Bethlehem. And there returned into Saul's mind, as though it were a dream that had faded out after waking, the memory of the hours when he had lain terrified and distraught in the gloom of his tent, and his only solace had been the music of David's harp-strings.

He said nothing of it, but talked long and earnestly with him, and questioned him. And David answered the king simply and openly, while Jonathan who had been absent from his father during his sickness, stood near at hand, his eyes fixed on David's face, as he mutely drank in every word he uttered. His heart welled over with wonder at his simplicity and fearlessness, and his soul went out to David. He loved him—as do all men who love—at first sight. And he continued to love him, friend with friend, until the last hour of his life.

So great was the love of Jonathan for David that he made a covenant of brotherhood with him, a covenant that in Israel knitted two friends together in mind and spirit closer even than if they had been sons of the same mother.

"Whatever thy soul desireth, that will I indeed do for thee," he said. And in token of it he stripped himself of the cloak which he wore, a cloak befitting the son of a king, and he gave it to David, and his armour also, even to his sword and his bow. And he girdled him with his girdle.

From that day forward Saul took David into his service

and made him his armour-bearer, and David returned no more to the house of his father.

When the king, with his captains and his army, laden with the spoil they had taken from the Philistines, returned in triumph from their camp above the valley of Elah and marched to Gibeah, a vast concourse of people gathered together to watch them pass.

And the women and maidens of Israel, clad in their brightest colours, scarlet and blue and purple, came out singing and dancing from all the towns and villages on their way to meet and greet King Saul, and to give him welcome.

To the clash of timbrel and of cymbal and the music of divers instruments they came dancing in two companies, scattering garlands before the king, singing his praises; and as the one company chanted their song of victory, so the other answered them again, shrill and wild and sweet; and the refrain of their song was:

"*Saul hath slain his thousands, but David hath slain his tens of thousands.*"

And Saul's heart sank within him. The words displeased him, and he thought, "To David they have given ten times the praise that they have given to me. What more is wanting to his glory than the kingdom itself?"

From that day forward he was filled with envy of David and looked at him askance. Nevertheless, to the joy and satisfaction of the people and of his own officers, Saul made him the captain of a thousand.

And David was renowned and beloved throughout Israel, for he bore himself wisely in all his ways, and the Lord was with him.